ECONOMIC CONTROVERSIES

Innovative and thought-provoking, the Economic Controversies series strips back the often impenetrable facade of economic jargon to present bold new ways of looking at pressing issues, while explaining the hidden mechanics behind them. Concise and accessible, the books bring a fresh, unorthodox approach to a variety of controversial subjects.

Also available in the Economic Controversies series:

Yanis Varoufakis, *The Global Minotaur: America, Europe and the Future of the World Economy*

Robert R. Locke and J.-C. Spender, *Confronting Managerialism: How the Business Elite and Their Schools Threw Our Lives Out of Balance*

Lorenzo Fioramonti, *Gross Domestic Problem: The Politics Behind the World's Most Powerful Number*

Heikki Patomäki, *The Great Eurozone Disaster: From Crisis to Global New Deal*

Richard Javad Heydarian, *How Capitalism Failed the Arab World: The Economic Roots and Precarious Future of the Middle East Uprisings*

ABOUT THE AUTHOR

LORENZO FIORAMONTI (@globalreboot) is Associate Professor and Jean Monnet Chair in Regional Integration and Governance Studies at the University of Pretoria (South Africa), where he directs the Centre for the Study of Governance Innovation. He is also Senior Fellow at the Centre for Social Investment of the University of Heidelberg and at the Hertie School of Governance, Germany, as well as Associate Fellow at the United Nations University. He is the author of several books about development policies, global and regional governance, alternative economies and social progress indicators, including *Gross Domestic Problem: The Politics Behind the World's Most Powerful Number* (Zed Books, 2013). He blogs at www.globalreboot.org.

HOW NUMBERS RULE THE WORLD

The Use and Abuse of Statistics in Global Politics

LORENZO FIORAMONTI

Zed Books

LONDON | NEW YORK

How Numbers Rule the World: The Use and Abuse of Statistics in Global Politics was first published in 2014 by Zed Books Ltd, 7 Cynthia Street, London N1 9JF, UK and Room 400, 175 Fifth Avenue, New York, NY 10010, USA

www.zedbooks.co.uk

Designed and typeset in Monotype Bulmer
by illuminati, Grosmont
Index by John Barker
Cover design: www.roguefour.co.uk
Printed and bound by TJ International Ltd, Padstow, Cornwall

Distributed in the USA exclusively by Palgrave Macmillan, a division of St Martin's Press, LLC, 175 Fifth Avenue, New York, NY 10010, USA

A catalogue record for this book is available from the British Library
Library of Congress Cataloging in Publication Data available

ISBN 978 1 78032 268 1 hb
ISBN 978 1 78032 267 4 pb

MIX
Paper from
responsible sources
FSC
www.fsc.org
FSC® C013056

Contents

Acknowledgements

After the publication of *Gross Domestic Problem: The Politics Behind the World's Most Powerful Number* I received a number of invitations to discuss the book throughout the world. I set out on a journey on which I encountered wonderful people: academics, journalists, radio hosts, activists and concerned citizens, who are committed to profound, sustainable and radical change. They asked questions, were keen to challenge conventional wisdom and were looking for new ideas to inform their work. So, my first thanks go to them, as they were a profound source of inspiration.

With Georg Mildenberger and Ekkehard Thümler of the Centre for Social Investment at the University of Heidelberg, I have reflected a lot on the role of civil society and markets in governance, while Maxi Schoeman, Mzukisi Qobo and Camilla Adelle at the University of Pretoria accompanied me in the intellectual journey that has culminated in the establishment of the Centre for the Study of Governance Innovation, where most of the topics you find in this book have finally found a research home. I would also like to thank various colleagues with whom I share concerns regarding issues that range from measurement of economic performance to sustainability and market dominance, in particular Saamah Abdallah and Tony Greenham at the New Economics Foundation; Lew Daly, who leads the sustainable progress initiative at Demos; Claudius Van Wyk of Transformation Strategies; Mark Swilling, director of the Sustainability Institute at Stellenbosch University; Patrick Bond of the Centre for Civil Society at the University of KwaZulu–Natal; and Sidney Luckett. Because of her commitment, friendship and intellectual guidance, I owe a lot to Susan George.

Ken Barlow, my editor at Zed Books, convinced me to finish this book in record time, as he believed that it would be a perfect complement to *Gross Domestic Problem*. He patiently reviewed the manuscript, corrected a number of mistakes and helped me improve the readability of the text, despite the complexity of the theme. My wife Janine has been a constant companion and an attentive reader of the manuscript. No offence to my colleagues, but she is the best intellect I know.

Finally I would like to thank my students, who have engaged me in fruitful and often challenging conversations, making me realize how important it is to teach with passion. They are full of ideas, but conventional teaching approaches tend to suppress their energy. I hope this book, like the previous ones, will further stimulate their free-thinking.

Needless to say, any flaws you find in the volume are mine alone.

To my children and to the world in which they will grow up

The politics of statistics

We make constant use of formulas, symbols, and rules whose meaning we do not understand, [which] have in turn become the foundation of the civilization we have built up.

F.A. Hayek, *The Use of Knowledge in Society*, 1945

The most important things cannot be measured.

W. E. Deming

In the romantic slapstick comedy *She's Out of My League*, the protagonist asks himself: 'How can a 10 go for a 5?' The plot revolves around a love story between an ordinary airport security guy named Kirk and Molly, a beautiful lawyer-turned-event planner. On a scale of attractiveness, she is a 'hard' 10 (gorgeous, smart and rich) and he is just a 5 (below average, skinny, working-class young man). Although Kirk is in love with Molly, and she is visibly interested in him, they act awkwardly as all odds appear stacked against them: a 10 can perhaps go with an 8 – as Kirk's friends explain – and a 5 might manage to reach a 7, but there is no way it can possibly work out between a 5 and a 10. Mathematics is no opinion: the distance is just too wide. The numbers' rule is clear. All side characters (Kirk's and Molly's families, their best friends and their respective ex-partners) agree that the relationship is impossible and actively conspire against it by trying to convince the two young lovers to give up. In an admittedly predictable (yet funny) spiral of events, the two protagonists grow distant from and suspicious of one another. Their interaction is unnatural, apparently insignificant events are blown out of proportion and misunderstanding becomes pervasive. The two lovers get confused. They no longer know what they feel for each other. The relationship collapses and each of them is brought back to their respective worlds. The 10s and the 5s cannot possibly be a happy couple. Or so it seems. In the end, of course, Kirk and Molly get together and live happily ever after. Despite the negative odds, love triumphs. Both protagonists overcome the number syndrome and let their hearts prevail. What appeared to be mathematically impossible is defeated by the irrationality of love. Romantic comedies are notorious for predictable and rather cheesy endings.

According to English statistician and biologist Ronald A. Fisher, statistics is 'the peculiar aspect of human progress', which has given 'to the twentieth century, its special character'.[1] Whether or not we agree with this statement, we cannot dispute that numbers largely run our societies. They have become driving forces behind our social, economic and political decisions. Just as with Kirk and Molly, numbers influence our behaviour and that of the people around us. We measure and compare every day. We continually assess ourselves based on general (and generic) scales of beauty, intelligence, smartness and success. We quantify everything, from income to sexual performance, quality of life and happiness. Our life is surrounded by numbers. We are so accustomed to them that we do not realize their power anymore.

Just take a look at the variety of specific thematic indexes and indicators produced by research organizations and private agencies in fields as varied as environmental policy, well-being and governance. My own count, which is undoubtedly reductive, is that there are over 300 aggregated indexes available for the social sciences, which account for tens of thousands of individual indicators. Such a figure does not even include all the numbers produced by governmental statistical offices. Moreover, such selection is grossly incomplete as it only deals with some specific sectors of research, such as development and governance, which are those I have covered in my own academic experience. It does not even incorporate the arguably endless list of numbers produced by natural scientists, engineers, doctors, architects and other representatives of 'hard' disciplines.

Every week, month or year, hundreds of think-tanks, non-governmental organizations (NGOs) and research centres the world over produce numbers to assess the state of the economy, the quality of life in cities, the competitiveness of firms, the speed of development in low-income countries, the quality of education, the service delivery in welfare systems, the amount of corruption ravaging societies and the performance of an endless range of institutions, just to name very few. They even measure apparently trivial economic aspects, such as the comparative cost of a Big Mac around the world, or the ease with which wealth can cross borders, the number of days it takes a firm to get a licence to operate in a given country, all possible country risks (from war to terrorism to economic instability), the ratings of banks, corporations and sovereign debt, tourism competitiveness, computer literacy, education attainment, global hunger, food insecurity and so on and so forth.

These numbers are used to assess development strategies, measure performance, inform policy-making and guide reforms. In a word, they drive global and national governance.[2] For instance, performance indexes have become key criteria to allocate foreign aid or investment, which gives them an enormous power to affect a country's economy. Credit ratings published by private agencies are perhaps the most visible example of the political and economic power of these numbers. Equally, the financial assessments published by the International Monetary Fund (IMF) can unilaterally coerce entire nations into obedience. In many sectors, the proliferation of numbers has blurred the distinction between public and private authority, in so far as the procedures established by governments are complemented by (and often enforced through) numerical benchmarks, ratings and rankings produced by companies, agencies, consultants, auditors and NGOs. To capture the impact of numbers in political and economic affairs, along with the integration of public and private forms of authority, various analysts have introduced terms such as 'meta-governance' and 'transnational private governance'.[3]

The range of application of statistical measurement is nowadays unlimited. There is no field in which numbers have not been able to exert dominance. Even sports are largely dependent on numerical examination, as experts fill up television shows with measurements of players' performance and strategic models. Take baseball, which is the best-known example of a sport whose tradition has been deeply intertwined with numbers. In his 1868 book *The Game of Base Ball: How to Learn It, How to Play It, and How to Teach It*, the father of modern baseball, Henry Chadwick, systematically applied statistical reasoning to the rules of what was soon to become the most popular sport in America. A former cricket reporter, Chadwick had a passion for statistics and produced the first baseball dataset in history. He listed all games played, including specific details such as the number and frequency of outs, runs, home runs, and strikeouts for hitters of prominent clubs. For him, certain statistics reflected real virtues, while others did not. He deprecated home run hitters (and the whole home run category) as overly 'showy' and lobbied hard to stop the practice of counting bases reached on field errors towards batters' averages, since these clearly did not demonstrate batting skill. He wanted to use statistics to revolutionize the game 'from the almost simple field exercise it was some twenty years ago up to the manly, scientific game of ball it is now'.[4] The power of numbers in baseball provided the narrative thread to the 2003 bestseller *Moneyball: The Art of Winning an Unfair Game*, which was then turned into a Hollywood film starring Brad Pitt. The focus of the book is on the strategy adopted by the Oakland Athletics (popularly known as the As), which used analytical, evidence-based, in-game statistical analysis (the so-called sabermetric, after the Society for American Baseball Research) to assemble a competitive team in spite of a limited budget. The central premiss of 'moneyball' is that traditional knowledge in the baseball community systematically misses out on important underlying factors, which make a critical difference between winning and losing a game. Factors such as stolen bases, runs batted in, and batting average, which have been typically used to gauge players and establish their salaries, are antiquated forms of valuing success for a team. By contrast, rigorous statistical analysis shows that other factors, such as on-base and slugging percentage, are better indicators of success, albeit not very spectacular for viewers. As such observations often flew in the face of traditional baseball knowledge, the As were able to recruit players that performed well according to these 'new' indicators for a relatively modest amount of money, as the baseball market was systematically undervaluing them. According to Harvard philosopher Michael Sandel, who discusses the A's systematic use of modern statistical models in his book *What Money Can't Buy*, the team 'brought to baseball what the new breed of quantitative traders brought to Wall Street – an ability to use computer-driven analysis to gain an edge over old-timers who relied on gut instinct and personal experience'.[5] Sandel analyses the case of the As to show the profound connection between statistical reasoning and markets, particularly in so far as quantitative methods can be used to produce more efficient pricing mechanisms and gain a competitive advantage against rivals. The As strategy succeeded for a time, as the team won the western division of the American League in 2002. But then moneyball became a victim of its own success when other teams jumped on the bandwagon and hired the most brilliant statisticians to help them outbid less wealthy competitors. Nowadays, the richest teams, from the Red Sox to the New York Yankees, make systematic use of computer-based statistical models to draw strategies and assess the value of players. The game itself has changed, as the power of numbers has taken over more instinctual components. Passion has somehow subsided to rigour. Paradoxically, 'money came to matter more, not less, in determining the winning percentage of major league teams'.[6] If there is one lesson that we can learn from baseball it is that the proliferation of numbers in virtually all sectors of our social and political life has directly or indirectly resulted in the unstoppable expansion of markets, despite the credibility blow dealt to them by the global economic crisis. This, in turn, has undermined the public sphere as an arena of participation and deliberation, in which ideas are discussed, debated and promoted.

This is what this book is all about. The next chapters will show how numbers have been used and abused in governance processes to entrench the power of markets and undermine public debate. By referring to research in the history of science, we will discuss in Chapter 1 how certain statistics came to be incorporated into policy-making processes. Indeed, the bureau-cratization of statistics is a defining character of modern states, in particular since the late 1800s, which saw the growth of public infrastructure works and the measurement of costs, tolls and taxes that this involved. After this general overview of the power of numbers, we will delve into the first empirical case: that of credit-rating agencies and their influence on global governance. Chapter 2 analyses the history of rating and the conflicts of interest characterizing the role of rating agencies in the evolution of public financial governance. By providing a thorough account of how credit rating came to be hardwired into national and international policies, the chapter shows that the incorporation of ratings into virtually every country's public governance has resulted in strengthening certain segments within the financial markets at the expense of democratic accountability. Chapter 3 then engages with the thorny issue of climate change mitigation, another fundamental area of global governance. In this field, the politics of statistics has triggered clashes between climate scientists and the so-called 'sceptics', in which each camp has used a set of numbers to prove different (when not opposite) truths. Various degrees of manipulation occurred in both camps and, ultimately, cost–benefit analyses were adopted to choose the best policies to mitigate the environmental consequences of industrial growth. These types of analyses, which rely on the monetization of costs and benefits through a set of critical assumptions and econometric models, have supported the establishment of carbon markets, offset schemes and emission trading. Chapter 4 delves into the delicate nexus between the politics of statistics and environmental governance by analysing new methodologies for the valuation of natural capital and ecosystem services. Although designed to 'correct' GDP by incorporating the costs of environmental degradation, some of these methods have encouraged the proliferation of financial markets for the natural world, with potentially dangerous consequences for the world's ecosystems. Finally, Chapter 5 looks at how certain types of measurements have affected the development aid sector and the global fight against poverty by reinforcing the appeal of tools borrowed from the business sector. Such a business-like approach to development has not only been confined to the way in which aid agencies nowadays measure impact and effectiveness in the so-called developing countries, but has also influenced how social change is promoted in industrialized nations, with perilous impacts on the role of civil society, the nonprofit and the modus operandi of philanthropic foundations.

This book does not dispute the importance of statistics for the improvement of society. Without statistics, policies would be simply dominated by impressionistic considerations and rhetorical arguments. Measuring is a fundamental component of human life. Our education, health care and housing – to name just a few fundamental areas of development – depend on measurements. At the same time, however, we should not credulously accept that numbers always reveal facts. In the social field, the incorporation of statistics is invariably driven by critical assumptions, which should be taken into account when taking decisions that affect society as a whole. More often than not, these assumptions are driven by a narrow econometric approach at the expense of more holistic considerations. We can measure the amount of time a couple spend together, the issues they talk about, the times they go out, how much they earn, how often they have sex and so on and so forth. Yet, the sum of all of these does not equate love, as Kirk and Molly have learned the hard way. Standardized tests may be useful in some schools, but they should not be seen as measures of education. Most performance assessments may help us identify gaps, but they hide more than they reveal. This is why a healthy society should be able to distinguish between policy areas in which measurement is useful, and policy areas in which it is not. There are limits to what we can measure. If we stretch our numerical reasoning too far, we end up oversimplifying reality. When this happens, our measurement tools become more important than what they measure. We end up wanting what we can measure, rather than measuring what we want. Pupils end up studying only what is relevant for the tests, couples focus on the quantity rather than on the quality of affection, and workers of all kinds become enslaved by productivity parameters imposed on them. In other areas, such as that of ecological governance, the natural world is monetized by auditors of all sorts who claim to do so with a view to protecting the environment. Ultimately, obsessive measurement can lead to the commodification of social relations and the natural world. In part, this is why markets have become so powerful in the era of measurement. Markets, as the locus of economic transactions, are more malleable to measurement. Their concepts, principles and functionings are extremely appropriate to economic and statistical categorization.

This book is about how numbers have been used to strengthen technocracy in some of the most critical fields of contemporary governance. It is about numbers reinforcing the grip of markets on our social and political life. In a word, it is about how numbers have curtailed public participation and rational debate, thus impoverishing our already battered and weak democracy.

CHAPTER 1

The power of numbers

Numbers saturate the news, politics, and life. For good or ill, they are today's preeminent public language – and those who speak it rule.

M. Blastland and A. Dilnot, *The Numbers Game*, 2009

Counting promotes the counter and demotes the counted.

Robert Chambers, *Whose Reality Counts?*

The Greek philosopher and mathematician Pythagoras of Samos was a deep believer in the power of numbers. Not only did he dedicate his entire life to the study of mathematics (still nowadays his theorem is a fundamental component of trigonometry), but he also developed an entire philosophy and religious system based on numbers. The cult of Pythagoreanism became quite popular in Magna Graecia (currently southern Italy), where the philosopher had established a 'Pythagorean brotherhood' in the city of Croton. The brotherhood took an active role in politics, proposing a number of reforms and promoting a culture of equality, including extremely progressive views on women and their role in society. Pythagoras saw for himself the role of philosopher–ruler, a concept that would later influence Plato's political thought, especially his masterpiece *The Republic*, in which he developed the idea of 'a tightly organized community of like-minded thinkers', who should 'provide guidance (even governance) for the polity in which they lived'.[1] According to the British philosopher Bertrand Russell, Pythagoras' view of numbers as the driving force behind nature deeply influenced Plato's philosophy and, as a consequence, most Western philosophical thought.[2] Pythagoras also inspired one of Plato's central ideas, 'that mathematics, and abstract thinking generally, including logic, can provide a secure basis, not only for philosophy in the modern sense, but also for substantial theses in sciences and in morals'.[3] Both Pythagoras and Plato were harshly criticized by Aristotle, who by contrast highlighted the crucial difference between form and matter and pointed out 'the equally important error of thinking that [numbers] can by themselves establish conclusions of substance about the physical world'.[4]

Although details about Pythagoras' life are scarce, we know that his use of numbers for political purposes was mainly based on persuasion. His models aimed at crafting and running the perfect society, in which conflicts and diversity of opinions were considered detrimental to stability and order. His political experience lasted about twenty years, a rather long period given the volatility of the political system at that time, but ended with a revolution. All the places sacred to his brotherhood were destroyed and most of his fellows got killed. Pythagoras himself had to flee Croton and died in exile. His legacy, however, exerted a lasting effect on a number of esoteric traditions, including the Freemasonry and Rosicrucianism, two secret societies established in the Middle Ages.

The Latin root of the word validity (*validitas*) is strength and force. The validity of a person as well as an argument is the capacity to command obedience. In a word, validity is power. But validity is also a fundamental concept in statistics, where it indicates the extent to which a measurement corresponds accurately to what it intends to measure. In social research, validity is defined in various ways (e.g. face validity, criterion validity, construct validity, etc.), which point to the need for measures to be as closely as possible aligned with the underlying phenomenon they wish to describe in order to produce any meaningful inference about real life. The key underlying assumption here is that statistics can have a significant impact on the way in which we experience the world and learn from it. In turn, this affects our decisions and how we govern ourselves as a collectivity. Validity is, then, essential for numbers to be truthful. At the same time, however, validity is about the power of persuasion, just as it was during Pythagoras' time.

Public statistics have been fundamental in ordering societies and supporting power structures. The first ever attempt at measuring a country's wealth (the forerunner of contemporary gross domestic product) was conducted in 1652 by the economist William Petty, as part of a land redistribution programme promised by Oliver Cromwell to his troops in Ireland. The survey was designed to serve the interests of the British government, whose main goal was to put its Irish problem to rest by expropriating the country's populace (especially its Catholic component) of productive land and turning it into a source of income for a permanent military occupation. Some historians have demonstrated the extent to which this statistical undertaking helped eradicate Ireland's indigenous culture,[5] while others have described it as a 'gigantic experiment in primitive accumulation'.[6] Petty's work was also instrumental in equipping government with new information to raise taxes and limit the amount of wealth owned by private individuals, a useful piece of intelligence to restrain local autonomy and avoid concentration of capital in the hands of potential opponents. The father of modern chemistry, Antoine Lavoisier, who attempted to draw up the first system of national accounts in France in the late 1700s, was an administrator of the powerful *Ferme Generale*, an outsourced customs and excise operation that collected duties on behalf of the king and reinforced the tax collection mechanisms of the *Ancien Régime*.[7] After the French Revolution, Napoleon Bonaparte wanted statistical offices to provide specific information on citizens with a view to making military conscription more effective, while strengthening the state's capacity to collect taxes and requisitions, as well as design better ways to manage the economy in wartime. During the Second World War, the national income accounts produced by the US Department of Commerce were systematically used to assess the feasibility of President Roosevelt's Victory Program and to coordinate the American involvement in the conflict.

In contemporary governance, international rankings have become crucial for the credibility of states in a globalized world. Research has shown that competitiveness indexes, such as those produced by the World Economic Forum, have reinforced neoliberal practices that increasingly change the role of governments from promoters of public interest to supporters of market expansion.[8] This trend has been reinforced by the integration of credit ratings into public policies and international treaties.[9] Various types of good governance indicators, including those focusing on state effectiveness, corruption and market openness, are important to define global hierarchies among states as well as international 'blacklists' of pariahs, while measures of economic performance (mainly through the calculation of GDP) are the leading parameters to design global governance institutions, from the G8–G20 to the composition of the Organisation for Economic Co-operation and Development (OECD) or the distribution of power at the World Bank and the IMF.[10]

French novelist Honoré de Balzac once argued that society is organized according to the instructions of statisticians, who hold significant sway in the rooms of power. Through numbers, 'Society isolates everyone, the better to dominate them, divides everything to weaken it. It reigns over the units, over numerical figures piled up like grains of wheat in a heap.'[11] Whether numbers are used to strengthen institutions or to promote reforms, their capacity to influence politics is probably unparalleled by any other social construct. Take the question of measuring a population, for example. In principle, counting people should not be particularly problematic. In fact, there are important political issues involved, as demographics can affect the outcome of elections and lead to a change in the distribution of resources. In the USA, for instance, various attempts have been made at correcting for the under-representation of homeless people or citizens with double residence.[12] Yet, as each correction has an impact on specific jurisdictions, racial or ethnic categories and the distribution of federal revenues, heated contestations have historically marred the issue. As James Madison had already written in 'Federalist No. 54',

> it is of great importance that the States should feel as little bias as possible, to swell or reduce the amount of their numbers. Were their share of representation alone to be governed by this rule, they would have an interest in exaggerating their inhabitants. Were the rule to decide their share of taxation alone, a contrary temptation would prevail.[13]

Numbers and politics

The relationship between statistics and politics (and political interests) has a long history. The forerunner of statistics was called 'political arithmetic', a discipline that emerged in England and France in the 1600s, which focused primarily on measuring demographic trends and life expectancy for urban planning purposes. Over time these calculations were systematically integrated into public decision-making, thus becoming one of the key components of state policy. The etymology of the word 'statistics' stems from such an inherent relationship between numbers and government: statistics became the science of using numbers to strengthen the state. And 'statists' were those conducting such numeric studies.[14] The first statists believed that by quantifying phenomena their models could help identify underlying patterns and thus tackle some of the most critical social problems their societies were facing. Behind the very philosophy of statistics, there was a sense that social reality was based on some social order, which numbers could reveal with powerful accuracy. Karl Pearson, the founder of modern mathematical statistics, fully embodied the 'positivist mania for quantification with vast social ambitions'.[15] For Pearson, the world was not made up of real objects, but of perceptions. Nature itself did not possess a definite form. Hence, the goal of science was to put nature in order through a clear method. In his magnum opus, *The Grammar of Science*, Pearson maintained that 'The field of science is unlimited; its material is endless, every group of natural phenomena, every stage of past or present development is material for science. The unity of all science consists alone in its method, not in its material.'[16]

Undeniably, Pearson's philosophy had more to do with managing the world than understanding it. As remarked by historian Theodore Porter, author of the book *Trust in Numbers*, quantification is 'a social technology'. Unlike modern mathematics, which has its roots in ancient geometry, emphasizes theoretical demonstration 'and was largely separate from the domain of number', arithmetic and algebra, which are the cornerstones of statistics, 'were born as practical arts'.[17] In modern societies, the process of quantification plays a central role in experimental practices. One of its main goals is 'to serve as a bridge between the material culture of the laboratory and the predictions derived from formal theory'. Although most of us believe that this theory-testing role is the decisive task of data quantification processes, this is often not true in practice: 'Researchers on topics that lack mathematical theory are often equally assiduous in reporting methods as well as results in quantitative form, and *filtering out findings that cannot be so expressed.*[18]

The application of this type of reasoning, permeated by the aspiration to order and signify social life, inevitably blurs the alleged distance between the subject and the object of investigation. In the real world, the way in which we measure things has an unavoidable impact on the things themselves. 'Social statistics describe society; but they are also products of our social arrangements', argues Joel Best, professor of sociology at the University of Delaware and author of *Damned Lies and Statistics*:

> The people who bring social statistics to our attention have reasons for doing so; they inevitably want something, just as reporters and the other media figures who repeat and publicize statistics have their own goals. Statistics are tools, used for particular purposes. Thinking critically about statistics requires understanding their place in society.[19]

Michael Blastland and Andrew Dilnot, former hosts of the BBC radio show *More or Less*, compare the way in which statistics are used in the social field to the Indian fable *The Blind Men and the Elephant*:

> It was six men of Indostan
> To learning much inclined,
> Who went to see the Elephant
> (Though all of them were blind),
> That each by observation
> Might satisfy his mind.[20]

As we know, although the men were really *inclined* to *learn* from *observation* (rather than theory), they could only touch one part of the elephant at a time. So, for the man who touches the side of the animal, the elephant is just a wall. For the one who touches the trunk, it is a snake. For he who touches the legs, it must be a tree, or a rope for he who touches the tail. And they 'disputed loud and long, / ... Though each was partly in the right, / And all were in the wrong!' Statistics are, by definition, static: 'Things have to keep static if you're going to count them', argues David Boyle, fellow at the New Economics Foundation and author of *The Tyranny of Numbers*: 'But real life isn't still.'[21]

According to the sociologist Paul Starr, winner of the Pulitzer Prize and co-editor of a volume on US demographics titled *The Politics of Numbers*, numbers are like photographs: they 'seem to arrest the flow of human activity and fix it for more detached inspection'.[22] While mere words resemble paintings, as they carry the need to be interpreted, numbers purport to represent reality as it is. In fact, though, 'statistics not only lend themselves to many interpretations; they contain them. And because statistics do not simply reproduce reality, statistical systems represent an independent factor in social life.'

As Blastland and Dilnot note, the problem is not just one of confusion and misunderstanding. As statistics are applied to policymaking, they generate all sorts of consequences, most of which we do not control: 'There is also a tendency for the parts we do not measure to do odd things when our backs are turned: while measuring the legs, the trunk starts to misbehave.'[23] In health care, for instance, performance assessments (and therefore the distribution of public funds) are generally associated with a limited set of indicators: for example, the number of patients surviving an operation versus the number of those dying while in hospital care. In the USA (and also increasingly in European countries), this has generated perverse incentives for doctors, who are less inclined to take on hard cases and prefer dismissing patients (or not booking them in altogether) when risks of failure are too high. Similarly, in the UK, where public hospitals have been assessed on waiting times, public investigations have identified a number of tricks, manipulations and other perverse

consequences that managers come up with, such as avoiding
follow-up visits. According to a 2003 parliamentary investigation
into one 'suspicious' hospital, the avoidance of follow-up visits
led to at least twenty-five patients going blind for lack of due
post-operation care.[24]

This politics of targets based on standardized assessments
has conquered most areas of public management, invading ter-
ritories where subjectivity and freedom were considered of utmost
importance. Nowadays, for instance, education is fundamentally
trapped within specific parameters of attainment. Schools are
rated on the basis of standardized tests and are encouraged
to compete with one another for public funding or to attract
wealthy students (and their families' donations). The No Child
Left Behind (NCLB) Act of 2001 was introduced in the USA
by a large bipartisan coalition, arguably animated by a genuine
interest to improve the way American public schools serve poor
children. The NCLB promotes accountability and performance
by making federal funds contingent on the acceptance of a system
of tests and sanctions, thus altering the operational philosophy of
schools around the country. According to critics, who include a
vast coalition of teaching professionals, civil society groups and
NGOs, the law is undermining public schools and the ability of
the public education system to serve poor and minority children.
In the volume *Many Children Left Behind*, a range of academics,
activists and teachers maintain that 'NCLB punishes rather than
helps poor/minority kids (and their schools)' and sustains an
agenda of privatization of public education, while the 'focus on
testing and test preparation dumbs down classrooms'.[25] A survey
conducted by Teachers Network in 2007 showed that for the
majority of teachers the emphasis of NCLB on high-stakes testing
did not work. Only 37 per cent of respondents found standardized
tests 'somewhat useful', while 42 per cent deemed them 'not at
all' helpful to their teaching. Moreover, over 40 per cent claimed

that these tests were encouraging them to use rote drill, and 44 per cent reported that standardized tests were pushing them to eliminate curriculum material not tested.[26] According to the National Center for Fair and Open Testing, standardized tests 'reward quick answers to superficial questions', 'do not measure the ability to think deeply or creatively in any field' and 'their use encourages a narrowed curriculum, outdated methods of instruction, and harmful practices such as grade retention and tracking'.[27] In late 2012, the Obama administration promised to revise and improve the policy, while granting waivers to more than thirty states.

Boyle notes that 'because it is so hard to measure what is really important, governments and institutions try to pin down something else. They have to. But the consequences of pinning down the wrong thing can be severe.' He mentions the case of school league tables in the UK, which have been introduced to instil competition among schools through the almighty power of standardized testing: 'The trouble was that schools concentrated on the test results to improve their position on the tables. That meant excluding pupils who may drag down the results, concentrating on the D grade pupils – the only ones who could make a difference in exam result league tables – to the detriment of the others.' And he concludes: 'If you choose the wrong measure, you sometimes get the opposite of what you wanted.'[28]

Trust in numbers

It requires a degree of coercion to establish valid measures in public life. For instance, enforcing common standards in the construction sector requires both compliance on the side of private firms and a disciplined labour force. At the same time, numbers are also potent ammunition for persuasion. Drawing on French philosopher Michel Foucault's analysis of the indirect means through which government exercises power, one may argue that the construction of 'objective' measures for evaluation allows not only for 'the possibility of being subject to regulation or control by someone else' but also for shaping 'one's own identity ... by self-knowledge and self-regulation'.[29] In a nutshell, the rule by numbers is more complicated than simple top-down coercion: it involves a significant degree of complacency and fundamentally shapes the way in which subjects behave. In short, it is a system of voluntary acquiescence. It thus becomes a key aspect of what Foucault identifies as governmental rationality, or 'governmentality' – that is, a technology to 'conduct the conduct' and affect behaviour 'from a distance'; in short, 'the right manner of disposing things' according to 'specific finalities' and 'multiform tactics'.[30]

Numbers are also fundamental in defining the modus operandi of modern bureaucratic systems of governance. New modes of knowledge have indeed been critical to the definition of an institutional body of decision-makers whose choices must be guided by parameters other than political discretion.[31] According to the forefather of modern bureaucracy studies, Max Weber, the essence of a bureaucracy is the power of technology, which leads to the marginalization of all irrational and emotional elements generally associated with political conflict – that is, human factors which escape the precision of calculation. The Weberian approach emphasizes 'the ways in which the ordering of public administration enabled distance, rationality, objectivity and authority – and a calculative machinery'.[32] As remarked by historian Theodore Porter, who has been studying the historical evolution of our society's trust in numbers, the process of quantification is inherently linked with the growth of bureaucratic administration. For legal and political reasons, administrative discretion was regarded suspiciously, 'so the regulators had little alternative but to search relentlessly for facts and to reduce them, if at all possible, to a few decisive numbers'.[33] Especially in pluralist democracies such as the USA, where interest groups competed for visibility and access to policymaking, the proliferation of statistics-based decision-making was instrumental to align the interests of government, business and society at large: 'Where values clash and consensus is elusive, numbers and the techniques that manipulate them are esteemed for their ostensible neutrality. With statistics, hotly debated issues can seemingly be turned into problems to be solved.'[34]

In the 1930s, amid the Great Depression, American statisticians and economists saw their role in public policymaking grow exponentially. A series of environmental disasters, in particular the exceptional Mississippi River floods of 1927, created excellent conditions for a massive use of statistics-based risk assessments for infrastructure projects, coupled with the first tentative studies to evaluate the costs and benefits of prevention policies. As the economic downturn kept on shrinking public budgets, new tools were introduced to guide the allocation of 'limited' resources and avoid political controversy. In 1936, the Flood Control Act for the first time introduced a cost–benefit analysis in public policy by stating that no flood-control programme would receive federal funding unless it was proved that its benefits would exceed its costs. Initially, cost–benefit methods were designed to encourage openness and neutrality in highly contested sectors, such as the prevention of environmental disasters and its correlation with public infrastructure projects and industrialization. And, of course, the credibility of numbers was couched in the rhetoric of professionalism, scientific neutrality and transparency. According to the senators who inserted the cost–benefit provision into the 1936 Flood Control Act, the experts in charge of the econometric analyses of these projects are 'honorable, straightforward, patriotic men' as the new system of evaluation requires 'an independent, nonpolitical, unprejudiced decision as to priorities'.[35] Because of their expertise and reputation, the offices tasked with crunching numbers began to enjoy a growing influence, which in turn was used to develop cosy relations with powerful private interests and corporations. According to Harold Ickes, secretary of the interior under Roosevelt, the bureaucrats in charge of the quantification process were 'the most powerful and ambitious lobby in Washington', strongly connected with military divisions and 'the perfect flower of bureaucracy'.[36]

During the 1960s and 1970s, the various models applied to measure costs and benefits and assess the effectiveness of public infrastructure projects were transformed 'from a collection of local bureaucratic practices into a set of rationalized economic principles'. In the American political context of 'systematic distrust' for government, the champions of statistical analyses introduced these tools in all sorts of fields, from the assessment of social welfare projects to the running of prisons, claiming 'almost universal validity' for econometric evaluations of public policies.[37] In particular, cost–benefit analyses and experimental testing procedures began to be implemented by a variety of subsidiary agencies and private firms, which sold their expertise to government departments or to companies tendering for public projects. As Porter underlines, during this phase there was a clear alignment 'between the interests of science and those of the state and large industries'. The Bureau of Standards, for instance, regularly encouraged a strict collaboration between government and the relevant industrial sectors, despite the notorious and unsuccessful appeal made by US president Ulysses Grant to Congress in 1877, in which he pleaded that private-sector testing and evaluations be separate from those required by the state: 'These experiments cannot be properly conducted by private firms, not only on account of the expense, but because the results must rest upon the authority of disinterested persons.'[38]

During the 1990s, new practices of quantified evaluation emerged as part of the 'audit explosion'. In addition to the regulation of private company accounting by financial audit, 'practices of environmental audit, value for money audit, management audit, forensic audit, data audit, intellectual property audit, medical audit, teaching audit, and technology audit emerged and, to varying degrees, acquired a degree of institutional stability and acceptance.'[39] According to Michael Power, author of *The Audit Society*, the practice of accounting further strengthened the focus on numbers and contributed to the 'myth structure of rationalized societies': 'The audit explosion has its roots in a programmatic restructuring of organizational life and a new 'rationality of governance'.[40]

Such a restructuring has afforded unprecedented influence to so-called experts – that is, individuals and organizations who produce data. In the words of German psychologist Gert Gigerenzer and his colleagues, authors of *The Empire of Chance: How Probability Changed Science and Everyday Life*, the authority of experts has been enormously enhanced by the incorporation of statistical and econometric calculations in public policymaking: 'Indeed, the explosion of numbers has created a new kind of expert, one whose claims rest more on information and formal techniques than on concrete experience and personal judgement. Not since Pythagoras has the prestige of numbers been so great, and this has been both a boon and a temptation to the new-style experts.'[41] The standardization procedures animating the work of these 'new' experts 'parallel the impartiality and rules of the modern bureaucrat', who seeks to exclude 'personal discretion and emphasize the consistent and even mechanical application of established procedures' across the board to avoid bias, the one aiming at truth to fact, and the other at fairness'.[42]

Most audit reports, however, do not communicate valuable information. They are not evidence-based, self-explanatory documentations for external users. By and large, such reports are self-contained, non-transparent records that fundamentally rely on a language of 'neutrality, objectivity, dispassion, expertise'.[43] What this means in practice is that full disclosure, transparency and accountability to the public at large are restrained via the expert certification. The audit process thus becomes a short cut, which is founded on our society's ingrained trust in experts, rather than a basis for a rational public deliberation: 'It is a dead end in the chain of accountability.'[44] In short, more numbers and more accounting do not necessarily equate with better accountability. To the contrary, they can reduce 'public curiosity and inquiry', which are compelled by the fact that the end users of professional audits are not the public at large, but 'a mythical reference point within experts' discourses'.[45] This is one of the many paradoxes of counting. Although the audit explosion has occurred in the name of accountability, 'giving an account is seen to be a way of avoiding an account', in so far as numbers stifle political and social discussion by purporting to provide incontestable facts.[46] Paradoxically, 'the audit society threatens to become an increasingly closed society, albeit one whose declared programmatic foundation is openness and accountability.'[47]

Experts who use numbers become the guardians of this social trust. The power of numbers and their guardians fundamentally upsets the principal–agent relationship underpinning social and political relations. Citizens, elected representatives and other stakeholders (the principals) are held hostage by experts (the agents). And the profound institutionalization of governance mechanisms based on numbers further reinforces itself, as 'we foster all kinds of ancillary certifications or guarantees of trustworthiness ... that are readily manipulated yet are now essential to principals who have abdicated their distrust to these new guardians.'[48] And we all trust people with numbers – even when we recognize how easy it is to fudge data for all sorts of purposes. In the field of academic research, hundreds of cases of manipulation are spotted every year, including in some of the world's leading universities. Most of them, of course, do not make headlines around the world. But some do. In 1986, for instance, the Nobel prizewinner biologist David Baltimore caused a global stir for getting involved in a case of allegedly fabricated data supporting new discoveries in the study of immune systems.[49] Although Baltimore was eventually cleared of all charges, the blow was felt in the discipline. In social research, too, there have been plenty of examples. Notorious is the case of historian Michael Bellesiles, who manipulated his 'unique' dataset about the distribution of small weapons across the American populace over centuries. His bestselling book *Arming America* was praised by the magazine *The Economist* and won Bellesiles the prestigious Bancroft Prize, before the academic community realized that his numbers were fake and forced him to resign.[50]

In 2010, Harvard economists Carmen Reinhart and Kenneth Rogoff, celebrated authors of the most influential historical account of financial crises, *This Time is Different: Eight Centuries of Financial Folly*, published a follow-up study for the National Bureau of Economic Research (NBER), which quickly became a reference point for all governments and conservative forces advocating for austerity programmes in Europe and America (both EU Commissioner Olli Rehn and US Republican Paul Ryan quoted the study). Their paper, titled 'Growth in a Time of Debt', employed time series data for 'forty-four countries spanning about two-hundred years' and '3,700 annual observations covering a wide range of political systems, institutions, exchange rate arrangements, and historic circumstances'.[51] Its main evidence-based conclusion was that countries should never surpass a 90 per cent ratio between debt and GDP, as this automatically triggers slow growth and the risk of a systematic recession. Then, in 2013, a young student from the University of Massachusetts Amherst was given the assignment of replicating the results of a famous paper in economic research. He chose

Reinhart and Rogoff's as their work was on everybody's mind due to its influence on the political management of the economic crisis. Yet, after several attempts, the student did not manage to replicate the results. Advised by his supervisors to contact the authors, he finally received the original spreadsheet and spotted numerous basic computation errors, including wrong averages, which largely undermined the results of the study.[52] Both Reinhart and Rogoff publicly apologized for the mistakes, yet stood by their overall conclusion, while Keynesian economists attacked them for misguiding policymakers.[53] Criticizing the results of the study and the justification it offered to the austerity policies which have been generating much popular discontent in America and Europe, the Center for Economic and Policy Research rhetorically asked: 'How much unemployment was caused by Reinhart and Rogoff's arithmetic mistake?' Daniel Hamermesh, professor of economics at the University of London, doubts that jobs were lost directly because of the policy applications of the study: 'but it provides an intellectual rationalisation for things that affect how people think about the world. And how people think about the world, especially politicians, eventually affects how the world works.'[54]

How could two renowned scholars commit such basic mistakes and get away with it for so long? How could they publish with the NBER, the most prestigious economic think-tank in the world, which prides itself on having been home to twenty-two Nobel prizewinners, and have nobody notice the wrong averages? National and international newspapers, as well as institutions such as the IMF, where both economists had worked before joining academia, glorified the two economists' work. How come nobody had spotted such gross errors? Of course, this issue seriously questions the credibility of the so-called peer review process and makes us wonder how many other studies out there, which influence policies everyday, suffer from similar bias.

And this is not just a problem in the USA. In Europe, the social psychologist Diederik Stapel, author of widely cited papers published in prestigious journals such as *Science*, admitted in 2012 to having 'adapted research data and fabricated research', 'not once, but several times', 'not for a short period, but over a longer period of time'. Arguably his entire research career, which had influenced educational programmes and policies in the field of social stereotypes, was based on fake numbers. In his recent memoirs *Ontsporing* (*Derailed*), Stapel describes the process of manipulating datasets with powerful narrative verve:

> I preferred to do it at home, late in the evening, when everyone was asleep. I made myself some tea, put my computer on the table, took my notes from my bag, and used my fountain pen to write down a neat list of research projects and effects I had to produce.... Subsequently I began to enter my own data, row for row, column for column ... 3, 4, 6, 7, 8, 4, 5, 3, 5, 6, 7, 8, 5, 4, 3, 3, 2. When I was finished, I would do the first analyses. Often, these would not immediately produce the right results. Back to the matrix and alter data. 4, 6, 7, 5, 4, 7, 8, 2, 4, 4, 6, 5, 6, 7, 8, 5, 4. Just as long until all analyses worked out as planned.[55]

As Stapel candidly admitted to the inquiry committee set up by his university: 'I did not withstand the pressure to score, to publish, the pressure to get better in time.... In a system where there are few checks and balances, where people work alone, I took the wrong turn.'

Numbers, markets and democracy

In his book *Chartism*, the Scottish social commentator Thomas Carlyle wrote that a witty statesman 'might prove anything with figures'. We all know the notorious aphorism 'There are lies, damned lies and statistics.' In the words of Gigerenzer and colleagues, if our societies have come to believe that statistics can prove anything, 'that is because they are so often (mis)used to *prove* things'. And when experts claim too much, 'it is the political and social system that permits, even encourages their pretensions'.[56] The French philosopher Jacques Ellul once wrote that 'modern man needs a relation to facts', which is a 'self-justification to convince himself that by acting in a certain way, he is obeying reason and proved experience'. But he was not referring to science. His focus of analysis was the meaning and forms of propaganda. In Ellul's understanding the use of numbers was essential 'to create an irrational response on the basis of rational and factual elements'.[57]

In order to be part of the social debate, individuals and groups have to produce numbers. Without numbers, arguments are viewed as lacking credibility and based on purely anecdotal evidence. As maintained by Best, 'Numbers are created and repeated because they supply ammunition for political struggles, and this political purpose is often hidden behind assertions that numbers, simply because they are numbers, must be correct.'[58] The media further amplify the degree of manipulation in this regard. The media are in desperate need for easy storylines. They are striving to report 'facts', and crude numbers are powerful marketing tools, as they catch the eye, stir controversy and simplify the job of a journalist, who does not need to dissect opinions and nuances. As recognized by a lecturer at the Graduate School of Journalism of Columbia University, 'I was trained to believe only in what is observable and quantifiable ... Journalists feel most secure with the batting average, the stock price, the body count, the vote tally.'[59]

Charles Seife, author of *Proofiness: The Dark Arts of Mathematical Deception*, cites the example of evaluations systems produced by the Pentagon during the Vietnam War, which used sophisticated computers to feed the media with all sorts of statistics to show that America was winning the conflict in the

Southeast Asian nation. But, of course, it was not: 'This sort of information is the raw fuel of journalism. It is what gives journalists their voices; without hard facts to pin our words to, we are powerless to express ourselves.'[60] As soon as a certain number appears on news reports, it takes on a life of its own, and it goes through a process of 'number laundering'.[61] Its dubious origins are immediately forgotten and, through repetition, it comes to be treated as a straightforward fact, 'accurate and authoritative'. Soon the trail becomes muddy: 'People lose track of the estimate's original source, but they assume the number must be correct because it appears everywhere.'[62]

Just as the Pentagon produced its bogus statistics to feed the propaganda of conservative US media, which cited the body counts, numbers of weapons captured and the head counts of troops to 'paint a rosy picture of the war', anti-environmentalist lobbies have been producing studies and statistical models demonstrating all sorts of phony connections, from the better environmental performance of gas-guzzling SUVs as compared to hybrid cars to the non-existence of global warming. The application of statistical reasoning has often paved the way to a form of systematic denial, which has been fed – especially in the USA – by powerful interest groups. Counterintuitive as it may seem, the production of statistical 'lies' has been meant not to convince ideological enemies, but to provide an arsenal of numbers to allies. When, in 2007, a marketing research group published a study showing that the notorious gas-guzzling Hummer H3 was more energy-efficient than the Toyota Prius (they reached such a conclusion by using a model that attributed the Hummer a longer lifespan and mileage capacity than the Prius, thus reducing the overall environmental impact of the former), anti-green pundits and global warming sceptics got re-energized. The bogus evidence made it quickly into mainstream media and the *Washington Post* hosted op-eds by climate-change deniers, calling for people to

buy a Hummer and 'squash a Prius with it'. As historians Naomi
Oreskes and Erik M. Conway show in their analysis of the power
of contrarian science in the field of medical and environmental
research, the media have been a complacent supporter of phony
numbers, as journalists have come to consider statistics as a
source of incontestable evidence.[63] Given that reporers are trained
to represent a neutral viewpoint, the production of numbers has
become a powerful weapon in the hands of those interested in
spreading doubts and slowing down reform in some critical fields,
such as the application of the precautionary principle to health
and environmental regulations: 'No matter how ridiculous one
side of the argument is, no matter how dependent it might be
upon proofiness, the press dutifully broadcasts it and amplifies
it, giving manufactured "facts" a life of their own.'[64]

The intimate relationship between media and numbers is best
exemplified by news reports' obsession with stock market indexes.
Until the 1980s, only specialized media outlets provided dedicated
information about national and international markets and very few
of them made any reference to stock indexes. For instance, the
Dow Jones Industrial Average (more commonly known as Dow
Jones), which is arguably the world's best-known stock index, was
invented in 1896; although popular among investors throughout
the twentieth century and enjoying temporary notoriety during
the Great Depression, it only entered the popular imaginary in
the 1990s, when generalist newspapers and television began to
introduce stock market information in their regular publications
and broadcasts. Similarly, the Standard & Poor's 500, formally
established in the 1950s, only rose to global fame in the early
2000s. The Nasdaq Composite began to operate in 1971, but made
global headlines only in the late 1990s, with the dotcom bubble.
Ever since, these numbers (along with a variety of national and
regional indexes) have become protagonists of virtually every
nation's public debate. Each and every day, our media feed us

with matrices and time series based on averages and estimates of stock markets' activity. Pundits of all sorts provide commentaries, while numbers scroll in the background. Animated graphs and sophisticated tables give these figures an additional aura of importance. The media systematically convey the impression that stock indexes are a public good, indicators of the health of a nation's economy. When trading volumes are low, it is a bad day for the country. When they are high, the media celebrate. And this affects society as a whole: when the indexes rise, we cheer; when they shrink, we mourn. But what do stock indexes actually describe? Far from being a public good, these numbers simply describe subsets of private market transactions. They only include companies that are publicly traded in the stock market, which are essentially a small fraction of the global private sector. Moreover, only the largest of these companies (in terms of overall stock value, not in terms of capital or labour force) are covered by such indexes. The Dow Jones, for example, has only thirty stocks; although it represents roughly a quarter of the value of the total stock market, it systematically excludes small and mid-size companies. Yet it is presented as the principal market barometer in the USA. The S&P 500 does better in terms of overall coverage, but since it is a market capitalization weighted index, it privileges larger companies. Finally, the Nasdaq only focuses on technology stocks. The same can be said about all stock market statistics. As these indexes are used to capture the capital of investors, they attract money that could otherwise be invested in small companies and local economies. In many parts of the world, the real economy is likely to suffer from stock index euphoria. Rather than being signals of economic development, these numbers skew the markets by reinforcing big capital at the expense of small and medium enterprises.

None of these indexes is a real indicator of market dynamism, let alone an indicator of economic health. Yet the media frenzy has succeeded at integrating these statistics into our social psyche, thereby strengthening the political grip of financial capitalism. Weber himself connected the power of numbers with the hegemonic affirmation of the capitalist ideology. He defined the capitalist establishment as 'one with capital accounting, that is, an establishment which determines its income yielding power by calculation according to modern book-keeping and the striking of a balance'.[65] Moreover, the popularity of these numbers has affected our understanding of value. Stock market indexes do not measure the actual value of companies. They reflect the projected exchange value of stocks; that is, how much investors would be willing to pay to purchase shares. They grow during booms, when investors feel confident, and collapse during busts. As underlined by Joel Kurtzman, former editor of the *Harvard Business Review*, 'No longer do institutions buy stocks to hold because they believe in the underlying value of the company.' Much to the contrary, they trade in and out of stocks, keeping their holdings for decreasing periods of time, with 'the aid of a few mathematical formulas'.[66] As argued by international political economist Ronen Palan, 'the numbers that we take to represent stock evaluations, profits and wealth no longer stand for "real" tangible goods, the numbers measure "power" as pure relations.'[67] Yet, thanks to their own numerical assertiveness and the lack of critical analysis by the media, these indexes convey the false message that actual wealth is being created when numbers are on the rise. In turn, we feel rich when the markets are euphoric, and we feel suddenly poor when this 'fake' wealth evaporates. Thanks to these numbers, we have all become unconscious stakeholders of the market society.

Some numbers are particularly insidious as they are inherently subtle. They do not present themselves in conventional statistical formats. They do not emerge out of complicated formulae. They are so straightforward that we forget they are numbers, abstractions, inventions. Prices are the perfect case in point. We are surrounded by prices. Most of us view the world through price tags. We let them define our decisions. Whether it concerns a holiday destination, a school for our children or a visit to our parents, we use prices as the fundamental parameter driving our choices. Prices have become the most powerful indication of value. Things are worth what they cost, or what we are willing to pay for them. As Oscar Wilde famously noted in *The Picture of Dorian Gray*, 'Nowadays people know the price of everything and the value of nothing.'

Prices are pervasive not only in our daily lives, but also in the way in which macro-economic statistics function. For instance, the most powerful indicator of all times, the almighty gross domestic product (GDP), is nothing else than the sum of goods and services measured in terms of market prices. I have discussed the politics of GDP in my previous book *Gross Domestic Problem*. Here it suffices to say that GDP is 'gross' in so far as it does not include the depreciation of assets utilized in the production process (such as machineries, tools, vehicles, etc.). Whatever is exchanged outside the market (e.g. within households, in the informal economies, through barter, etc.) does not count. In addition, GDP disregards the value of the natural resources consumed in the process of economic growth, as these are obtained free of charge from nature. Moreover, it does not even consider the economic costs of pollution and environmental degradation, which are obvious consequences of industrial development. All these important omissions make GDP a very selective (some may rightly say myopic) measure of economic performance. Household services, for instance, have a fundamental economic impact even though they are not priced and exchanged in the market. If governments had to pay for the innumerable services rendered at the household level (from child and frail care to education), our economies would arguably grind to a halt. According to a recent study, which estimated the value of household production in the USA, the various productive activities carried out within homes accounted for over 30 per cent of economic output every year from 1965 to 2010 with a peak of 39 per cent in 1965, declining to 25.7 per cent in 2010.[68] In many countries, the 'odd jobs' and the goods and services exchanged informally provide the necessary subsistence to millions of people and often constitute the backbone of the real economy, although they do not feature in GDP. Similarly, disregarding the input of natural resources just because they are not priced by nature makes us forget that economic growth is only possible because of a continuous provision of 'capital' from our ecosystems. Agricultural production would not be attainable without clean soil, water, air and other essential natural processes. Industrialization would have not been achieved without the fossil fuels, hydrocarbons and energy sources made available by the planet. When these resources are depleted, however, we risk endangering not only economic progress, but also the very natural equilibrium that makes life possible. Accounting 101 tells us that profit equals income minus 'all' costs. As GDP systematically disregards key sectors in the economy and neglects critical costs, no reasonable businessman would use it to run a company. Yet it has become the key parameter to run entire societies. As mentioned in an article published by the *OECD Observer*,

> If ever there was a controversial icon from the statistics world, GDP is it. It measures income, but not equality, it measures growth, but not destruction, and it ignores values like social cohesion and the environment. Yet, governments, businesses and probably most people swear by it.[69]

The application of pricing mechanisms to design public policy has a long history, which dates back to the development of modern engineering in Europe and in the USA, as the building of infrastructure required numerical assessment tools with a direct bearing on tax collection. Quantitative public management became a rather common practice in the second half of the 1800s, especially in the pricing of public works, to assign tenders, and for the calculation of tolls citizens had to pay to use bridges and railroads. For instance, the French engineer Jules Dupuit was among the first to introduce concepts such as diminishing marginal utility in the calculation of fares for rail travel. Dupuit believed the certainty of mathematical reasoning to be essential for good political economic analysis. The proper role of the lawmaker, he explained, is to 'consecrate those facts demonstrated by political economy'.[70]

Friedrich August von Hayek, the forefather of free-market economics, was the first to develop a comprehensive theory of prices as indicators – that is, signals of information. As he wrote in 'The Use of Knowledge in Society', an influential article published in the *American Economic Review* in 1945, the price system is 'as a kind of machinery for registering change, or a system of telecommunications which enables individual producers to watch merely the movement of a few pointers, as an engineer might watch the hands of a few dials'.[71] According to Hayek, society is 'a system in which the knowledge of the relevant facts is dispersed among many people'. And in this kaleidoscope of partial information, 'prices can act to coordinate the separate actions of different people in the same way as subjective values help the individual to coordinate the parts of his plan.' Yet, despite his enthusiasm for the communicative power of prices, Hayek recognized that a price is just 'a numerical index which cannot be derived from any property possessed by that particular thing, but which reflects, or in which is condensed, its significance in view of the whole means–end structure.'

Following Hayek's definition of prices as information signals, economists Fischer Black, Myron Scholes and Robert Merton developed sophisticated formulae to predict prices in all sorts of financial interactions, particularly in the derivative markets. The Black–Scholes–Merton model, which earned its creators a Nobel Prize in 1997, soon became the be all and end all of pricing methods in global finance. As the world economy grew increasingly financialized, prices became perfect substitutes for values and financial markets were turned into the elective space for the allocation of resources, thus affecting our governance model and the way in which society assesses wealth.

That is, until September 2008, when the world of perfect pricing collapsed. As recognized by former chairman of the Federal Reserve Alan Greenspan in a notorious hearing at the House Committee of Oversight and Reform, 'A Nobel Prize was awarded for the discovery of the pricing model that underpins much of the advance in derivatives markets. This modern risk management paradigm held sway for decades. The whole intellectual edifice, however, collapsed.'[72] And that was just the beginning of a global financial crisis that has since spanned the world and turned into the most devastating recession since the Great Depression. Yet the grip of prices on our societies is unchallenged by the economic chaos produced by the financial world and, more than ever, the power of numbers has been reinforcing markets in an age of crisis.

Prices are indexes. They are aggregate parameters defined by the encounter of supply and demand, in a context of scarce resources. In theory, prices should by and large correspond to the marginal utility that goods and services bring to individual consumers. Actually, in most real economies, prices are not at all (or only partly) constituted by the preferences and priorities of consumers. In general, prices are easily affected by dynamics that are external to the virtuous match of supply and demand, which include taxation, subsidies, lobbying, cartels, monopolies, not to speak of political allegiances that can afford certain industries preferential treatments not available to other competitors. As prices (and money) depend on credit, the discount rates of financiers, investors, bankers and insurers largely determine what things are worth. Our economies are, more than ever, determined by the preferences of a few.

Prices and markets go hand in hand, as the former are indicators of an exchange value. What has a price tag on can – by definition – be bought and sold. So, the pervasiveness of prices has resulted in the growth of markets well beyond the conventional boundaries traditionally associated with profit-based interaction.[73] We now have carbon prices and their relative emission markets. We have financial models applied to the nonprofit sector. We have offset markets and prices for biodiversity, carbon emission and forestation. We value human life based on the rates provided by insurance policies. Economic concepts such as cost–benefit, willingness to pay, replacement costs and return on investment are dominating our governance models, both locally – where most of our public institutions have adopted managerial formulas borrowed from business – and globally – where market-based mechanisms have been introduced to deal with issues such as climate change and environmental degradation. Some recent research has also shown how principles of numerical organization – that is, the representation of wealth through the synthesis of numbers – facilitate the movement of capital in the offshore economy, thus reinforcing global divides between the super-rich and the rest, as well as undermining the capacity of states to sustain their welfare systems.[74]

In 2004, while president of Harvard, the economist Larry Summers celebrated the triumph of numbers in society. He commended Moneyball for having become the most predictive model of success in baseball and maintained that 'what's true of baseball is actually true of a much wider range of human activity than has been the case before':

In the last 30 years, the field of investment banking has been transformed from a field that was dominated by people who were good at meeting clients at the 19th hole, to people who were good at solving very difficult mathematical problems that were involved in pricing derivative securities. The field of environmental regulation has substantially given way in its actual application from people who were committed activists and attorneys to people who were skilled in performing cost–benefit analyses. The presidential campaigns that at one time put out the call for a group of bright lawyers to staff them, now put out the call for bright economists and bright MBAs to staff them. And I could go on and on with these examples, suggesting that the kind of analytical techniques that come out of social science are finding more and more widespread application.[75]

The global market 'turn' has been strengthened by the un-fettered trust in numbers. As is the case with Adam Smith's invisible hand – that is, the founding hypothesis of market efficiency at allocating resources and resolving complex distributional issues – there is nowadays a generalized 'belief that numbers will finally start to work 'automatically', by themselves, so to speak'.[76] But numbers do very little on their own. They hide conflicts, do not solve them. They conceal politics and oppression by masking them with a cloak of inevitability. There is no doubt that numbers are important tools for the progress of knowledge and the improvement of governance. At the same time, they can be powerful instruments in the hands of those who would like to preserve the status quo.

CHAPTER 2

New global rulers:
the untameable power of credit rating

There are two superpowers in the world today in my opinion. There's the United States and there's Moody's Bond Rating Service. The United States can destroy you by dropping bombs, and Moody's can destroy you by downgrading your bonds. And believe me, it's not clear sometimes who's more powerful.

Thomas Friedman[1]

When S&P or Moody's speak, that's not the voice of 'the market'. It's just some guys with an agenda, and a very poor track record. And we have no idea how much effect their actions will have.

Paul Krugman[2]

Credit ratings are among the most powerful numbers in global affairs. Their reach knows virtually no limit. Corporations, banks, insurance companies and even sovereign states need ratings to operate. Although they are usually expressed through alphanumerical characters, ratings are no different from any other measurement, indicator or index. In many regards, in fact, ratings are the most distinctive example of the global power of numbers. Moreover, since the outbreak of the global financial crisis, ratings sit at the intersection of a kaleidoscope of forces determining the politics of statistics. Indeed, there is no other field in which the conflicts of interest, the power of technocrats and the influence of markets are so evident. Think of this. Five days before the bankruptcy of the energy giant Enron in 2001, the major credit rating agencies considered its bonds to be 'investment grade'.[3] Three days before the bankruptcy of the investment bank Lehman Brothers in 2008, its bonds were given the highest possible grade by the major agencies. Even on the morning of its collapse, credit analysts thought Lehman Brothers to be worth a good investment.[4] The insurance giants American International Group and Washington Mutual held prime ratings until the moment they collapsed, triggering massive public bailouts. A report by the US Congress found that rating agencies had no incentive 'to assign tougher credit ratings to the very securities that for a short while increased their revenues, boosted their stock prices, and expanded their executive compensation'.[5]

In January 2011, the Financial Crisis Inquiry Commission appointed by the American government reported that the leading credit rating agencies were 'essential cogs in the wheel of financial destruction':

> the mortgage-related securities at the heart of the crisis could not have been marketed and sold without their seal of approval. Investors relied on them, often blindly. In some cases, they were obligated to use them, or regulatory capital standards were hinged on them. This crisis could not have happened without the rating agencies. Their ratings helped the market soar and their downgrades through 2007 and 2008 wreaked havoc across markets and firms.[6]

Funnily enough, though, rating agencies had warned against the inaccuracy of their assessments: 'Any user of the information contained herein should not rely on any credit rating or other opinion contained herein in making any investment decision', reads the disclaimer at the bottom of all reports published by the largest agency in the world.[7]

But what is a credit rating agency? It is a 'company that assesses the debt instruments (bonds and other securities) issued by firms or governments and assigns "credit ratings" to these instruments based on the likelihood that the debt will be repaid.'[8] These organizations rate the creditworthiness of debt issuers and evaluate the investment risk – that is, the likelihood of default or repayment irregularities. They publish regular reports assigning bonds a set of grades, from AAA (prime grade) to D (in default), which provide comparable risk estimates in order to overcome problems of information in financial markets. As companies (that is, the borrowers) always possess better information about their own financial profile than any external investor (that is, the lender), rating agencies try to bridge this 'asymmetry' by looking at the nuts and bolts of a borrowing institution and producing an assessment of its financial credibility. The level of risk determines the interest rate for the investment and, consequently, the cost of debt and the debtor's access to new investments. Moreover, ratings determine the eligibility of debt for the portfolios of certain institutional investors, due to national regulations that restrict investment in speculative bonds. Likewise, regulators use credit ratings to ascertain the strength of the reserves held by insurance companies.

As a result, these agencies have an enormous influence on global capital flows and, inevitably, on global governance. Nowadays, three big agencies (the so-called Big Three), Standard & Poor's, Moody's Investor Service and Fitch Ratings, control over 95 per cent of the global rating market. At the moment of the collapse of Wall Street, Standard & Poor's (S&P) controlled roughly 40 per cent of the market, Moody's about 39 per cent and Fitch another 16 per cent.[9] As the last is mostly working in specialized markets, Moody's and S&P effectively form a duopoly in the global rating sector.[10] Such a skewed distribution of market access makes it virtually impossible for any large company or government interested in attracting foreign investment to operate without these agencies' stamp of approval. Rating agencies are a powerful example of what political scientist Colin Crouch has termed 'giant firms': they are both multinational – with branches all over the world – and their numbers exert market dominance. Given the lack of regulation at the global level, these firms are in a position to set their own standards and thereby determine regulation in the global economy.[11]

Rating agencies are 'odd beasts' in global governance: they are private firms with public purposes – 'hence the term credit rating *agencies*, not credit rating *firms*' – but they are fully private in terms of ownership, employees and revenues.[12] Some authors see the regulatory role of rating agencies as a clear instance of the ongoing 'privatization of world politics'.[13] The private governance function of these companies can thus be interpreted as an indication of the long-term shift in the locus of authority, especially within the realm of the global economy: private actors have become the 'real players' while the authority of states continuously declines and their autonomy weakens.[14] For some, rating agencies should be 'more properly viewed as quasi-government entities'.[15] For others, rating processes have generated a system of 'governance without government',[16] making these powerful producers of numbers 'de facto private makers of global public policy'.[17] No matter what specific view one endorses, it is clear that their power curtails the capacity of states and other public authorities to support public policy interventions not in line with market diktats.[18] This chapter traces the history of ratings and how these numbers became an all-powerful weapon in contemporary global politics.

Credit rating agencies:
from market analysts to oligopolists

Credit rating agencies (CRAs) have not always been as influential as they are today. In order to understand their privileged position, it is necessary to look at the evolution of the global financial architecture over more than a century.[19] Their story begins at the crossroads of the nineteenth and twentieth centuries in America, when US corporations grew in number and size, especially those building long-distance railroads. While previously funded through local savings, the scale of industrial development soon required an increasing amount of capital, which could no longer originate exclusively within the circles of local investors. Other, more distant markets needed to be tapped into. But, of course, these new investors did not have first-hand knowledge of what they were investing in and, before putting their money into any new venture, they demanded some form of third-party assessment of the risks associated with their investment. It was because of this growing demand – on the one hand, investors interested in buying bonds with a greater degree of certainty and, on the other, companies aiming to enlarge the spectrum of their potential funders – that credit agents found their niche.[20] The financial analyst Henry Varnum Poor was among the first to cater systematically to this growing hunger for more precise analysis of the type of industrial development under way. In 1868, his *Manual of the Railroads of the United States* provided the first systematic account of the sector: 'their mileage, stocks, bonds, costs, earnings, expenses, and organizations; with a sketch of their rise, progress and influence'.[21]

During the early years of operation, CRAs concentrated on rating companies operating in the field of railroad, tracks and rolling stock. They assessed debt instruments, such as bonds and securities, issued by firms and assigned 'ratings' based on the likelihood of debt repayment. These publications were sold to investors, thus making credit rating originally a relationship between the agencies and the investors' community.

CRAs have played a major part in the US financial system since 1900, when the analyst John Moody published his first market assessment, titled *Moody's Manual of Industrial and Miscellaneous Securities*, and established John Moody & Company, the first rating agency.[22] For a few decades, ratings were nothing more than private assessments, no different from any other form of consultancy provided to investors. Born out of a need in the burgeoning industrial world of the late nineteenth century, the power of credit agencies increased with the shift affecting the financial industry in the interwar period, especially the banking sector. Traditionally, banks had been the primary source of funding for firms and corporations. They were the link between lenders (mostly private savings, i.e. deposits) and borrowers. Credit defaults (and the risk thereof) were shouldered by them and usually did not affect depositors. Therefore banks 'acted as hybrid institutions of collective action, between the state and the market', controlling the risk and reducing 'the uncertainties for the political authorities, as well as for borrowers and lenders'.[23] Yet the increased downward pressure on capital costs experienced during and after the Great Depression incentivized direct market participation for banks (in form of financial and investment products) and eventually decreased their role as mediators between lenders and borrowers. As a result, such 'disintermediation' transformed banks from agents of self-regulation to market participants. The decentralization of capital allocation (away from banks), directly connecting borrowers and lenders, accentuated the problem of asymmetrical information in the market and thereby strengthened the role of rating agencies.[24]

In 1936, the Office of the Comptroller of the Currency institutionalized ratings by mandating that banks must hold bonds rated at least low-to-medium risk. This regulation was introduced to keep banks from engaging in 'speculative investments' with public money, but had the indirect effect of giving CRAs power over banks' bond holdings by assigning to their ratings the 'force of law'.[25] Four agencies were given this quasi-institutional role: Standard Statistics Bureau, H.V. and H.W. Poor & Co. (these would later merge to become S&P), John Moody and Company, and the Fitch Publishing Company.

This position was further entrenched in 1975 when the Securities and Exchange Commission (SEC),[26] the institution tasked with overseeing financial markets in the USA, mandated that brokers honour their capital requirements with highly rated assets.[27] Since the SEC was concerned that unaccredited agencies might inflate the market of ratings, they came up with the concept of 'nationally recognized statistical rating organization' (NRSRO) and granted this status to the three largest agencies, the so-called Big Three: Moody's, S&P and Fitch Ratings. From then on, only their ratings would be acceptable for public regulation purposes. Other financial regulators followed suit, so that 'these three firms' judgments of bonds' safety came to be *official* determinants of the bond portfolios of most major American financial institutions.'[28]

In theory, CRAs should enhance the efficiency of financial intermediation by redressing the informational asymmetry between lenders and borrowers.[29] Economists like describing this issue in terms of principals and agents – that is, those investing the money and those tasked with making the investment bear fruit.[30] In this view, rating agencies are described as 'neutral' institutions, which gather and provide information in an objective and technical way to market participants. This view also mirrors the preferred self-image of the rating agencies themselves. For instance, according to the Securities Industry and Financial Markets Association, a group of investment bankers, a credit rating agency 'objectively analyzes the credit worthiness of a company or security'.[31]

For the first few decades of their existence, CRAs earned their money by rating bond-issuing corporations and charging subscription fees to investors.[32] By and large, this made agencies accountable and transparent to the investment community. Such a state of affairs changed in the 1970s, mainly because of a series of developments in the international political economy. With the collapse of the Bretton Woods system and the ensuing global liberalization of financial capital markets, the demand for credit ratings grew exponentially, as these helped investors assess and compare the creditworthiness and associated risks of financial instruments in the global market. Consequently, CRAs enlarged their portfolios from the assessment of corporations to the rating of a wide range of financial products, which would soon become their main source of revenue. Unlike the evaluation of flesh-and-blood industries (which is often referred to as the 'real economy'), the study of the financial industry required a significant level of abstraction that increased the complexity of ratings and made methodologies less intuitive and open to scrutiny. In the meantime, as it had become increasingly hard to prevent investors from sharing ratings (which threatened the capacity of CRAs to sell them as copyrighted material), the agencies' business model took a fundamental U-turn, moving away from subscription fees to rating fees. In this new arrangement, rated corporations began to pay for the CRAs' assessment, while investors got reports for free.

Needless to say, the new business model triggered conflicts of interest at all levels. With corporations paying for their own ratings, CRAs had an incentive to give inflated assessments in order to satisfy and keep their customers. In theory, the issuer-pays model should have its fail-safes: as CRAs compete for reputation in the investment community, they should refrain from giving inflated grades that would then result in a weakening of their credibility. Yes, in theory. In fact, the oligopolistic distribution of power in the field, with the overarching dominance of only three agencies, has ever since reduced the degree of competition and, by contrast, has encouraged common strategies and cartels. Although there are now several NRSROs in the USA, assessing millions of debt issues, only the Big Three have the power to unbalance markets and states. The lack of competition in this sector is accompanied by high barriers to entry and is demonstrated by the oligopolists' high profit margins. Before the financial meltdown, between 2005 and 2007 S&P operating profit rose by 73 per cent compared to the three-year period ending in 2004.[33] Investigations into their rating practices of the past few decades – prior to the 2008 housing bust – have revealed that factors such as 'the drive for market share, pressure from investment banks to inflate ratings, inaccurate rating models, and inadequate rating and surveillance resources' have resulted in deficient and questionable ratings.[34]

Behind the numbers: a shady business

One question strikes to the core of the CRAs' work: what is the risk that investors will not get their money back (plus their promised interest) when investing in a bond or other type of obligation? As risk managers, CRAs come up with apparently sophisticated systems to turn 'risk' into a measurable output. They look at the assets' characteristics and quality.[35] They conduct interviews with informants, insiders and other so-called experts. After an initial assessment, they inform the issuer of a tentative rating, providing the latter with an opportunity to appeal. Although rating scales vary across CRAs, they follow a very similar model based on alphanumeric symbols. The Big Three use AAA to indicate prime-grade investments. Investments above BBB (or Baa for Moody's) are considered 'investment grade'. The closer to C, the more speculative the ratings become. For S&P and Fitch, D is default. Although they take the form of letter symbols, these ratings are scores assigned by analysts, whose methodology is not open to scrutiny. After the rating is issued, the agency monitors the rated bonds, potentially upgrading or downgrading them, or putting them on a 'watch list'. As regulations oblige issuers to write lengthy prospectuses outlining their portfolios, many investors simply rely on the CRAs' ratings as a 'Good Housekeeping Seal of Approval'.[36] The power of brevity, exemplified by the CRAs' scores, prevails over the complexity of financial analyses. Markets use ratings as a guide for investment, resulting in the fact that the credit rating alone is often considered enough to decide to buy or sell bonds.

CRAs guide and shape investors' decisions, thus creating an institutional framework that steers market behaviour. As is often the case with numbers in governance, most investors trust the ratings 'with a surrendering of individual judgment', and believe in their authority 'based not on the merits of any particular pronouncement, but on a belief in the rightness of the authority itself'.[37] CRAs shield themselves behind the reputational argument. For example, S&P claims that 'reputation is more important than revenues'.[38] Moody's once stated that 'we are in a business where reputational capital is more important' and that 'what's driving us is primarily the issue of preserving our track record. That's our bread and butter.'[39] Yet, some critics have argued that 'the reputation argument only works when a large fraction of the CRA income comes from other sources than rating complex products', which is no longer the case.[40] Others have maintained that, as ratings do not look at other noteworthy aspects such as liquidity or price volatility, they are not designed to comprehensively guide investment decisions.[41]

It could also be claimed that rating agencies merely follow markets that have already identified problematic debtors. Several empirical studies have concluded 'that ratings have little or no informational value added compared to market signals'.[42] Markets appear to move slowly when a sovereign debt rises, but can also at times act rapidly – and imprudently. Consequently, the rating system simply relies on the 'trust in the trust' that others will also use the agencies' assessments to guide their decisions, which is why snowball effects occur so frequently.[43]

As early as 1985, the sociologist Harrison White argued that, due to rising specialization in the financial industry, there is a tendency towards control reversal: 'the principal comes under the control of the agent after the latter becomes a specialized purveyor'.[44] The core problem is that CRAs interfere with the assumed rational, atomistic and therefore independent choices of capital allocation made in a decentralized market. CRAs have the power to shift capital flows, transcending the 'atomistic cognitive behavior of the single transaction'.[45] As a result, ratings can easily become self-fulfilling prophecies, as CRAs strongly influence the choices of millions of small and large investors.[46] In addition, such ratings are frequently pro-cyclical and therefore reinforce business cycles artificially.[47] Due to their size and market power, CRAs can distort the credit market in ways that exceed their role as information providers.

Complicating matters, agencies claim that their ratings are opinions. CRAs under threat from prosecution in the USA have repeatedly invoked the constitutional First Amendment and charges against them have been dropped on the grounds that ratings are protected as freedom of speech and expression.[48] Rating agencies like to compare themselves to publishing companies and financial journalists who are merely issuing opinions.[49] As a result, the treatment of rating agencies has been paradoxical: regulatory standards are predicated on credit ratings, but there has been little direct oversight of how the ratings are made.[50] As underlined by a discussion paper of the UN Conference on Trade and Development (UNCTAD), rating agencies 'provide little guidance as to how they assign relative weights to each factor'.[51] It is also quite difficult to establish clear connections between the general criteria they use and the actual ratings. The 'opinion' enjoyed by the ratings has largely exempted CRAs from satisfying minimum transparency and accountability requirements applied to traditional forms of investment advice, which 'has helped shield rating agencies from private litigation for inaccurate or misleading statements'.[52] Moreover, 'Investors have not historically invested large resources in improving rating agencies' behaviour perhaps because there was insufficient transparency on the way CRAs operated to facilitate this.'[53]

The major CRAs make their profits by payment from the private issuers that they assess, which provides them with a powerful incentive to give out good ratings as this ensures the issuer will return to them the next time, instead of looking for another agency.[54] As a general practice, investment banks have 'shopped around' for the best ratings and sometimes even played 'one rating agency against another when informally consulting them to achieve high ratings'.[55] In essence, CRAs purport to achieve two main objectives, which are very often mutually exclusive: maximizing profit and objectively gauging the performance of their clients, who in turn determine the agencies' profits. This creates a bias, making the main goal of objectivity much harder to achieve. As revealed by W.J. Harrington, a former senior analyst at Moody's, top managers are ultimately in control. They would say to the analysts: 'Time's up, let's convene in a committee and we'll all vote "yes".' Issues brought up by analysts would be dismissed or simply parked, saying 'Let's make a note of that' or 'I am glad you're raising it', but nothing would happen.[56]

Because of the payment structure, the issuers of debt (as the client) can exercise significant influence on the agency (as the service provider). In a survey of 1,956 investment professionals carried out by the CFA Institute in 2008, 11 per cent said 'they had seen a credit rating agency change a bond grade in response to pressure from an issuer, underwriter or investor'.[57] Roughly half these respondents maintained that the pressure took the form of a threat 'to take future ratings business to other' rating agencies. The CFA survey went further to reveal that many respondents felt the most harmful conflict of interest results 'from the payment structure' under which rating agencies operate. Obviously, debt-issuing organizations have an interest in achieving the highest possible rating. As they pay for their assessments, they have the upper hand. It thus comes as no surprise that all the major CRAs gave Enron their highest ratings before the company filed for bankruptcy in 2001. As Enron's top management feared that lower ratings would jeopardize its imminent takeover by the energy company Dynergy, it pressed for a good assessment, and the CRAs seemingly cooperated.[58] When, in 2004, the food multinational Parmalat's collapse revealed that the company had 'cooked the books' with the support of some financial advisers and the collusion of rating agents, the EU called for more stringent rules.[59] The European Commission and the European Central Bank set out to report on ratings agencies' conflicts of interest over advising institutions on how to package debt, while also awarding them AAA ratings, as well as on their failure to alert investors to dangers in the subprime mortgage market.[60] Most of these plans, however, fell by the wayside, as they were deemed unnecessary by the Committee for European Banking Supervisors.[61]

Commenting on the methodologies adopted by most CRAs, some insiders have confirmed that the assessment process surpasses simple review and evaluation, and often takes more 'personal' twists. It seems to be common practice for reviewers to meet with their clients to discuss options for maintaining a certain rating or even upgrading it. As recalled by a former president of the Federal Home Loan Bank in Chicago (a bank traditionally awarded a AAA rating by both Moody's and S&P), visits from the representatives of rating agencies were a common routine. 'They'd say, "Here's what it's going to cost." I'd say, "That's outrageous."

They'd repeat, "This is what it's going to cost." Finally, I'd say, "OK." With no ratings, you can't sell your debt.[62] Some CRAs were also accused of blackmailing their clients with the threat of an immediate downgrade should they switch providers.[63] In 2007, at the Hearing of the US Senate Permanent Subcommittee on Investigations, an anonymous managing director of Moody's Investors Services rhetorically asked,

> [W]hy didn't we envision that credit would tighten after being loose, and housing prices would fall after rising? After all most economic events are cyclical and bubbles inevitably burst. Combined, these errors make us look either incompetent at credit analysis, or like we sold our soul to the devil for revenue, or a little bit of both.[64]

The politics of ratings and the global financial crisis

The range of products analysed by CRAs has grown along with the diversification of financial markets, expanding from commercial bonds to companies as a whole, to sovereign debt and finally to the myriad new debt instruments introduced in the past decades, most notably securitizations, including the infamous collateralized debt obligations (CDOs) and credit default swaps (CDS).[65] CRAs reaped a bonanza in fees from the late 1990s on, as they worked with financial firms to manufacture CDOs based on subprime mortgages. Ever since, S&P, Moody's and Fitch have been winning up to three times as much in fees for grading these securities as they charge for rating ordinary bonds.[66]

Also, with the increasing integration and globalization of financial markets, what was formerly a US phenomenon became a global standard. Since the 1990s, CRAs have penetrated international markets virtually everywhere. CRAs' offices have mushroomed across Europe and Asia. Obtaining a rating from any (or both) of the two dominating firms, S&P and Moody's, is by now deemed indispensable by debt issuers all over the world, especially in less industrialized countries.[67] In Latin America, after the 1980s debt crisis, the growing bond market drove up the demand for sovereign credit ratings.[68] Being issued by developing economies, these obligations carried a certain risk but also high returns, which propped up the need for third-party information about these countries' financial credibility. In April 2002, the then secretary of state Colin Powell announced that the US government was planning to help African countries obtain sovereign ratings, as this would help economic growth by giving 'courage to capital'.[69] Just a month later, the United Nations Development Programme (UNDP) launched a partnership with S&P to support the introduction of systematic sovereign credit ratings throughout Africa. In 2003, it hosted the first African Capital Markets Development Forum in cooperation with the New York Stock Exchange and the African Stock Exchanges Association.[70] While originally sovereign issuers (that is, states) did seek ratings to contemplate debt issuance, over time the attribution of high ratings became a matter of international status. It helped governments profile themselves globally as transparent and accountable investment partners. Through ratings, countries around the world strived to 'gain "stamps of approval" from international capital markets'.[71]

CRAs do not derive their current influence solely from the trust of market participants. States, too, have actively advanced and institutionalized them by integrating ratings into financial regulations. According to some observers, rating agencies 'are granted reference status both by widespread market practice and by public regulation'.[72] By deflecting their own due diligence responsibilities in the regulation of global financial markets, public authorities have for the most part referred to the judgement of private CRAs to determine the eligibility of collateral for central banks and assess the investment decisions of public and sovereign wealth funds.[73] As early as the 1930s, US pension funds were only allowed to hold assets in proportion to their relative ratings; since then, whenever a quality assessment of debt is needed, US financial regulators have resorted to the evaluations of the CRAs.[74] Across the American economy, credit ratings have been used to increase the risk sensitivity of investment restrictions for certain financial institutions (e.g. banks and insurance companies), to define differential disclosure requirements for issuers of rated bonds, and to adjust capital reserve requirements for commercial and investment banks.[75] In the European Union, a similar trend was encouraged by the 1993 Capital Adequacy Directive, which specified that companies must set aside more capital for their non-investment grade holding. Specifically, the Directive established that the default risk associated with financial instruments traded within the EU must be evaluated 'by at least two credit-rating agencies recognized by the competent authorities', or alternatively 'by only one such credit-rating agency' so long as they are not rated below investment grade by other agencies.[76] Given the strong cartel tendencies of the major CRAs, it comes as no surprise that ratings were generally in line with the authorities' requirements.

The influence of rating organizations has been further under-pinned by the Basel Accords, a series of inter-banking regulations set out by central bank governors outlining requirements and recommendations for the banking industry. In particular, the Basel II accord (established in 2004) created an international standard to control how much capital banks need to put aside to guard against various types of financial and operational risks. Originally designed to protect the international financial system from the cascading effect of major banks' collapse, it generated a distorted system of control and assessment by ultimately giving CRAs the power to determine banks' net capital reserve require-ments; that is, how much capital a bank must set aside in reserves against potential losses.[77]

Nowadays, issuers are legally obliged to seek a rating in order to sell their bonds and get access to international capital markets, which makes credit ratings extremely valuable to them not because of the information they possess, but rather because they grant a regulatory licence of sorts. According to the financial news agency Bloomberg, the reach of CRAs 'extends into virtually every corner of the financial system. Everyone from banks to the agencies that regulate them is hooked on ratings.'[78]

The use of CRAs' assessments in financial market regulation thereby effectively becomes the abdication of regulatory authority to a privately controlled oligopoly for the provision of an information public good. Their informal status as de facto regulators, bestowed by governments in order to avoid what free-market economists viewed as 'messy regulation' and 'costly oversight', has morphed into an instance of gross public negligence. As a consequence, the resulting regulatory failure by national and supranational authorities has exacerbated the continuous failure of markets, which is now amplified by the global integration of banking systems. This set of policies has resulted in CRAs becoming much more than the original intermediaries purported to facilitate the exchange of information and decrease transaction costs. As states have 'outsourced many regulatory functions to rating agencies', the latter have become the most powerful market gatekeepers in the world.[79]

Some attempts at reforming the sector were put in place both in the USA and in Europe, but little change occurred in terms of regulatory and market access practice. In 2006, the US administration passed the Credit Rating Agency Reform Act, which made the SEC responsible for oversight in the sector.[80] The same year, the EU revised its directive on capital adequacy by reframing the role of credit agencies, while confirming the obligation of investment firms to trade in highly rated products.[81] Furthermore, the European Securities and Markets Authority was entrusted with launching investigations, conducting inspections, proposing fines and prohibiting operations. Throughout the world, CRAs are also subject to the 2004 Code of Conduct Fundamentals for Credit Rating Agencies adopted by the International Organization of Securities Commissions. Yet adherence is voluntary, which safeguards 'the independence of CRAs or their ability to issue timely ratings opinions'.[82]

That the Big Three had retained all their power and influence in spite of public authorities' efforts at reforming the sector became all the more evident with the eruption of the financial crisis in 2008 and the ensuing sovereign debt crisis in both the US and Europe. Because of their lag in modifying ratings following legislation developments and the 'abruptness of unexpected downgrades' of state bonds, CRAs were able to throw markets out of balance and fundamentally affect the public finances of the world's major economies.[83] In 2011, S&P took the unprecedented step of 'removing the United States government from its list of risk-free borrowers', a downgrade that elicited the indignation of the Obama administration.[84] The US government attacked the agency, arguing that 'the company had made a significant mathematical mistake' and, in cooperation with the SEC, launched an investigation on the S&P's 'overwhelmingly positive ratings of mortgage-backed securities during the housing boom'.[85] State investigators also looked at cases in which the company's analysts wanted to award lower ratings on mortgage bonds but were overruled by their managers. For the SEC, rating agencies 'just abjectly failed in serving the interests of investors'.[86] In 2013, the Department of Justice filed civil fraud charges against S&P, 'accusing the firm of inflating the ratings of mortgage investments and setting them up for a crash when the financial crisis struck'.[87]

The historic US downgrade was not based just on purely financial assessments, but rather on a general evaluation of

Washington's political strategy, a type of assessment that one would not expect from financial analysts. In their justification for the downgrade, S&P's analysts wrote:

> More broadly, the downgrade reflects our view that the effectiveness, stability, and predictability of American policymaking and political institutions have weakened at a time of ongoing fiscal and economic challenges.[88]

So governments had not only given ratings 'the force of law', but also a say over nations' political strategies. In Europe, the Big Three set out to downgrade countries such as Greece, Ireland and Portugal to 'junk status' in spite of the several bailout plans put forward by European authorities throughout 2010 and 2011. A heated debate erupted in the EU, championed by Michel Barnier, the commissioner for internal markets and services, who lashed out at CRAs, arguing that '[w]e need to rebuild our political sovereignty so we're not subject to the sovereignty of the markets'.[89] Also former German chancellor Helmut Schmidt maintained that '[s]ome rating agencies have taken the politically liable governments in Europe hostage'.[90]

In order to rein in the power of CRAs, a number of proposals were laid out by the European Commission, including the need for financial firms to rotate the agencies they use every three years, for analysts to step down from an account after four years, and for agencies to be prevented from rating products or institutions where their shareholders have a financial interest. Moreover, it was decided that sovereign downgrades would need to be notified to governments at least twenty-four hours before they are made public (as opposed to twelve hours, as was previously the case) and could only be issued after markets closed.[91] As it was felt that repeated downgrades revealed an 'excessive speculation by the U.S. agencies over European debt', some went so far as to propose the constitution of a Europe-based credit rating agency.[92]

Even the chairman of the European Commission, José Manuel Barroso, took issue with the rating agencies:

> It is quite strange that the market is dominated by only three players and not a single agency is coming from Europe. It shows there may be some bias in the market when it comes to evaluation of issues in Europe, that Europeans know better than others.[93]

When in October 2011 Moody's downgraded Italy for the first time in over two decades, it legitimized its decision by arguing that fiscal consolidation remained 'vulnerable to the high level of uncertainty around economic growth in Italy and elsewhere in the EU'.[94] Within a few weeks the Italian government was forced to its knees. The then prime minister Silvio Berlusconi, whose grip on power had endured civil society protests, strikes and a number of judicial processes for corruption and prostitution over a period of seventeen years, had to bend to the authority of rating agencies and resigned. On 13 January 2012 (soon dubbed the Eurozone's 'black Friday'), S&P downgraded nine European countries, stripping nations such as France and Austria of their coveted AAA rating.[95] Public institutions in Europe tried to prosecute CRAs on several grounds, including accusations of manipulation directed against S&P former president Deven Sharma.[96] As the Euro-crisis deepened a draft European Commission paper on rating regulation suggested that CRAs should be forbidden from issuing downgrades of sovereign debt in cases of financial distress.

Such attempts at altering the position of CRAs were met with hostility by the industry. In the USA, ratings agencies refused to give ratings to bond issuers, effectively halting their issuance. The situation was fixed in the short term with the SEC waiving the rating requirement for the time being. In Europe, the Big Three responded by placing all countries of the Eurozone on negative credit watch, spooking investors and adding further tensions to an already fraught situation. Then, in July 2012, Moody's directly targeted Europe's powerhouse, Germany, shifting its outlook from positive to negative.[97]

Policymakers were finally realizing that, due to negligent regulations put in place by governments and central banks, CRAs had become deeply hard-wired into banking and financial market regulations. Governments had made themselves unable to act when successive rating adjustments triggered a cascade of second-order write-offs throughout nations and continents. On the one hand, CRAs' increasing capacity to affect national and supranational policymaking effectively resulted in a narrowing down of the legitimate sphere of government intervention.[98] On the other hand, their approach to financial stability clashed with politicians' short-term preoccupations, resulting in perverse mechanisms of financial punishment when social justice reforms were proposed and of approval when austerity measures were introduced. Rating decisions reinforced social distress in Europe, given that '[h]igher interest rates on government borrowing mean more taxpayer money gets paid to financial investors rather than being spent on popular public services and investments'.[99] So, instead of contributing to solving the sovereign debt problem, rating agencies seemed set to worsen social conditions throughout the world.

For borrowing countries, a rating downgrade has negative effects on their access to credit and the cost of borrowing. Furthermore, the lowering of a credit score by a CRA can create a vicious cycle, as not only do interest rates for that country increase, but other contracts with financial institutions may also be affected adversely, causing, in response, further expenses and reductions in creditworthiness.[100] According to some, rating agencies provide a good example of agents manifesting 'tunnel vision'. By 'producing "certainty equivalents" rating agencies contribute both to absorbing and to (re)producing uncertainty', instead of strengthening financial stability.[101]

The behaviour of CRAs during financial and economic crises is essentially conservative; that is, they either downgrade or at most confirm previous scores.[102] A rating downgrade, or threat of downgrade, weakens the financial position of the state as issuer of debt obligations. Worse scores are an official recognition that the state's debt has become riskier, which is compensated by an increase in rates of return for those obligations. Higher rates of return hinder treasuries' ability to refinance the stock of existing debt, to issue new debt, to tackle short-term macroeconomic shocks through fiscal policy, and to manage short-term investments aimed at increasing fiscal revenues to repay debt. Since tax income is cyclical, it is considered less reliable by CRAs, which generally prefer privatization and austerity measures – that is, liquidation of public resources and reduced spending.[103] The influence of the state over the market is increasingly restricted, while market mechanisms are sought to provide ever-larger shares of hitherto public services.

Although sovereign ratings are provided without a fee for the country, there are nonetheless perverse incentives involved. Having missed the crisis in 2007/08, and the Latin American and Asian debt crises as well as the default of Enron and other fraudulent corporations before that, rating agencies have become overly sensitive to market movements, to the extent that they are erratic in their evaluations. Moreover, inflation of optimistic ratings during booms and abrupt downgrades during busts raise suspicions of corrupt practices.[104] This is particularly problematic when these agencies sell advisory services to the same clients to whom they sell ratings, as in the case of advising a government on how to structure a security and then rating it on the basis of those recommendations.

The global financial crisis has confirmed that rating agencies are potent political actors. CRAs not only provide information but help construct the context in which corporations and public bodies make decisions.[105] Rating agencies are not the neutral, technical and objective arbitrators they presume to be. Instead, they organize, coordinate and 'make' capital markets in the first place by controlling information and shaping judgements. At the very least, they possess a formidable 'epistemic authority', arguably like no other private institution in the world.[106] Their numbers influence macroeconomic policies. Their assessments can doom entire countries and their peoples.

Ratings and irrationality

CRAs are important to investors not because of the informational function they fulfil, but rather because market participants believe CRAs' numbers to be consequential: that is, they believe that they will influence the behaviour of *other* investors. Public expectations of CRAs as revealing some type of 'truth' about financial flows and creditworthiness are falsely grounded on a rationalist understanding of market behaviour.[107] When looking at how markets operate, it becomes clear that financial actors are much more influenced by their expectations of how other market participants react than evidence-based analysis. This endogenous perspective, first voiced by Keynes in the late 1920s, implies that market participants are focused on anticipating what other traders are likely to do, in order to derive profits from predicting moves and subsequent market changes.[108] Markets are generally not interested in finding a good or a better investment. They do not care too much about distinguishing between evidence and rumours. If they believe that enough investors will believe the rumour, then the latter becomes evidence – enough, that is, to switch investment plans and sell stocks or bonds. Social and psychological drivers of financial markets, such as fads, herd mentality and other features of collective irrationality, clearly upset the ideal of purely self-regulating efficient markets and help explain the ever more frequent rise of irrational exuberance. This is what Keynes termed 'animal spirits', naturally and periodically giving rise to financial crises.[109] Nobel prizewinner Paul Krugman argues that CRAs' ratings promote markets' irrationality and, as such, should be disregarded for the purpose of regulation. He believes that, instead of relying on market agents for self-regulation, policy-makers should work towards the establishment of reliable rules and steering mechanisms to avoid market failures.[110] A number of experts and consultants (including analysts within the derivatives industry) have supported the idea of abolishing ratings as a way of 'weaning investors and regulators off' what appears to be 'like a drug'.[111] Even the free-market think-tank Cato Institute advocates for policymakers to stop using ratings for regulatory purposes, recognizing the 'de facto oligopoly' in the sector.[112]

According to UNCTAD, 'ratings tend to be sticky, lagging markets, and overreact when they do change', which aggravates financial crises and contributes to cross-country contagion.[113] During the 1997–98 Asian crisis, for instance, rating agencies reinforced boom-and-bust trends by lagging instead of leading events and by overreacting during critical phases, thus amplifying cycles.[114] Studies looking at the role of CRAs during the Mexican crisis in the mid-1990s also concluded that negative announcements on sovereign ratings from the largest agencies significantly raised bond yields and stock market volatility and thus contributed to destabilizing international capital flows.[115] As we have seen, downgrades often result in fewer investors wanting to purchase government bonds, thus triggering higher yield rates. This spike is then reflected in higher interest rates for future auctions, making the borrowing even more costly and thereby contributing to an increasing budget deficit, which in turn can lead to a further downgrading, starting the spiral once again.

According to the agencies, such sluggishness in adjusting ratings is justified by their aim of providing long-term perspectives rather than immediate assessments. This strategy implies that CRAs will always have a delay in perceiving that any particular reform is not just the initial part of a reversible cycle, but instead the commencement of a sustained process. As a result, a country's effort to improve its financial situation, for instance, might be long undermined by a persistently negative (though incorrect) outlook on its capacity to service its debt. This situation reinforces the view that the numbers produced by CRAs do not really provide any informational added value, but simply impact investors unilaterally, hindering the state's ability to recover from negative shocks and forcing it to embark on austerity measures that may turn out to have a limited impact on markets' recovery while putting a sizable burden on the population.

Historically, less than 1 per cent of investments with AAA ratings experienced outright default. But after the housing bubble burst in the USA, 'a vast majority of securities with AAA ratings incurred substantial losses; some failed outright.'[116] About 80 per cent of the CDOs that were rated AAA by S&P's between 2005 and 2007 were downgraded below investment grade in the turmoil of the US real estate crisis.[117]

The US Senate's investigation panel came to the conclusion that overly positive ratings supported market soar, then 'sudden mass downgrades ... were the immediate trigger for the financial crisis'.[118] The chief economist at the Organization for Economic Cooperation and Development declared that CRAs 'express judgements that speed up trends already underway' and concluded: 'It is like pushing someone who is standing on the edge of a cliff.'[119]

In spite of their evident realization of the power of CRAs, public regulators have continued relying on ratings to design policies aimed at curbing the global financial crisis. The Federal Reserve's Term Asset-Backed Securities Loan Facility, which financed the purchase by taxpayers of some trillions of new securities to sustain the economy, based the acquisition of these loans 'on the condition they have triple A ratings'. [120] Moreover, the Fed accepted to buy commercial paper directly from companies, 'only if the debt has at least the equivalent of an A-1 rating, the second highest for short-term credit.' Because of these decisions, which once again put CRAs at the centre of financial market regulation, it was estimated that the Big Three may have enjoyed as much as $400 million in fees, coming from taxpayer money, in 2009. During the 2008 economic collapse, Moody's alone reported revenue of $1.76 billion, a profit margin of 41 per cent.

In Europe, a 2009 directive made registration with the Committee of European Securities Regulators mandatory for CRAs intending to operate in the EU market. [121] Key additional provisions included prohibiting rating agencies from providing advisory services, preventing them from rating financial instruments if they do not have sufficient quality information, and forcing them to disclose their models, methodologies and key assumptions. As recognized by the news agency Bloomberg, public institutions have taken numerous steps to find a way out of the deepest recession in recent history. Yet 'no one has taken steps that would substantially fix a broken ratings system.'[122]

In the opinion of Peter Fischer, managing director and co-head of fixed income at the New York-based BlackRock, the largest publicly traded asset management company in the USA, rating agencies should simply be replaced. While at the beginning of the twentieth century, when equities were thought to be complicated and bonds were viewed as simple, it appeared to make sense to have a few rating agencies set up to tell us all what bonds to buy: 'But flash forward to the slicing and dicing of credit today, and it's really a pretty wacky concept.'[123] In his view, the entire licensing process is flawed, as it gives a few companies complete control over markets and regulations. By eliminating public licences, rating agencies would become just like equity analysts, paid for their opinion directly by investors.

Economic thinking is completely comfortable with the concept of risk. Indeed, risk is quantifiable: it can be measured and, therefore, controlled. Whoever controls risk can predict the future. And those who predict the future are the new rulers. By contrast, uncertainty implies subjectivity. It is the realm of guessing, where common sense and rules of thumb are the only parameters to guide decisions. Uncertainty can be defined as pure possibility, which cannot be trapped into numbers. And without numbers, which convey a sense of authority, there is no political influence. In the realm of uncertainty and subjectivity, everybody is equal. According to the economist Frank Knight, the founder of the free-market Chicago School, uncertain conditions make it impossible for agents to assign probabilities and anticipate evolutions.[124] For one of his historical opponents, John Keynes, uncertainty eliminates the power of numbers, as it prevents the forecasting of such things as prices, war or future interest rates.[125] In spite of their opposing views on political economy, both Knight and Keynes agreed that uncertainty is a constant facet of economic activity, providing opportunities for profit while inevitably exposing markets to the possibility of losses. It is perhaps this open entrepreneurial spirit, marked by unforeseeable possibilities, that rating agencies have tried to tame by resorting to apparently complex calculations aided by shady statistical methodologies. Through the apparent objectivity of mathematics, they have purported to transform uncertainties into risks.[126] Undoubtedly, a certain progress in computing technologies has enabled them to diffuse the margins of indeterminacy with a view to translating more contingent events into statistical probabilities.

In economics, risk is typically associated with optimal equilibria. It is a function of fancy models, which can get you published in peer-reviewed journals or hired by multi-billion-dollar hedge funds. Uncertainties are simply unknown risks. As such, they will never get you anywhere. Risk managers are well respected and remunerated. Uncertainty specialists, just like wizards, exist only in fairy tales.

The rating process is at the core of a risk society. Through the apparently scientific neutrality of numbers (or alphanumeric characters, in the case of ratings), it conveys a false sense of control and predictability. Even Moody's concedes that 'credit rating is by nature subjective' and that 'any attempt to reduce credit rating to a formulaic methodology would be misleading and would lead to serious mistakes.'[127] Similarly, the former president of S&P recognized that ratings are too enmeshed in regulatory frameworks. He pleaded with the SEC to get rid of references to rating companies in regulations as he felt that 'there's too much risk of being overused and inappropriately used'.[128]

In the end, it may be argued that CRAs are simply products of a society unable to deal with the unbearable lightness of uncertainty. CRAs have thrived because they have been extremely crafty at using the 'objectifying cloak of economic and financial analysis'.[129] They have been hiding behind numbers 'when it is easier than justifying what may, in fact, be a difficult judgment'.[130] By resorting to catchy computations, which hide the fundamental sketchiness of data collection, these agencies project an idea of reality that corporations, politicians and investors have traditionally found very comfortable. Through their ratings, CRAs have in fact provided a false sense of confidence, which has suited policymakers and ultimately explains their eagerness to invest these 'opinion makers' with unprecedented authority. Yet, socio-political events do not readily lend themselves to being captured as a numerical probability. This is why crises reveal the underlying fiction of risk management and catapult societies back onto the playing field of uncertainty.

In their political manifestation, CRAs' ratings have thrived in an age marked by a short-sighted narrative: that of the obsolete and dysfunctional state being overtaken by the victorious and effective capital market. In the world designed by ratings, which quickly collapsed under the irrationality of financial distress, it was the politics of numbers, not the politics of citizens, which decided how to govern our societies. Ultimately, the power of ratings is a function of the impoverishment of democracy.

As discussed in the previous chapter, it is not only the manipulation of numbers that skews governance processes, but also the inherent trust in measurements and in those who produce them. In many regards, the rating agencies perfectly exemplify our society's trust in numbers and the burgeoning power of auditors. In the next chapter we move from the financial world to that of the politics and economics of climate change, where numbers have provided munitions for heated contestations between climate scientists and the so-called sceptics, ultimately rewarding market forces through the adoption of policies based on a narrow conceptualization of costs and benefits.

CHAPTER 3

Fiddling while the planet burns: the marketization of climate change

Public policy could itself become the captive of a scientific-technological elite. The prospect of domination of the nation's scholars by ... project allocations, and the power of money is ever present – and is gravely to be regarded.

Dwight Eisenhower

Although the politics of statistics and the power of numbers in global governance are most powerfully exemplified by the role of credit rating agencies, there are many other critical areas where measurements have taken centre stage in informing public policy. Environmental governance, and in particular the climate change debate, has been the field in which fully fledged 'stat wars' have been waged in the past forty years, with different camps using numbers, measurements, models and indexes to pursue opposing agendas. In this field, too, just like in that of ratings, a burgeoning industry of auditors has taken centre stage, with an enormous quantity of money to be made.

These four decades have been characterized by growing concerns regarding the overall state of the world's environment, with a series of high-level summits inaugurated by the United Nations

Conference on the Human Environment (usually referred to as the Stockholm Conference) in 1972 and the World Commission on Environment and Development, better known as the Bruntland Commission, which published the first report on sustainable development in 1987.[1] With the creation of the Intergovernmental Panel on Climate Change (IPCC), established by the World Meteorological Organization and the United Nations Environment Programme in 1988, scientists from all over the world began to work on collating information with a view to generating consensus on the state of the planet's climate. Their main goal was to review piles of numbers and clarify whether the globe was warming or not. Politicians waited for statistics to move forward, so scientists felt pressed to prove, beyond any reasonable doubt, that global warming was really happening. At the same time, a series of think-tanks and contrarian scientists began to produce alternative research with the aim of debunking the work conducted by the IPCC. In parallel, economists of all sorts introduced a variety of models to estimate the pros and cons of climate-change-inspired reforms, triggering debates, controversies and profound contrast within the social sciences. Among them, the battle of numbers saw a profound division between those who advocated action and those who demonstrated the economic advantages of inaction. Much was at stake, as environmental groups, social movements and various voices in civil society started calling into question the very foundation of the development model pursued by advanced economies since the Industrial Revolution.

During these years, the politics of numbers sealed the intimate connection between market approaches and the environment, eventually accepting – albeit indirectly, as we will see – the proposals put forward by climate sceptics and the fossil fuel industry. Narrow economic reasoning and some of its traditional methodologies, especially cost–benefit analysis, were introduced in climate change governance with a view to identifying acceptable equilibria between the interests of markets and those of nature. The apparent neutrality of numerical models ultimately led to a marketization of the climate debate, in which concepts such as sustainable development, cap and trade or green growth became linguistic devices to strengthen the grip of markets on the alleged transition to a low carbon society.

Environmental scepticism and the rise of cost–benefit analysis

In their book *Merchants of Doubt*, historians Naomi Oreskes and Erik M. Conway provide a detailed analysis of the connections between some industrial lobbies, conservative 'think-tanks', private foundations and the so-called environmental sceptics, particularly in the USA.[2] They show the tentacular reach of this 'industry of denial' and its impact on American political institutions. Ever since the 1970s, this industry's strategy has been to stir controversy in areas where scientific consensus was reached (famously, for instance, in the research on the link between cancer and tobacco smoke) and to manufacture doubt. The overall objective of their 'counter-science' has been to oppose governmental regulation in a variety of fields and protect consolidated industrial interests, especially in the fossil fuel sector and in the military–industrial complex, which they did – for example – by providing scientific reports backing President Reagan's strategic defence initiative (popularly known as the Star Wars plan). Championed by the Tobacco Institute, this strategy was consistently adopted throughout the past decades to derail reforms in the field of, among others, acid rain, the ozone hole and climate change. The main promoters of this view have been powerful scientists such as the physicist William Nierenberg, who had been involved in the Manhattan Project during the Second World War; Fredrick Seitz, the former president of the US National Academy of Sciences and

NATO consultant; US Navy scientist Siegfried Fred Singer; and climatologist Patrick (Pat) Michaels, research fellow at the libertarian Cato Institute and author of books like *Meltdown: The Predictable Distortion of Global Warming by Scientists, Politicians, and the Media.* All of them have been, in one way or another, connected with fossil fuel lobbies and the military–industrial complex, and played a pivotal role in informing the environmental policies enacted during the Reagan administrations (1981–89) and George H.W. Bush's tenure (1989–93). Among other activities, Nierenberg and Seitz co-founded the George C. Marshall Institute, a powerful conservative think-tank established in 1984 to support Reagan's nuclear defence plans against the criticisms of progressive scientific organizations such as the Union of Concerned Scientists. In the following years the Institute moved on to fund 'alternative' research disputing the carcinogenic nature of tobacco smoking (including passive smoking), the cause and consequences of acid rain and the depletion of the ozone layer.[3] Fred Singer consulted for oil companies such as Exxon and Shell and for military corporations such as Lockheed Martin, before joining the University of Virginia, where he founded the Science and Environmental Policy Project, an advocacy group disputing mainstream scientific consensus on environmental problems. In an interview with CNN's Fareed Zakaria, Pat Michaels admitted that roughly '40 per cent' of his income and research funds comes from the petroleum industry, triggering accusations by US policymakers that he had 'misled' Congress in a testimony before the Energy and Commerce Committee held in 2009.[4]

For the past few decades, a dense web of foundations and think-tanks has been actively supporting the environmental sceptics in the USA, whose controversial stance has been further amplified by complacent media, some of which have given credit to unorthodox views intentionally, while others have simply played by the so-called 'fairness doctrine', a code established in 1949 in conjunction with the rise of television that requires broadcast journalists to dedicate equivalent airtime to opposing parties in the coverage of controversial issues of public concern.[5] According to sociologists Riley Dunlap and Aaron McCright, who contributed a chapter on the theme to the 2011 *Oxford Handbook of Climate Change and Society*, the 'climate change denial machine' revolves around a handful of business groups (including fossil fuel giants such as ExxonMobil, the American Petroleum Institute, the Western Fuels Association and natural resources industries such as the National Mining Association and the American Forest and Paper Association), which have provided systematic funding to think-tanks such as the George C. Marshall Institute, the American Enterprise Institute, the Cato Institute, the Competitive Enterprise Institute and the Heritage Foundation.[6] Their lobbying and research work over the past decades has been successful at creating an aura of 'doubt' about the scientific consensus on climate change, its causes and impacts. In a few instances, they have also succeeded at initiating more popular movements, such as the Global Climate Coalition (a business campaign opposing reduction in greenhouse gases) and the American Coalition for Clean Coal Electricity (recently renamed America's Power).

Although their arguments have been refuted innumerable times by the scientific community, the sceptics' most significant (and enduring) success has been the popularization of utilitarian reasoning as the best way to deal with policy decisions in environmental governance. Their intimate connections with the Reagan administration allowed them to shape not only the president's views on environmental issues, but also his inclination to adopt a market-based approach to the resolution of any potential trade-off between business interests and ecological concerns. These scholars were instrumental in forging a broad consensus among policymakers (which is still dominant today) that environmental protection (and preservation) should not be seen as a fundamental value for the promotion of human well-being, but rather as an obstacle to economic development. By framing the three components of sustainability (economic, social and environmental) not as mutually reinforcing, but as in constant trade-off with one another, they called for the systematic application of utility-based criteria to guide policy decisions. Fred Singer himself, for instance, was among the first to champion the use of cost–benefit analysis in dealing with environmental problems. Cost–benefit analysis is a comparative measurement of the costs and benefits associated with a particular decision, project or government policy, which has nowadays become common practice for the ex-ante assessment of environmental policies in most countries. To be comparable, costs and benefits must be expressed in monetary terms and adjusted for a particular time horizon. As often costs and benefits occur at different points in time, especially in fields such as environmental protection (where costs are borne by present generations and most of the benefits enjoyed by the future), economists apply discount rates for future benefits: in theory, this should make it possible to equalize the time difference and gauge if overall benefits outweigh overall costs (the so-called 'net present value'). When costs outweigh benefits (measured in terms of market prices), economic rationality calls for inaction: it would make economic sense simply to do nothing. In a 1979 report on the costs and benefits of air pollution control commissioned by the Mitre Corporation, a leading force in the US military apparatus, Singer took exactly such a position, arguing for 'a conservative approach to air pollution control' and making the case for alternative options to 'lower national costs'.[7] In 1982, he was rewarded for his contribution to the application of cost–benefit methodologies in the field of environmental assessment and invited to join President Reagan's Acid Rain Peer Review Panel, which was chaired by his friend and fellow sceptic William Nierenberg.

There are numerous conceptual and methodological problems with cost–benefit analysis, which almost invariably lead
to contrasting outcomes and endless disputes among those who
use this method. Take, for instance, the results of cost–benefit
studies dealing with global warming mitigation. According to
the famous review on the economics of climate change carried
out by LSE professor Nicholas Stern for the UK government in
2006, the benefits of strong and early action on climate change far
outweigh the costs of not acting. For the review, climate change
would cause a loss of between 5 and 10 per cent of GDP every
year, while the costs of introducing measures to avoid most of
the harm would amount to roughly 1 per cent of global income.
However, alternative calculations produced by other economists,
including Nobel prizewinner William Nordhaus, reached opposite results.[8] One study carried out by the Cato Institute sets
the bar much higher, arguing that emission cuts would only be
worth it in the event of climate change reducing GDP by at least
10 per cent a year.[9] Yale professor Robert Mendelsohn, following Nordhaus's reasoning that society should balance marginal
mitigation costs with marginal damages, maintained that '[c]osts
borne in the present are more burdensome than costs born in the
future', which led him to the obvious conclusion that the current
generation should only invest in climate change mitigation policies
that earn 'the same rate of return as competitive investments in
a myriad of market sector alternatives'.[10] Interestingly, in a paper
published in April 2008, Stern rebutted his critics by pointing
out a traditional weapon employed by environmental sceptics: that
is, that '[u]ncertainty, and the prospect of resolving some of it in
the future, is often used as a justification for delaying action'.[11]
He added that results of the IPCC's Third Assessment Report in
2007 vindicated his claim that bold reforms were needed as soon
as possible and emphasized that, while economists seem willing
to accept high risks as they fall primarily on future generations,

'most people would find this conclusion unethical'. Then he conceded that his review probably erred, but on the side of caution: 'We underestimated the risks ... We underestimated the damage associated with temperature increase ... and we underestimated the probabilities of temperature increases.'[12]

The discount rates on which the very concept of cost–benefit analysis is based are, ultimately, personal value judgements made by researchers.[13] In general, economists are fond of assigning a lower value to benefits occurring in the future because they assume that income will be higher then, which, in view of the principle of diminishing marginal utility, should make it easier for future generations to bear the costs of lower consumption. They also assume that technological progress will find more efficient ways to address environmental problems. Moreover, their models give priority to the utility of people living in the present (inherent discounting), thus rejecting values such as intergenerational solidarity and long-term sustainability.[14] As Berkeley economist and former deputy assistant secretary of the US Treasury Brad Delong puts it, there is a fundamental 'flaw in our reasoning' as we are 'impatient in the sense of valuing the present and near-future much more than we value the distant future' and always prefer 'a bird in the hand to two in the bush'.[15] Indeed, no matter how 'elegant' some cost–benefit models may seem, the fact remains that no one can measure how much future generations will value decisions we take today or, by contrast, how much we value the benefits that future generations will enjoy because of our decision to bear certain costs in the present.

Due to all these assumptions, Singer's contribution to the Acid Rain Panel's report in 1984 concluded that it was simply too difficult to quantify the costs and benefits of air pollution control (he actually ventured into an infamous off-the-cuff estimate of 'one-billion dollar solution to a one-million dollar problem' without providing any information as to how he had computed such figures), although in 1979 the White House Council on Environmental Quality had already estimated the economic benefit of clean air at US$ 21.4 billion – *a year.*[16] He suggested, instead, adopting a market-based system of transferable emissions credits, in which government would simply need to set a maximum allowance (today we would call it a 'cap') and sell these rights to companies, which would use them or trade them for a financial return.[17] In the end, this is exactly what the Bush administration did. Following Singer's advice, the US government launched the first large-scale trading scheme in the world, which was established in 1990 with a view to curbing emissions of sulphur dioxide, the gas responsible for acid rain. In 2003, the Environmental Protection Agency quantified the overall cost of acid rain provisions for the previous decade at about US$8.8 billion per year, while estimating benefits at the tune of more than ten times as much (between US$101 and US$109 billion per year), thus debunking Singer's early analysis. Despite all its flaws, Singer's approach would ultimately be victorious in the battle of ideas on environmental governance. Indeed, the rapid diffusion of emission trading schemes since the adoption of the Kyoto Protocol confirmed the global appeal of the sceptics' main argument: avoid regulation at all costs and let the market rule.

Climategate: twisting numbers for the climate

In the years from the adoption of the Kyoto Protocol to the outbreak of the global economic crisis, climate change gained centre stage in international politics, with a series of high-level summits and growing commitments made by governments and political leaders across the globe, despite the sceptics' attempts to convince public opinion that science was inconclusive. In 2007, the IPCC shared the Nobel Peace Prize with former US vice president Al Gore, by then one of the leading activists in the fight against global warming. Global campaigns such as those organized by the environmental coalition 350.org galvanized millions of people in all continents. The election of Barack Obama to the White House, coupled with a large majority of Democrats in both branches of Congress, seemed to reassure the world that the USA was finally ready to commit to an international binding treaty, after almost two decades of opposition to any form of international cooperation. Meanwhile, the nations of the world were negotiating a new treaty to replace the Kyoto Protocol and all eyes were on the preparation of the United Nations Framework Conference on Climate Change, which was to take place in Copenhagen in December 2009. Then came the 'climategate' affair, which shed a dark shadow over the tenability of some numbers produced by climate scientists to demonstrate the planet's warming. As most policy and economic analyses (including the Stern Review) relied on data produced by climate scientists, what better way for sceptics to discredit the source of all forecasts and bring controversy into the picture?

For most of his academic career, Phil Jones was a productive, but rather obscure climate scientist. Since 1998, he had been the director of the Climatic Research Unit at the University of East Anglia, in the UK. Jones worked quite closely with the British National Weather Service to gather information from thousands of meteorological stations around the world. He was in charge of the so-called instrumental temperature record; that is, a time series of temperature fluctuations of the global land surface and oceans dating back hundreds of years. In 2001, his studies of the planet's temperature were featured rather prominently in the Third Assessment Report of the IPCC and then, in 2007, his work deeply influenced the conclusions of the Fourth Assessment Report, which stated that 'warming of the climate system is unequivocal', and that 'most of the observed increase in global average temperatures since the mid-20th century is very likely due to the observed increase in anthropogenic greenhouse gas concentrations.[18]

Then, quite abruptly, Jones's relatively uneventful life was steamrollered by a scandal of global proportions. On 19 November 2009, the server of the Climate Research Unit was hacked and thousands of emails and documents were stolen. The hacked information was sent to a handful of climate sceptics' websites, including Climate Audit, arguably one of the best-known dissident blogs in the field, developed by Steve McIntyre, a Canadian mathematician and former mining consultant with links to the Competitive Enterprise Institute, a think-tank that had long disputed the validity of official data on global temperatures. Jones's private correspondence was dissected and then fed to the Internet. Thousands of websites and social networks started to relay the content of these documents and, finally, the media broke the news.[19]

Jones's emails were embarrassing, to say the least. In some messages, he regularly instructed collaborators and colleagues to avoid putting their data in the public domain, lest they may be used by opponents. This was in clear violation of scientific openness and of the UK Freedom of Information Act, which granted access to scientific studies to all those interested. He lamented that McIntyre and his co-author, the economist Ross McKitrick, had been after his data for years: 'If they ever hear there is a Freedom of Information Act now in the UK, I think I'll delete the file rather than send to anyone.'[20] Other messages revealed the collusion of climate scientists to 'pressure journal editors who published work questioning the climate science-consensus' and to keep some more critical analyses out of the IPCC official reports, 'even if we have to redefine what the peer-review literature is'.[21] Jones's deputy, Keith Briffa, admitted in an email that he had worked 'hard to balance the needs of the science and the IPCC, which were not always the same'.

They complained to the Royal Meteorological Society when it requested that all authors of its journals publicize their data. Jones threatened not to submit 'any more papers to any RMS journal'. In an email dated 3 January 2009, Mike McCracken of the Climate Institute raised concerns that predictions regarding the warming of the planet's temperature may be wrong. He suggested thinking of a backup plan by arguing, for instance, that sulphates were causing global cooling: 'Otherwise, the skeptics will be all over us – the world is really cooling, the models are no good, etc. And all this just as the US is about ready to get serious on the issue.'[22]

Quite astonishing were the entries retrieved from the journal kept by Ian Harris, the researcher and programmer in charge of updating the Unit's datasets. In the so-called 'Harry ReadMe File', Harris pointed out the presence of missing cases that weakened statistical correlations: 'What the hell is supposed to happen here? Oh yeah – there is no "supposed", I can make it up. So I have :-).' He went on, lamenting 'the hopeless state of our databases', in which 'there is no uniform data integrity, it's just a catalogue of issues that continues to grow as they're found.' He concluded:

> You can't imagine what this has cost me – to actually allow the operator to assign false WMO codes!! But what else is there in such situations? Especially when dealing with a 'Master' database of dubious provenance (which, er, they all are and always will be).[23]

The most compromising message, however, was sent by Jones himself. In conversations with Michael Mann, Raymond Bradley and Malcolm Hughes, distinguished authors of a 1998 paper published in *Nature* that analysed global-scale temperature patterns, he boasted the use of some methodological 'trick' to hide the decline in temperatures over the previous five decades.[24] Jones, Mann and colleagues argued that these statements were taken out of context and largely misinterpreted.[25] Yet Jones's admissions cast doubt over the reliability of the most popular icon of the climate change debate, the so-called hockey stick graph. Developed by Mann and his colleagues, the hockey stick graph shows the average temperature over the past six centuries, by plotting data gathered via instruments against reconstructions based on the varying widths of tree rings from ancient trees, a proxy for the variation of temperatures in the past.[26] According to their calculations, there was little or no variation in global temperatures until the late 1800s. Then, in the twentieth century, numbers go up, thus causing a sharp rise in the graph, just like the blade of a hockey stick. For many, not only in the scientific community, the graph shows quite intuitively that mankind, ever since the Industrial Revolution, has somehow managed to alter an otherwise stable climate pattern.

This was what climate sceptics had been waiting for. In their view, it proved that climatologists had been tinkering with their data to show that temperatures were on the rise, a conclusion notoriously disputed by a spate of critics. Among them was the influential Frederick Seitz, founding chairman of the sceptics' stronghold, the George C. Marshall Institute, who in a 1996 editorial in the *Wall Street Journal* had harshly criticized the IPCC report by affirming that 'in my more than 60 years as a member of the American scientific community, I have never witnessed a more disturbing corruption of the peer review process.'[27] Sceptics argued that the so-called 'hacker' was in fact an internal source who, unhappy with the methods employed by the research unit, decided to act as a whistle-blower.[28] McIntyre and McKitrick, who had written a number of papers contesting the validity of the hockey stick graph and the conclusion that the last century had been experiencing extraordinarily high temperatures, felt vindicated.[29]

In a few days, Jones's mailbox was stormed by abusive emails, some of them threatening his life and those of his family.

Embarrassed and worried, Jones stepped down. In an interview with the *Sunday Times*, he confessed to having considered suicide.[30] Several official investigations were launched. The most important of them was undertaken by the House of Commons' Science and Technology Select Committee, which concluded that there was no real case against Jones and his team. The group of scientists had adopted a debatable communication style, but no evidence of omission or manipulation was found.[31] In 2010, Jones was indeed reinstated in his academic capacity, although with another job, after a further investigation found no fault with the 'rigour and honesty as scientists' of Jones and his collaborators.[32] It conceded, however, that the Climate Research Unit had not lived up to the spirit of openness that is generally expected of scientists, mainly because of their resistance to share information and data. Michael Mann was also subject to an investigation by Penn State University, where he was director of the Earth System Science Center. The panel that reviewed his case concluded that there was no evidence of data falsification or destruction, and that Mann had not engaged in any misuse of privileged or confidential information. Yet it left open the question of whether the scientist 'deviated from accepted practices within the academic community'.[33]

The damage was done. Never mind that no evidence of malfeasance was found. Never mind that researchers were able to resume their work as planned. And, most importantly, never mind that the scientific validity of their contribution to the study of global warming was confirmed by the international community. As the media had jumped on the bandwagon of 'climate bashers', what should have been treated as a minor public relations issue became a historic opportunity to sling mud at decades of scientific research. For example, the IPCC was accused of having suppressed critical chapters in its *Fourth Report*. Although the IPCC denied such allegations, a number of errors were identified in its publications, forcing the UN secretary general Ban Ki Moon to call for an independent review.[34] Given that American scientists had been involved in the suspicious email exchange, Republican members of the US Congress called for a criminal investigation by the Department of Justice. They maintained that the implicated climatologists had been 'manipulating data and knowingly using flawed climate models to reach preconceived conclusions' and, as a consequence, the IPCC consensus that 'anthropogenic emissions are inexorably leading to environmental catastrophes' had been irremediably compromised. They also called on the US Environmental Protection Agency to review its stance on the risks associated with greenhouse gases, suggesting that the so-called endangerment finding, which states that industrial and motor emissions threaten the public health and welfare of current and future generations, 'should be thrown out'.[35]

As remarked by the magazine *Nature*, 'huge damage has been done to the reputation of climate science, and arguably to science as a whole.'[36] The very name 'climategate', widely adopted by the media to describe the incident, undoubtedly contributed to creating an aura of suspicion and manipulation, as if climate scientists – in their dark university rooms and laboratories – had been orchestrating a fear-mongering plan to take control of environmental governance. Quite expectedly, conspiracy theories abounded. A much-downloaded report published by the Science and Public Policy Institute (SPPI), a think-tank opposing 'prodigious economic or political sacrifices for the sake of negligible benefits', maintained that the Climate Research Unit 'had conspired in an attempt to redefine what is and is not peer-reviewed science'.[37] It called for these 'climate criminals' to be 'imprisoned for their fraudulent tampering with scientific data, and for their suppression of results uncongenial to their politicized viewpoint' and concluded that 'the manufactured non-problem of "global warming" should be put on hold forthwith, and no further public policy measures should be instituted at any future time.' The author of the report, the British commentator Christopher Monckton, used to be a scientific adviser to prime minister Margaret Thatcher in the 1980s and had made himself infamous for his views on AIDS, against whose spread he recommended 'to screen the entire population regularly and to quarantine all carriers of the disease for life'.[38] In what appeared as a coordinated attack against mainstream scientific findings, the SPPI launched a series of smear campaigns, including a public call for the suppression of the IPCC and the arrest of Al Gore. With the support of another sceptics' institution, the Center for the Study of Carbon Dioxide and Global Change, they gathered evidence from what they claimed to be more than 1,000 scientists from more than 600 institutions in more than 40 countries to demonstrate what they believed to be the fallacies in the IPCC's consensus on the trend of global temperatures. Their latest book is aptly titled *The Many Benefits of Atmospheric CO2 Enrichment*.[39]

The timing of climategate could have not been more propitious for the sceptics and the lobbies they represented. Just a few weeks after the hacking, world leaders met in Copenhagen to discuss the future of the Kyoto Protocol. The 17th Conference of Parties (commonly dubbed COP17) turned out to be a colossal disappointment for environmentalists and concerned citizens. Not only did the international community reject the possibility of a common long-term agreement, but ever since all international summits have turned out to be no more than very expensive opportunities to postpone the problem. The USA, the stronghold of environmental scepticism, also saw a sharp decline in the public's concern with climate change. In 2008, 71 per cent of American citizens believed that global warming was happening. By 2010, however, this number had dropped to 57 per cent (with those who did not believe in climate change at 20 per cent from 10 per cent in 2008, and those who were uncertain increasing to 23 per cent).

Among those who believed in climate change, however, only 59 per cent were 'very' or 'extremely sure' that it was happening, about a 13 per cent drop from 2008. Similarly, only about half of Americans were 'worried' about climate change, while in 2008 the same belief was held by 63 per cent of the population.[40]

One of the think-tanks that has profited most from the climategate controversy is the Copenhagen Consensus Center (CCC). Founded in 2002 by the 'sceptical environmentalist' Bjørn Lomborg, the Copenhagen Consensus comprises a small group of researchers, with a wide network of collaborators, including several economists of Nobel fame. According to its mission, the CCC 'improves knowledge and gives an overview of research and facts within a given problem, which means that the prioritization is based on evidence'. The reference to 'evidence' is of course a powerful one, but no further specification is made as to what such evidence would consist of. The Center purports to shy away from ideology and political agendas, by relying exclusively on numbers and economic reasoning. Through a systematic use of cost–benefit analysis, they present themselves as the new frontier of global problem-solving. In 2008, through the input of a panel of five well-known economists (including free-marketeer Jagdish Baghwati and Austrian economist Vernon Smith), they came up with a list of the best and worst ways to fight climate change. Quite expectedly, the best ways focused on non-regulatory approaches, such as technological innovation and climate engineering, including carbon sequestration. They also recommended a wider use of technology transfers from more industrialized to less industrialized countries and funding for climate adaptation – that is, projects aimed at preparing societies to deal with harsher climates, instead of focusing on social justice proposals for mitigation, such as the introduction of carbon taxes in rich countries to deal with the climate debt. In a paper published in 2009, the CCC dished out a series of numbers to make its point.

It estimated that the welfare loss induced by climate change in the year 2100 would be in the same order as losing a few percentage points of income: 'That is, a century worth of climate change is about as bad as losing one or two years of economic growth.'[41] Why bother then? Their conclusion was that climate change should not be a priority for policymakers, at least not yet. Specific measures should only be introduced later on, when the costs for society will be more acceptable.

According to its founder, the CCC promotes evidence-based reflections on climate change by championing 'an economic approach to the environment'.[42] As a consequence, they privilege solutions that are based on the monetization of resources. For instance, to address food scarcity while preserving biodiversity, they stress the importance of increasing agricultural yields through research and development, 'making it possible to feed more people with less land'.[43] They estimate that with a $14.5 billion annual infusion into research it is possible to achieve a 20 per cent higher annual growth of crops and 40 per cent higher growth for livestock, which over the next four decades should reduce pressure on nature and thus help biodiversity. In total, the alleged benefits will be in the order of $53 billion: 'for every dollar spent, we will do about 7 dollars worth of good both for biodiversity and climate.'

In 2012, the CCC published a new 'consensus', outlining the most important global challenges for the years to come. For climate change, which they ranked at the bottom of the list, the CCC experts recommended spending just a small amount of public money (roughly $1 billion) to explore new frontiers in climate engineering, such as Stratospheric Aerosol Injection (whereby a precursor of sulphur dioxide – the gas causing acid rains! – is continuously injected into the stratosphere, forming a layer of aerosols to reflect sunlight) or Marine Cloud Whitening (whereby seawater is mixed into the atmosphere to make the clouds whiter and more reflective). They also asserted that the economic impact of climate change is grossly overstated. In their view, the most negative impacts will be felt in agriculture and tourism, 'where nations will lose, on average, about half a percent of GDP from each by mid-century'. However, they pointed out that people adapting to changes in their environment would avoid much of this damage. Farmers will choose plants that thrive in the heat. New houses will be designed to deal with warmer temperatures: 'Taking adaptation into account, rich countries will adapt to the negative impacts of global warming and exploit the positive changes, creating a total positive effect of global warming worth about half a percentage point of GDP.' Once again, no big deal. Much to the contrary, climate change may turn out to be an economic blessing for all.

The use of economic reasoning, with its claim of neutrality, can be quite alluring. In fact, the reliance on cost–benefit analysis is a fundamentally macabre exercise, which overly simplifies the multidimensional character of social problems and makes us blind to the persistence of power structures that oppose the resolution of longstanding global problems. In the next sections, we see why.

Markets for climate

One of the main accusations sceptics advance against climate scientists is that their conclusions on the state of the planet's temperature have led to the creation of a moneymaking industry composed of 'green economy' investors, carbon trading markets and offset schemes. A report by climate sceptics points to this issue in a rather straightforward and aggressive way:

> all 'global-warming' profiteers who are making money out of carbon-trading or 'green investment' or UN climate boondoggles of whatever kind should be warned, and clearly warned, that now that the basis for their profitable activities is known to be

hollow and fraudulent, they themselves will be indicted, pros-
ecuted, and jailed for fraud, and their profits confiscated as the
fruits of money-laundering.[44]

It is at least ungenerous (and, in some respects, offensive) to
link climate scientists with speculators in the green industry.
Climatologists have highlighted a problem (i.e. the rising temperature of the planet and the concentration of greenhouse gases),
but have never taken a stance on what would be the best policy
to tackle this issue. In fact, the 'green growth' paradigm has
been invented by business and policymakers (and their economic
advisers), not by climate scientists. Most investment in this field
is actually coming from the very polluting corporations (from
oil companies to extractive industries) that have long benefited
from climate denialism and deregulation. The petroleum and coal
industries are largely in control of carbon markets throughout
the world, and are also responsible for most of the investment
in climate engineering (e.g. carbon capture and storage). For
many of them, climate change has become a lucrative business.
As we have seen, climate sceptic Fred Singer was an influential
champion of market-based solutions to address environmental
concerns. The policy he supported, the Acid Rain Program,
became the first large-scale system of emissions trading in history,
which the rest of the world would use as an example to design
market-driven mitigation policies for climate change. Carbon
markets are nowadays available in most continents, including the
European Union, North America (e.g. the Regional Greenhouse
Gas Initiative and the new California cap-and-trade mechanism,
the largest in the USA), New Zealand, Australia, Japan (in the
city of Tokyo) and China.[45]

There are various mechanisms for the design of an emissions
trading scheme. The most general distinction is between 'cap
and trade' and 'baseline and credit'. In the former case, public
authorities set a specific cap on emissions (e.g. by gauging the

limit of greenhouse gases acceptable to avoid climate change's disastrous effects) and then allocate or auction an equivalent number of allowances to polluting companies, which are free to use them as permits or trade them in the open market. In a baseline and credit system, specific performance targets (also known as 'notional baselines' set against business-as-usual estimates) are given to polluting companies, which can generate tradable credits by beating their emissions targets.[46]

Advocates of these mechanisms claim that trading systems are more efficient and flexible than top-down regulatory policies (like, for instance, a carbon tax) because they capitalize on companies' inherent drive for innovation.[47] Unlike across-the-board regulations, which affect all industries in the same way, emissions markets are seen as building on ingenuity and comparative advantages, thus providing incentives for compliance. Companies that innovate more quickly and effectively can sell their permits to less innovative businesses, which are therefore given more time to catch up, thus allowing for a flexible and gradual transition to a low-carbon economy compatible with internal market dynamics. Moreover, trading would give entrepreneurs 'the freedom to choose how to deal with their polluting activities' by deciding 'not only the extent of reductions that is cost-effective for their operations but also how to reduce emissions in order to reduce permit costs'.[48] This would ensure that emissions are reduced at the most cost-effective location and that a clear price for carbon emissions is produced organically from within the market, instead of being imposed from the outside. It is also assumed that trading schemes lower regulatory costs because, once established, the market will run according to its own internal supply and demand.[49] Moreover, these systems are said to reduce the dangers of regulatory capture – that is, the process whereby private interests control public oversight bodies – given that in a trading scheme markets basically control themselves.[50]

Despite a number of alleged virtues, emissions-trading schemes have evolved into precarious and potentially dangerous mechanisms, practically outweighing most (if not all) of their presumed strengths. In several cases, they have simply marketized climate change, turning it into another opportunity for speculation and financial hazard. Possibly nowhere is the vulnerability of the carbon market felt as strongly as in Europe, which is home to the largest trading scheme in the world. The European Union's Emissions Trading System (ETS) was launched in 2005 as one of the founding pillars of the EU's widely heralded approach to the fight against climate change. The scheme, which includes all twenty-seven Member States plus Norway, Iceland and Lichtenstein, is already into its third iteration, whose cycle will be concluded in 2020, when the EU is set to meet its reduction targets under current UN-backed protocols. The ETS covers over 11,000 factories, power stations and other types of installations (collectively responsible for 40 per cent of Europe's total emissions), and in January 2012 was extended to the civil aviation sector.[51] Despite having been presented as a global best practice by EU authorities, the ETS has been grossly flawed ever since its inception. The initial allocation of tradable allowances (Phase 1, from 2005 to 2007) was marred by lax targets, generous dispensations to powerful interest groups and overallocation of permits.[52] Intense lobbying by the fossil fuel industry took place in Brussels and in European capitals, where the actual volume of allocations was being decided upon.[53] According to the think-tank Open Europe, European governments 'handed out permits for 1,829 million tonnes of CO_2 in 2005, while emissions were only 1,785 million tonnes'.[54] The scheme proved a source of windfalls for Europe's worst corporate polluters, as free-of-charge allocations were based on each industry's historic emissions (a process known as 'grandfathering') and gauged against their future projections, inevitably rewarding bad performers.[55] In Germany, which is the most polluting nation in Europe and accounts for the largest carbon emissions market, the environment minister accused the country's four biggest energy companies – Eon, RWE, Vattenfall and EnBW – of profiteering from the ETS at the expense of consumers by stoking earnings up to €8 billion in 2006.[56] The environmental organization Greenpeace dubbed the ETS 'a licence for polluters to print money', arguing that relying on future emissions projections (which can be easily inflated by the industry) resulted in handing out permits for free that were then sold for profit.[57]

In 2006, when such loose targets and overallocations were confirmed, the price of emissions credits crashed in a matter of days, from the official price of roughly €30 a tonne (which was considered the minimum to achieve reduction targets) to a meagre €9 a tonne. Then in mid-2007, the nominal value of permits plummeted to zero, with the carbon market grinding to a halt.[58] According to the accounting firm Ernst & Young, the ETS created volatility in carbon prices rather than encouraging sustainable investment in renewable energies. Contrary to its alleged objectives, 'the scheme has encouraged the short-term trading of positions to optimise return and minimise financial risk.'[59]

The tenability of the emissions market is also affected by new policies. For instance, when the EU sells additional permits to raise revenues aimed at funding green energy programmes, this inevitably adds to an already inflated market.[60] Moreover, revised regulations on energy efficiency also result in emissions reductions, which are however not incorporated into the pre-existing cap, thus leading to additional drops in the price of carbon. As prices are by nature unstable (as they are affected by various market and non-market dynamics), investors have projected a significant surplus of 'hot air' of some 845 million extra permits by the deadline of 2020, against a planned cap that year of 1.8 billion.[61]

In a memorandum submitted to the UK Parliament in 2009, David Newbery, research director of the Electric Policy Research Group at the University of Cambridge, confirmed that the ETS 'cannot deliver the predictable and stable carbon price needed for long-term low-carbon investment decisions'.[62] In 2004, the UK secretary of state for trade and industry Patricia Hewitt had already written to then European Commission president Romano Prodi to complain about the way in which the ETS was set up and managed by Member States. She warned that 'allocations beyond need are in effect gifting companies a free asset' and that there was 'a very real risk that overallocation will mean that little or no trading occurs', so that 'the credibility of the trading mechanism could be undermined, and the EU and its Member States would need to find other less flexible and more costly regulatory instruments to meet [their] obligations'.[63] With the sale of new permits in Phase 2 (2008–12), prices once again hovered around €30 for some time, but then dropped to less than €10.

In 2012, the European market lost a third of its value (from US$148 billion to about US$100 billion), increasing pressure on European governments to provide additional support. In December 2012, the EU sold 5.58 million carbon permits (as part of Phase 3) at a value of €6.45 million, way too low to prod firms into making serious investments towards a low carbon economy.[64] As the European Commission recently recognized, plummeting carbon prices may actually reverse the trend of emissions cuts and lead to investments in high-emitting technology.[65] Moreover, constantly low prices have also shifted the perceptions of investors in the market, who are no longer willing to buy allowances for more than €10 per tonne.[66] Finally, on 16 April 2013, when the European Parliament rejected a proposal to reduce carbon credits for the coming years, the price of carbon fell about 50 per cent, to €2.63 from nearly €5, in ten minutes. With these prices, all analysts agree, the ETS is actually discouraging investment in alternative energies, making it more profitable to support 'dirty' industries.[67]

The ETS's curse, however, did not end with its pricing debacle. When the market volume peaked in mid-2009, with several hundred million allowances traded at an ever-descending value of around €12 per tonne, the Europol (the Europe-wide police force) began an investigation, which led to the discovery that 'as much as 90 per cent of the entire market volume on emissions exchanges was caused by fraudulent activity, undermining the very viability of the ETS'.[68] More than a hundred people were arrested for a crime known as 'missing trader' (a form of Value Added Tax evasion) and losses for Europe's tax revenues were quantified at around €5 billion across eleven countries. The Europol report highlighted two major problems with the system: the intangible nature of carbon markets (which makes them similar to speculative financial markets, in which public authorities have limited control and tracking capacity over money flows) and the registration procedures for carbon traders (which were lax and mainly based on self-monitoring, thus increasing the risk of money laundering).[69]

The ETS has proven particularly vulnerable to internal shocks, speculation and organized crime. A series of 'phishing attacks', involving emails prompting users to reveal their identification codes, led to the shutdown of national registries throughout Europe in 2010. Financial hackers also managed to access servers of firms and sell allowances on the 'spot' market, which allows for the instantaneous trading of permits in exchange for cash. The spot market increased 450 per cent over 2008, totalling 1.4 billion tonnes, and in 2009 spot volumes went up by 75 times. The first 'theft' occurred in Germany in 2010, but public authorities turned a blind eye. Then, in 2011, allowances stolen from several countries totalling over €30 million caused spot trading markets, which account for about 20 per cent of the sector, to close for several days.[70] Only then did governments call for a thorough investigation.

The numerous flaws of the ETS have alarmed environmental groups, which point out that much of the EU's leadership in the fight against climate change may be the result of an auditing trick, masked by numbers that simply do not add up in the real world: financial operations that are not mirrored by the trend in actual mitigation targets. As pointed out by the WWF, 'there's so much credit around, it's undermining the European emissions trading system and allowing the EU to keep emitting while still claiming to meet reduction targets. [I]t could mean Europe is actively making climate change worse, not better.'[71] Similarly, the think-tank Open Europe has described the ETS as 'an environmental and economic failure'.

Such issues have been compounded by other market-based applications, particularly carbon offsetting mechanisms, which have added further risks and distortions to the fight against climate change. Carbon offsets allow corporations and individuals to pay for reductions in greenhouse gases that are made else-where. Offsets are quantified in metric tonnes of carbon dioxide equivalent (CO_2e), certified by accredited institutions and then traded in the form of 'credits', just like in a conventional emis-sions trading scheme. Ever since the establishment of the Kyoto Protocol in 2005 the offset industry has grown exponentially. The Clean Development Mechanism (CDM), which is an inter-national framework established by the Kyoto Protocol, is the world's largest offset programme in terms of geographical scope and volume and the second largest carbon market. To date, the mechanism has issued over 1.14 billion credits. In 2007 its value was estimated at over US$33 billion.[72] Yet, just like the ETS, the price of CDM offsets has collapsed 90 per cent year on year to around 40 cents in 2012, roughly 10 cents below 'what analysts say it costs developers in fees to get issued with credits and well below costs involved in investing in carbon-cutting equipment'.[73] Nowadays, it is very easy to offset the emissions generated by one's daily commuting, by vacations and holidays or by any other type of economic activity simply by clicking on any of the thousands of dedicated websites and paying via credit card. Cleaning one's ecological footprint has never been so easy and cheap.

For the offset market to have any consequence, the certification process is paramount. If an offset claims to have reduced greenhouse gas emissions by a certain degree, then this needs to be reflected in real reduction.[74] However, determining business-as-usual baselines – that is, measurements of what would be the emission scenario in the absence of the offset project – is subject to numerous methodological and conceptual challenges. How does one distinguish between reductions that would have occurred anyway and those that are made possible only by the existence of an offset scheme? This is what experts call the principle of additionality: a genuine offset must be a reaction to a market incentive and must therefore occur *in addition* to what would happen anyway. One can distinguish between two types of approach to determine additionality: a project-specific and a standardized one. Project-specific methods are based on an evaluation of the proposed outputs of the offset scheme, which are then discounted from the outputs of the most viable and probable scenario (against a variety of benchmarks) in the absence of carbon markets. Standardized methods, by contrast, simply assess offset projects against a predetermined set of criteria, which usually require that the project must not be mandated by law, must involve a specific pre-approved technology, and must have an emissions rate lower than most others in its class.[75]

Another essential parameter is that of permanence: emission reductions must be permanent if they are to result in a genuine offset. Indeed, if emissions are released back into the atmosphere, the overall amount of greenhouse gases would grow rather than diminish. The issue of permanence is quite crucial for offset schemes, but particularly for those projects (which are often the majority) in which emissions have been sequestered through processes that may be reverted over time. A case in point is reforestation (re-establishment of existing forests) or afforestation (creation of new forests). While there is broad consensus that planting trees helps capture emissions, in the medium to long term the decay of forests and fires would result in more emissions being injected back into the atmosphere, thus cancelling out the assumed benefit of the offsets. Similarly, geological sequestration (e.g. carbon capture and storage) is at risk of leakage, especially if one takes into account the possibility of subterranean dynamics. Offset auditors have developed a variety of market-based mechanisms to measure and pre-empt the risks of reversal, including the purchase of specifically designed insurance policies, the development of reserve 'buffer pools' of credits and the issuance of temporary credits that must be recertified or replaced in the future. However, all these additional guarantees increase costs and slow down trade volumes.

Because of criteria, benchmarks and quantification methodologies, the entire offset industry relies on the third-party certification of so-called Designated Operational Entities (DOEs) – that is, specialized auditors that run evaluations, carry out measurements and certify the credibility of offset projects so that they may be marketed in a cap and trade system. In the case of the CDM, these are independent auditors accredited 'to validate project proposals or verify whether implemented projects have achieved planned greenhouse gas emission reductions'.[76]

In spite of the fundamental role they play, the accreditation standards for DOEs are quite generic (e.g. they have to posses sufficient human resources and experience in financial reporting system), the only constraint being that to qualify as a DOE a company should not have any pending 'judicial process for malpractice, fraud and/or other function incompatible with its functions as a designated operational entity'.[77] In order to safeguard impartiality, a DOE is required to work 'in a credible, independent, non-discriminatory and transparent manner', and in cases in which different sectors in the company serve different clients must 'clearly define the links with other parts of the organization, demonstrating that no conflicts of interest exist' and show it is not involved 'in any commercial, financial or other processes which might influence its judgement or endanger trust in its independence of judgement and integrity in relation to its functions'. When conflicts of interest arise, then DOEs are expected to clarify how these can be managed. They are also expected to promote a 'culture' of impartiality throughout the management structure and publicize their policy on their website. The only institutional requirement is for DOEs to establish an internal 'impartiality committee' which reports to top management.

Basically, these organizations are expected to monitor themselves. Public authorities assume that, by virtue of an unspecified culture of impartiality, auditors will do their job with no undue influence. Once again, the overall principle of self-regulation prevails in the governance of climate mitigation. The adoption of numerical models and quantification procedures, mostly developed by financial banks and audit firms, gives a false impression of neutrality. As is the case with credit ratings or with the discount rates in cost–benefit analysis, the assessment of additionality, permanence and future risks of reversal is, ultimately, a subjective assessment.[78] And when subjectivity reigns in a field characterized by growing financial resources, then conflicts of interest are bound to occur. DOEs can be easily corrupted by their clients into offering certifications that are skewed. As most DOEs are also financial auditors, they might find themselves validating clients to which they are providing other types of consultancy. Sectoral acquaintances and common networks also create conditions for risky 'familiarity' among DOEs and their counterparts. Finally, intimidation is always possible, whether it happens overtly or secretly. As reported by the professional service firm Deloitte (one of the Big 4 global audit firms, with Ernst & Young, KPMG and PWC, all involved in the offset market), because of the 'lack of regulation and enforcement agency regarding both verifiers and carbon offset providers, there's a high risk of fraud in these voluntary carbon markets'.[79] PWC climate service experts have also noted that there are situations in which 'project proponents are motivated to try and raise money before the project gets up and running', which means that one ends up 'selling credits before they actually exist'. Moreover, as 'there is not a global registry for carbon credits', companies 'could sell the same credit into several different markets'.[80]

Given the lack of a credible external enforcement system to guarantee the impartiality of DOEs and the essential subjectivity of their assessments, it is not surprising that cases of poor auditing and outright misbehaviour have abounded. In 2007 a study commissioned by the WWF called into question the role of independent auditors, showing that many CDM projects suffered from poor quality and did not lead to emissions reductions.[81] In 2010, a new study found no improvement in the work of evaluators assessing more than 900 offset projects in developing countries. On a scale between A (best) to F (worst), the maximum grade obtained (only by a single evaluator) was a paltry D.[82] The report concluded that attempts at providing additionality had miserably failed: 'Due to the shortcomings in project evaluation, large amounts of non-additional CO_2 certificates might be awarded. This might lead to a boosting of global emissions, quite contrary to the intended reductions for which the system was put in place.'

In 2010 alone, the UN Climate Change Secretariat was forced to suspend four DOEs after evidence of wrongdoing. One of these companies, the German Tüv Süd, a giant in the field of climate accounting, responsible for 21 per cent of the 395 million tonnes verified until then, was found guilty of not following procedures and granting 'a positive validation opinion to some projects even though it had concerns about additionality'.[83] Interestingly, Tüv Süd was the only D-rated auditor in the 2010 WWF report. According to a 2012 survey conducted by Point Carbon, the outlook for CDM investments 'is gloomy'.[84] Most offset projects take place in China and India, where analysts report a growing number of instances of corruption and fraud in emissions reduction projects. Moreover, many investors 'plan to decrease or completely stop investing in CDM projects'. The report published by the High-Level Panel on the CDM Policy Dialogue has also recognized that the offset market is 'imperiled'.[85] They acknowledge the fall in prices (70 per cent in 2012 alone) and project further decline in the coming years. Public and private investors alike 'are losing confidence in the CDM market' and mitigation targets 'are so modest that they no longer create strong incentives for private international investment', thus weakening the 'global carbon market technical capacity'.

Conclusion: when numbers become dangerous distractions

As both the ETS and the offset schemes demonstrate, the reality is very different from the numbers underpinning market-based policies. Echoing the case of credit rating agencies, power positions, informational asymmetries and conflicts of interest are common phenomena in real life. The capacity of powerful corporate interests to affect the rules of the game is unmatched by other sectors in society, be it public interest groups or non-governmental organizations.[86] And the rise of renewable energy companies has not yet changed the market dominance of the fossil fuel industry. According to Transparency International, the lobbying investment of oil and gas firms in the USA surpassed that of the clean energy sector by a factor of eight in 2009. In the EU, the policy positions of business groups largely outweigh those presented by environmental groups.[87] Just like the financial sector, the new carbon markets are prone to all sorts of aberrations, including fraud and criminal activities. Some analysts estimate that total climate change investments in mitigation will reach the staggering figure of US$700 billion by 2020, with a projected annual public investment of at least US$250 billion per annum. In such a gigantic financial market, the risk of malfeasance is extremely high, particularly due to the level of 'complexity, uncertainty and novelty that surrounds many climate issues', including 'what should count as a forest, or how to establish additionality', while 'tools to measure the environmental integrity of carbon offsets are relatively untested'. [88]

The various actors pulling the strings of the climate denial machine have been animated by a variety of motives. Arguably, the fossil fuel industry's main goal has been to keep its grip on power by steering the policy agenda. By providing timely counter-evidence to policymakers, while funding most of their electoral campaigns, the petroleum and coal conglomerate has virtually held the US political system hostage, while extending its tentacular reach to the rest of the world. Possibly no country nowadays, from China to Russia and Brazil, is immune from the immense pressure exerted by fossil fuel business. For this powerful corporate complex, any delays in (or obstructions to) environmental regulations mean prolonged privileges and advantages. For the scientists carrying the flag of scepticism, there have been rewards in terms of funding and prestige. As controversy around climate issues has grown over time, most of these unorthodox 'experts' have enjoyed unprecedented media coverage. Their papers, books and films (e.g. *Cool It*, the film documentary featuring Lomborg) have become popular among a wide audience, including those citizens looking for some evidence that business-as-usual works just fine. It pays to be against the mainstream, when you are supported by the most powerful and rich corporations in the world. While climate-change advocates are swimming in an ocean of collective scientific research, which makes them largely unknown as their individual contribution is just a small piece into a huge jigsaw puzzle, contrarians have enjoyed their comfortable position in a small pond of counter-propaganda. In a normal world, scepticism should have been relegated to the cultural curio shops, as is the case with creationism and Holocaust denial. But when journals, newspapers and television fall into the controversy trap, then the pond is elevated to ocean status. Both sides are given the same airtime and access to the public. That is when benefits become immense. Visibility turns into pay cheques, speaking fees and royalties. And, in a world of marketized academia, celebrity can get you a job at the most prestigious universities.

Dunlap and McCright maintain that, never mind the variety of motives behind these groups and individuals, 'the glue that holds most of them together is shared opposition to government regulatory efforts'.[89] While the claims of contrarian scientists invariably evolve over time, the theme of 'no need for regulations' remains constant: 'A staunch commitment to free markets and disdain of governmental regulations reflect the conservative political ideology that is almost universally shared by the climate change denial community.'[90]

Utilitarian reasoning has been their most powerful weapon. Whereas their scientific claims (e.g. climate change is a hoax, it is not caused by humans, it may not be that bad for the planet) have been proven wrong time and again, their econometric models have become mainstream in the economics of climate change. Cost–benefit analyses and market-based instruments are now the founding pillars of environmental policymaking. Discounting the future is an accepted approach to the monetization of marginal utilities. Carbon trading is broadly viewed as the most cost-effective response to climate change.[91] Climate accounting has become a burgeoning industry worth billions of dollars and offset schemes have mushroomed across more and less industrialized nations. Thousands of companies (and millions of well-meaning people) buy and sell carbon credits every day. Who are the main beneficiaries of all these new financial markets? Mostly fossil fuel corporations and banks, the very institutions responsible for the global climate and financial crises. Windfall profits have been made by polluting industries through emissions trading (mostly in 'progressive' Europe), while investment and commercial banks have been in charge of designing most (if not all) existing trading facilities. Meanwhile, the price of carbon has plummeted to ridiculously low values, generating enormous losses in tax revenues for governments and demanding additional public resources (a form of 'carbon bailout'), at a time when public authorities throughout the world are in unprecedented financial distress.

Has this at least contributed to abating CO_2 emissions? There is much doubt about that, as accounting systems are sketchy and ultimately controversial. The numbers published by international authorities such as the International Energy Agency, for instance, are gathered by polluting industries (e.g. oil, coal and gas corporations, cement companies, construction industry, manufacturers, etc.) as part of their carbon reporting requirements, which raises doubts about the accuracy and validity of the final data. In any case, according to the Emissions Database for Global Atmospheric Research, global emissions of CO_2, which is the main cause of global warming, have continued to grow over the past decade. In 2012 (the most recent report available at the time of writing), they increased by 3 per cent, 'reaching an all-time high of 34 billion tonnes'.[92] Currently, there is an estimated total of 420 billion tonnes of CO_2 in the atmosphere 'cumulatively emitted due to human activities'.

The apparent neutrality of cost–benefit analyses hides an important underlying reality. Although economic reasoning tends to treat all costs as equal, in real life this is not necessarily true. Costs are not spread equally in society. In general, decisions that spread costs proportionally to capabilities are seen as fair. In some instances, it may even be appropriate to concentrate costs on certain categories rather than others. In deciding between two alternative ways of bearing costs, the overall total may matter less than how it is distributed. For instance, a society may legitimately select a more expensive governance option whose costs are distributed fairly (in terms of proportionality and capabilities) instead of a cheaper one in which distribution is viewed as unfair. If certain industries have benefited more from traditional arrangements and competitive advantages, it would be fair to ask them to bear most of the costs for the transition to a low carbon (or, ideally, a no-carbon) economy. Cost–benefit analyses, by contrast, spread costs across societies uniformly and, ultimately, place greater emphasis on the 'cheapest' alternatives. Invariably, this mode of reasoning rewards business.

The ETS, just like most trading schemes, may very well be the most cost-effective option on the table. But cost-effective for whom? Definitely for the fossil fuel industry: as we have seen, it has resulted in a redistribution of resources from the public to the private sector. But was it also cost-effective for citizens? Probably not, as most energy utilities simply charge the higher costs of buying permits to their clients' energy bills. While the ETS produced a big plus on the books of business, it generated a minus in the budgets of households.

In the battle of ideas for environmental governance, sceptics have ultimately been victorious. Their cost–benefit analyses, which turned everything into numbers, and numbers into prices, have had a long-lasting impact on our societies. They have been a dangerous distraction for the international community, leading the world into a vicious circle of market supremacy and ecological collapse. Although there has been evidence of anthropogenic climate change since at least the 1960s (and scientific consensus since the late 1980s), the world has been waiting. Waiting for economics to do the trick. Waiting for accountants to do their measurements and for auditors to certify them. Forgetting, however, that nature does not follow economic models and, more importantly, does not sign off on auditors' checklists.

While this chapter has focused on how the politics of statistics has paved the way for market-based approaches to climate change mitigation, the next chapter will delve into another critical sector of environmental governance, namely the valuation of natural capital and ecosystem services. Both sectors are indeed closely related. We may say that, if the marketization of climate change has now become a reality through emissions trading and offsets, the introduction of similar 'markets' for the preservation of nature may ultimately lead to the financialization of the natural world. As is the case with carbon markets, numerical models lead us to think that we can price anything. But in trying to measure the price of nature – even if with the genuine intention to preserve it – our generation is treading on a rather treacherous terrain populated by speculative markets, investment ventures and private auditing companies.

CHAPTER 4

Measuring the unmeasurable: the financialization of nature

To measure the unmeasurable is absurd and constitutes but an elaborate method of moving from preconceived notions to foregone conclusions. The logical absurdity, however, is not the greatest fault of the undertaking: what is worse, and destructive of civilisation, is the pretence that everything has a price or, in other words, that money is the highest of all values.

E.F. Schumacher, *Small is Beautiful: A Study of Economics as if People Mattered*, 1973

The only common measure the nature of things affords is money.

Jeremy Bentham

The spread of economic reasoning and market approaches has not been confined to the controversial field of climate change mitigation. It has become a dominant trend in the way in which we interact with nature as a whole. There are two fields in which methods for the monetization of non-market phenomena have seen an unexpected and unprecedented growth in the past few years: natural capital and ecosystem services. The difference between these two accounting areas is rather fictitious. One way to describe it is to say that natural capital accounting aims to measure the depletion of environmental 'capital' consumed in conventional economic process (as measured in terms of GDP), while ecosystem accounting tries to measure the economic values of natural services in general. As a field of economic research, natural capital/ecosystem accounting has emerged out of the need to assess the complex interaction between human economic systems and nature, as the latter regularly provides essential services to mankind, which are however not delineated by property rights and market dynamics.

As we have seen in Chapter 1, the national income accounts on which GDP is based neglect the economic value of a number of non-market goods, including unpaid work, the gift economy, all forms of 'prosumerism' (that is, people producing for their own consumption) and natural resources. Critics point out that official metrics of economic performance treat natural resources as disposable income while they should instead be treated as capital which is not renewable and must be replenished if the process of economic growth is to go on. Their argument is that if Mother Nature was to be properly valued and incorporated into the calculations of economic performance, we could not avoid recognizing how critical its services are to economic welfare.[1] Such recognition would result in very different macroeconomic policies, in which environmental preservation would come to occupy centre stage. With this objective in mind, since the 1980s pioneers in the field of economic performance metrics have been producing measures of 'genuine progress' and 'green' accounting. They have developed various methodologies to take into consideration the value of natural non-renewable resources consumed during economic processes with a view to subtracting it from GDP, just like capital consumption is subtracted from 'net' estimates of domestic product.[2] In 1992, the US Bureau of Economic Analysis began to work on a set of satellite accounts to capture the economic impact of subsoil mineral resources. Two years later, however, the US government halted the initiative, as some of the findings were being attacked by the extractive industries, and called for an external evaluation. A high-level panel chaired by William Nordhaus and made up of some of the most renowned experts in the field of national income accounting, including Robert Eisner, who in the 1980s had developed a 'total income' system of accounts, concluded that measuring natural resources and the environment was 'an important goal'.[3] In their final report, published in 1999 and titled *Nature's Numbers*, the panel recommended a phased approach, focusing primarily on constructing forest accounts and then moving on to agricultural assets, fisheries and water resources. Nevertheless, they recognized the methodological challenges involved in developing these new accounts: 'The process will require resolving major conceptual issues, developing appropriate physical measures, and valuing the relevant flows and stocks.'[4]

In general, these methods of accounting have aimed to achieve a double goal: on the one hand, to reform the international system of national accounts by taking into consideration the derivation of income from non-sustainable consumption of natural resources and other environmental services; on the other hand, to produce numerical information about the economic value of natural ecosystems with a view to emphasizing how important nature is to human well-being and economic growth. As remarked by economist Simon Hicks in the 1940s, any measure of income should gauge the capacity of individuals (or societies) to produce wealth without undermining future capacities to consume ad infinitum.[5] But if contemporary income measures are mostly based on an unaccounted depletion of non-renewable ecosystemic resources, it results that such consumption patterns are not sustainable in the long term. In the words of Robert Repetto and his team, who in 1989 conducted one of the first studies of how natural resources may be integrated in national income accounts, 'A country could exhaust its mineral resources, cut down its forests, erode its soil, pollute its aquifers and hunt its wildlife and fisheries to extinction, but measured income would not be affected as these assets disappeared.'[6] According to a 2013 study measuring the world's genuine progress, global GDP growth correlated to general improvements in human welfare up until 1978. After that date, increases in economic growth (at the aggregate level) led to the deterioration of human, social and natural equilibria.[7]

Natural capital adds to human well-being in multiple ways, which are systematically neglected by official GDP statistics. It produces goods that are marketed, as is the case with most products in the agricultural sector. It also produces ecological services and amenities that directly contribute to economic growth and human welfare, such as water provision, soil fertilization, pollination, which however are not channelled through markets (e.g. nature provides us with water free of charge). At the same time, there are economic processes that have a negative impact both on human welfare and on natural capital. Waste production, pollution and contamination are consequences of economic growth which are detrimental to the environment and harmful to human beings. As human welfare is a function of much more than the consumption of economic goods and services, then the fundamental role played by nature cannot be disregarded. But can nature be priced? What are the inherent methodological and conceptual problems with that? Do other political agendas hide behind such an apparently benign attempt to 'value' nature? This chapter looks at how the politics of statistics has affected the global debate on the conservation of biodiversity. It discusses the historical evolution of key methodologies to translate nature into numbers and also dissects the strengths and weaknesses of existing approaches. As this book is mainly concerned with the political role that numbers play in governance, the chapter argues that such new trends in the field of natural capital accounting and ecosystem services have the potential to spiral out of control. As investment banks, private auditors and a varied range of consulting companies become interested in these new 'markets', there is a serious risk that what was initially a genuinely good cause (i.e. 'valuing' nature to preserve it) may actually lead to the financialization of the world's natural wonders.

Measuring the value of nature: statistical evolutions in global governance

In 2007, world leaders gathered for the G8 in Heiligendamm, Germany. They endorsed, among others, a proposal submitted by their environment ministers to 'initiate the process of analysing the global economic benefit of biological diversity, the costs of the loss of biodiversity and the failure to take protective measures versus the costs of effective conservation'.[8] They wanted to develop a clear and sound cost–benefit analysis of environmental governance objectives, based on indisputable numbers and reflecting accurate prices. Not ideas, not generic goals, but crude statistics that, in the form of market values, would be easier to integrate into economic planning and also resonate more widely with society's focus on economic growth. This initiative resulted in a study coordinated by the European Commission and the German government on 'the economics of ecosystems and biodiversity' (commonly known as TEEB), which presented a state-of-the art collation of monetary valuation techniques with a view to defining a common framework for policy application.[9] In the introduction, the project's report acknowledged the complexity and the importance of the task at hand:

> [W]e are still struggling to find the 'value of nature'. Nature is the source of much value to us every day, and yet it mostly bypasses markets, escapes pricing and defies valuation. This lack

of valuation is, we are discovering, an underlying cause for the observed degradation of ecosystems and the loss of biodiversity.[10]

As interest in the valuation of natural capital grew, more institutions joined in. In 2010, the World Bank launched the 'Wealth Accounting and Valuation of Ecosystem Services' (WAVES), a global partnership to build consensus on a common methodology to measure the economic value of natural resources.[11] WAVES' main objective is 'to promote sustainable development by ensuring that the national accounts used to measure and plan for economic growth include the value of natural resources'. It focuses specifically on building synergies between public and private sectors to include natural capital considerations in the strategic choices of the corporate world. The Bank's approach to natural capital accounting builds on its decade-long work on new measures of 'total wealth', which have been inspired by 'the ideas of the classical economists, who viewed land, labor, and produced capital as the primary factors of production'. One of the key indicators employed in these studies is the so-called adjusted net savings, better known as genuine savings, which purports to be a measure of sustainability by looking at how much countries provide for the future.[12] Total wealth indicators, such as the Inclusive Wealth Index backed by the UN, distinguish between produced capital (including the sum of machinery, equipment, infrastructure and urban land), natural capital (including land resources, forests and sub-soil assets) and intangible capital (a wide array of assets such as human capital, quality of institutions and governance). In a report titled *Where is the Wealth of Nations? Measuring Capital for the 21st Century*, the Bank asserted that 'in poorer countries, natural capital is more important than produced capital', thus suggesting that the careful management of natural resources should become a fundamental component of development strategies, 'particularly since the poorest households in those countries are usually the most dependent on these resources'.[13] It must be underlined, however, that these types of indicator adopt a 'weak' sustainability approach, which states that the depletion of natural resources can be offset by, for instance, an equivalent investment in other fields. As a consequence, the removal of a park to build a kindergarten would result in a perfectly balanced sheet, with no negative impact on sustainable development or, in economic terms, with a net opportunity cost for future generations equivalent to zero. In this model of accounting, what we take away from nature is rebalanced by what we invest in human development.

It was only in 2012, though, that the UN Statistical Commission adopted the first international standard for the valuation of natural capital: the System of Environmental-Economic Accounting (SEEA).[14] The origins of SEEA date back to the revision of the system of national accounts in the late 1980s and early 1990s, when historic shifts in the world's political and economic arena (from the end of the Cold War to the growth of globalized markets) led to a major revision of UN accounting standards, with new guidelines being published in 1993.[15] At that time, UN reviewers rejected the call for an outright revision of GDP because of their reluctance to add any further imputations to the national accounts. In their motivations, they criticized environmental advocates for trying to impose 'normative measures' on calculations of economic performance.[16] They also maintained that, since natural resources are not 'purchased' from Mother Nature, whatever valuation one may come up with would inevitably be artificial and controversial. Hence, better no valuation at all than a distorted one. They distinguished between depletion (of natural resources) and depreciation (of man-made assets): unlike the first, the second refers to consumption of goods 'whose production has already been fully accounted for in the system'.[17] UN statisticians did not recognize nature as a factor of production (in line with mainstream neoclassical economic thinking), thus making traditional national accounts unsuitable for environmental accounting.

For the same reason, the next round of reform in 2008 discarded the possibility of taking into account natural capital depletion. This revision process reaffirmed the principle that a 'necessary condition' for an activity to be treated as productive is that 'it must be carried out under the instigation, control and responsibility of some institutional unit that exercises ownership rights over whatever is produced'.[18] For example, the natural growth of stocks of fish in the high seas not subject to international quotas is not counted as production, given that no proprietary institution manages the process and the fish do not belong to any organization or company. By contrast, the growth of fish in fish farms is treated as a process of production and therefore adds to GDP. Also the 'natural growth of wild, uncultivated forests or wild fruits or berries' is excluded from production, whereas the 'cultivation of crop-bearing trees, or trees grown for timber or other uses', is counted in the same way as the growing of annual crops. Similarly, the 'deliberate felling of trees in wild forests' and 'the gathering of wild fruit or berries, and also firewood' counts as production.[19] Following the same logic, 'rainfall and the flow of water down natural watercourses' are *not* processes of production, whereas 'storing water in reservoirs or dams and the piping or carrying of water from one location to another' *all* constitute a positive increment to national income.

While the subtraction of natural capital depletion from official GDP statistics encountered resistance among UN statisticians, much easier was to incorporate it into the system of satellite accounts, a parallel set of calculations covering, among others, indicators to gauge the scope of the informal sector, tourism (which is only marginally captured in GDP accounts) and unpaid work.[20] It was in this area that the SEEA was developed as a complementary system of accounts. The SEEA provides a general framework for the standardization of assessments dealing with the direct physical flows of materials and energy between the economy

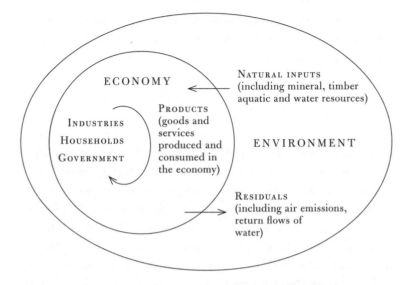

FIGURE 4.1 Conceptualizing nature's contribution to the economy
Source: UN Statistical Commission et al., *System of Environmental-Economic Accounting*.

and the environment, the stocks of environmental assets and the economic transactions related to the environment. As depicted in Figure 4.1, the SEEA views natural capital and ecosystems as factors of production and measures their contribution to specific economic activities. In its language, conceptual framework and methodology, the SEEA mirrors the logic of the GDP accounts by extending them to the assessment of nature's contribution to economic growth.

Due to its exclusive focus on the material benefits deriving from the *direct* use of environmental assets as natural inputs to the economy, the SEEA is not a comprehensive framework for the assessment of ecosystem services in general. The SEEA only provides 'guidance' on the valuation of renewable and non-renewable natural resources and land *within* the asset boundary of national income statistics as reflected in GDP. It does not aim to measure natural assets and related stocks and flows that go beyond traditional systems of national accounts. At the time of writing, the development of an ecosystem assessment methodology was still under discussion at the UN level. They had planned the publication of a report on 'experimental ecosystem accounts', which would deal with the measurement of both material and non-material (as well as direct and indirect) benefits to humanity as a whole. Yet they clarified that it would 'not be a statistical standard, but will provide a consistent and coherent summary of the state of the art of using a systems approach to the measurement of ecosystems'.[21]

In the SEEA, the scope of valuation is limited to economic actors. Following the GDP accounts, which are based on clear production and property boundaries, it only measures the benefits that accrue to economic owners, defined as 'the institutional unit entitled to claim the benefits associated with the use of an asset in the course of an economic activity by virtue of accepting the associated risks'.[22] In the case of environmental assets, such benefits are recorded in the form of 'operating surplus from the sale of natural resources and cultivated biological resources', as rent earned on 'permitting the use or extraction of an environmental asset', or in the form of 'net receipts' (i.e. excluding transaction costs) when an environmental asset is sold (e.g. sale of land). When market prices do not exist for such 'transactions', the estimation of values must be based on conceptual assumptions and numerical models, for which SEEA makes a series of recommendations. Whenever possible, direct observations of the prices of assets traded in real markets should be used to price similar assets that are not traded. For example, information on sales of land, timber and minerals may be used to estimate the value of similar goods that have not (yet) been sold. Another method may be to look at replacement costs, especially for natural assets that cannot be or are not commonly traded. According to this approach, the value of a natural asset is equal to the current acquisition price of an equivalent new asset, after deducting its depreciation. Just as the price of a second-hand car corresponds to the cost of a new car minus the depreciation of value over the course of its life and mileage, 'this approach may be applied to estimate the value of the stock of cultivated biological resources that are fixed assets, for example, orchards.'[23]

When these two approaches are not possible (because, for example, there are no relevant market transactions or acquisition prices), the SEEA recommends adopting a mathematically more sophisticated (yet fundamentally elusive) method, which bases the price of natural flows on the discounted value of future returns, as is the case with conventional cost–benefit analysis, which we have already encountered in Chapter 3. The discounted value of future returns is commonly referred to as the Net Present Value (NPV) and 'uses projections of the future rate of extraction of the asset together with projections of its price to generate a time series of expected returns'.[24] In line with conventional economic thinking, which assumes that returns earned in the present are worth more than those earned in the future, the stream of expected returns is discounted to reflect 'the value a buyer would be prepared to pay for the asset in the current period'. Moreover, to ensure that the valuation is aligned to the general concept of market prices, the UN statisticians advise auditors of natural capital to apply a market-based discount rate equal to the assumed rate of return on produced assets. For the NPV approach, indeed, an asset with no expected returns has no value in economic terms. However, since expected returns are, by definition, not observed in reality, only estimations and projections can be made, thus shifting the entire argument from statistical accounting (which is often portrayed as the art of neutral collection of data) to financial analysis (which is the realm of value judgements and risk assessment). But SEEA was written after the 2008 financial crisis and its authors are aware that private markets 'may not be sufficiently developed to provide robust estimates of these specific rates of return'. Thus, in what appears more like a policy recommendation based on anecdotal evidence rather than sound economic analysis, they suggest using real-life rates of return such as 'government bond rates'.[25] In their opinion, the return on investment produced by the possession of natural resources should be roughly equivalent to that of sovereign bonds. Evidently, the report must have been written before the sovereign bonds downgrades experienced by most advanced economies since 2011.

Looking beyond the models' apparent neutrality, the UN Statistical Commission recognizes that all these approaches are problematic and fundamentally subjective. It also admits that its framework intentionally rejects the attribution of value to 'all of the benefits that may accrue to current and future generations', thus refuting the adoption of 'what might be regarded as social valuations of environmental assets'.[26] In addition, its narrow focus on specific property boundaries and direct input to the economy neglects the broader societal implications of natural capital. UN statisticians agree that a better methodology should apply 'social discount rates' in the valuation of environmental assets, rather than market-based discount rates, given that the former reflect 'broad and long term value to society as a whole' while the latter are computed 'solely in relation to their value to a present day extractor'. And so they conclude, albeit in a marginal note, that one of the main arguments supporting the use of social discount rates is that these 'place higher relative importance on income earned by future generations', whereas estimates of NPV using market-based discount rates 'do not value future generations'.[27]

Putting a price on ecosystems

In 1997, a team of researchers led by ecological economist Robert Costanza of the University of Maryland made the first attempt at producing an estimate of the total value of ecosystem services

– that is, the worldwide variety of processes that nature provides for free to economic activity, from water supply to pollination. In a paper published in *Nature*, they gathered all studies available to date and estimated the overall value of the entire biosphere to be (on average) US$33 trillion per annum.[28] At the time, this figure was almost twice the value of global GDP, which hovered around US$18 trillion a year. The researchers were animated by genuine environmental concerns. They were, of course, aware that many people believe that 'valuation of ecosystems is either impossible or unwise' and that 'we cannot place a value on such "intangibles" as human life, environmental aesthetics, or long-term ecological benefits.'[29] Yet their conclusion was that, in the absence of any clear and transparent valuation, ecosystems will continue being given 'too little weight in policy decisions', ultimately compromising 'the sustainability of humans in the biosphere'.[30] In a follow-up study published in *Science* in 2002, they concluded that the net benefits of nature conservation worldwide (measured in terms of NPV) outweighed the costs by a margin of 100 to 1.[31] Each dollar invested in the preservation of natural ecosystems would yield one hundred times in financial returns. From an investment point of view, no financial bubble or speculative derivative could ever produce so much money. As remarked by some commentators, 'even in the heady pre-Sept. 11 days of the dot-com craze, numbers like this would have made any day trader giddy.'[32] But what was behind these numbers?

As exemplified by the evolution of the SEEA framework, valuation methods for natural capital are fraught with fallacies and risks. These are further compounded when the field of analysis is expanded to include the arguably endless variety of ecosystem services, which must be valued not only in terms of their direct contribution to economic growth in certain sectors (as the SEEA does) but also (and more importantly) in terms of their overall impact on humanity's well-being. In their pivotal research, Costanza and colleagues acknowledged the 'conceptual and empirical problems inherent in producing such an estimate'.[33] Their approach was inevitably simplistic. They calculated average value per hectare of seventeen types of service across sixteen biomes – that is, geographically defined areas of the planet characterized by similar climatic conditions – and then multiplied this value for the extent of the terrestrial surface. As it turned out, much of the data was missing. In their paper, for instance, they could not find valuation studies for some major biomes such as deserts, tundra, ice/rock and cropland. They also remarked that estimates inevitably result in a 'static snapshot' of what, in fact, is a very complex, non-linear and interdependent system. Moreover, the monetization frameworks assume that there are no 'sharp thresholds, discontinuities or irreversibilities in the ecosystem response function', which is 'almost certainly not the case'.[34]

There are also critical issues of scale that limit the policy and societal impact of studies monetizing ecosystem services. Take the infamous figure of US$33 trillion. Is that a high or a low figure for an average citizen or a policymaker? Even a simple question such as this proves very difficult to answer. Although some people may find it hard to make sense of such an enormous volume of money (just as much as they struggle to fathom the scale of the global economy), a closer look reveals that the figure may actually be extremely low. If nature is worth the equivalent of two global GDPs, then some may conclude that, in the worst-case scenario, should ecosystems collapse entirely, it would be enough to triple the world economy to replace all natural capital. If all workers were to produce three times as much and if all companies were willing to commit to triple production targets, then mankind could do without nature. We could successfully replace rainfall, pollination, water sources and so on. Nothing short of a very cheap bailout of nature. Would that be possible? Many of us would recoil at such an idea, considering these extrapolations just some type of economic extravagance or outright political madness. Twice the global economy? Even three, four, fifty times as much would still be a foolish 'underestimation of infinity'.[35] Point taken. However, a calculation that leads to infinity would never trigger policy reforms. It would simply be a generic statement with no real teeth in practice. As often happens, when figures are much higher than our daily experience (quadrillions, light years, infinity), we fail to grasp their actual magnitude. And when numbers are too 'big' to comprehend, then it is unlikely that policies will change. But when they are relatively small, there is the opposite risk.

Because of this inevitable valuation dilemma, many observers have maintained that the ambition to monetize ecosystems (or, as is often put, to put a price on infinity) is both impossible and unwise. There are obvious reasons to be suspicious of a utilitarian calculation of economic value applied to 'intangibles' such as human life, environmental beauty or long-term ecological benefits.[36] Since the publication of the *Nature* paper, numerous ecological economists have questioned various technical aspects of the methods for the valuation of ecosystem services, especially the reliance on a mix of scattered surveys and estimates of replacement costs, which are further undermined by the always-present risk of double counting.[37]

There exist a variety of methodologies to monetize ecosystems. Some of these assess the value of environmental 'goods' indirectly, by tracking prices in related markets. For instance, hedonic methods applied to the price of housing stock are used to estimate the value of local environmental quality. Take the case of two flats. They are roughly the same size and quality, but one is located near a park (and is therefore more expensive) while the other is not. What would then be the estimated price of the park? An algorithm based on price differential between the two flats answers this question. Similarly, the travel costs incurred by visitors have been used as proxies of the value of recreational areas, while the costs borne by people who try to protect themselves against environmental risks (e.g. drinking bottled water, medical expenses, etc.) have been employed to monetize the value of ecological preservation.[38] Most techniques, however, are more 'direct' and follow the conceptual frameworks of the so-called 'willingness to pay' (WTP) approach, a survey method that tries to estimate prices as a function of the willingness of potential buyers to acquire certain goods. To the distaste of many genuine environmentalists, the WTP was developed by marketing research and ultimately popularized by big corporations, as a rather mainstream approach used to gauge pricing decisions in the development of new products. Companies usually adopt WTP to develop an optimal pricing strategy (and thus outcompete rivals and increase their market share), to forecast market response to price changes, to model demand functions and to measure the added value of a brand to a specific product vis-à-vis an unbranded baseline product. The underlying principle is that, when we buy something, we base our assessment on a series of 'objective' and 'subjective' parameters. Some of the objective parameters include functionality, newness, usefulness and the like. Some of the subjective parameters include its desirability and social status, given that not everything that we buy has a use-value. Moreover, the act of buying does not happen in a vacuum but is part of a complex social dynamic characterized by traditions and expectations. Our WTP is based on all these parameters, and when the market price equals (or approaches) our criteria then we are likely to make the purchase. This is why companies compete to know as much as possible about consumers' preferences. They collect data on our shopping habits, they want to know what we look for when we surf the Internet and what goods we cherish. If they could read our WTP on our foreheads, they could set prices accordingly and see their sales skyrocket. In their marketing strategies, however, they are not simply passively guessing how much we would be willing to pay for a given good. They are actively influencing our mental processes of valuation, mainly via advertisements and branding. They want our WTP to mirror their expectations and profit margins. In this continuous mutual exchange, measuring WTP becomes both a heuristic task and a psychological battle.

Most WTP methods can be divided into two main groups: those based on revealed preferences and those relying on stated preferences. Among the first we find experiments such as Vickrey auctions, in which participants submit sealed bids without knowing the valuations of the other bidders, similar to the online proxy bidding auctions popularized by, among others, the website eBay. In these experiments successful bidders are requested to buy the good for the bid price, although the price is set on the level of the second best bidder (second price auctions).[39] A similar experiment involves participants simultaneously submitting offer prices, with the sale price randomly drawn from a distribution of prices ranging from zero to the commonly agreed maximum price.[40] Bidders whose bids are greater than the sale price receive a unit of the item, but only pay an amount equal to the sale price. Both auction mechanisms are designed to encourage participants to disclose their true valuations, a principle which is generally defined by economists as incentive compatibility: as their acquisition of the auctioned good is not based on the highest possible bid, participants have an incentive not to gamble against the process (overbidding).

In the second group, we find survey-based techniques in which participants are either asked to rank their WTP for a certain set of items (e.g. a preference structure) or directly invited to identify a minimum–maximum prince range. In some cases, limited resources and time constraints make the use of focus groups preferable to more bottom-up techniques such as experiments and surveys. Expert judgements, in this regard, become 'a heuristic to assess customers' willingness to pay as well as to provide generic estimates of demand in response to different price levels'.[41] As a matter of fact, it is widely recognized that survey approaches to measure the WTP are fundamentally problematic and unstable. Respondents do not have an incentive to reveal their true preferences as a number of other considerations come into play. For instance, some may tend to overstate prices because of 'prestige effects' or so as not to appear 'stingy'.[42] By contrast, they may attempt to quote artificially lower prices, since many people perceive their role 'as conscientious buyers as that of helping to keep prices down'.[43] Buyers have little capacity to estimate the price of a product, especially if it is not a high-frequency purchase, which can lead to a sudden change in the declared WTP once respondents learn what the actual market price is.[44] Quite often, personal interviews can result in contradictory results and even reversals.[45] Moreover, market researchers are aware of the irreconcilable schism between hypothetical pricing and actual purchasing: even when respondents reveal their WTP, this does not automatically translate into actual purchasing behaviour.[46] In many cases, it is easier to decide whether the specific price for a product is acceptable rather than directly assign one.[47] Apparently insignificant technical tools, such closed-ended questions (in which respondents choose among prices posted by the interviewer) or open-ended formats (in which respondents have to come up with their own estimates), yield very different results.[48] Unsurprisingly, closed-ended dichotomous options (that is, only two alternatives to choose from) tend to produce more reliable results. Also indirect surveys, in which respondents are presented product profiles with varying prices and are asked to indicate whether they would purchase the good at that price or not, produce very different and inconsistent results across respondents.[49]

All these difficulties with estimates of WTP are common in conventional marketing fields. Even more complicated is when markets do not exist, as is the case with ecosystem services. In this context, the process must be simulated through so-called contingent valuations: instead of setting prices to estimate buyers' willingness to pay, the latter is used to gauge the former.[50] Thus, in the absence of a real-life price against which to check the results of the survey, what people are willing to pay becomes the de facto price of nature. The first published reference to this methodology appeared in the late 1940s, when researchers mentioned the possibility of conducting surveys based on the WTP to measure the financial 'returns' of preventing soil erosion.[51] It was only in the 1960s, though, that contingent valuations began to be used more systematically in studies focusing on a diverse range of topics, from the value of nature reserves to the right to hunt waterfowl and the value of duck hunting permits.[52] Contingent valuations began to be used also in research dealing with non-environmental issues, such as policies to reduce the risk of death from heart attack, prevention of respiratory disease and improved information about grocery shop prices.[53]

In the 1980s, contingent valuation methods were also incorporated into policy reforms, especially in the field of natural damage assessment, which stirred significant debate within academic and business circles. An interesting case was the establishment of the Comprehensive Environmental Response, Compensation and Liability Act of 1980, also referred to as CERCLA or, more commonly, as the Superfund law, which gave US government agencies the right to sue companies for damages to the natural resources for which they were trustees (which included lakes, streams, forests, bays, marshes, land masses and the like) and established that contingent valuations may be used to provide estimates not only of direct damage to users, but also of implications for society as a whole. Then, in March 1989, the supertanker *Exxon Valdez* ran aground on Bligh Reef in Prince William Sound, Alaska, spilling 11 million gallons of crude oil into the sea, causing the hitherto worst environmental disaster in the history of America. Following public outrage, the US Congress passed the Oil Pollution Act and contingent valuations made it for the first time into the litigation field.[54] The National Oceanic and Atmospheric Administration was tasked with the job of defining a methodology to monetize damage, and a blue ribbon panel of experts, led by Nobel laureate economists Kenneth Arrow and Robert Solow, carried out a review of the pros and cons of contingent valuation methods. Most business associations, championed by the American oil and mining sector, fought against the legitimacy of contingent valuation methods, as they believed that such 'subjective' methods would only be used to support expansive regulation and large damage awards. Much to their surprise, this was not the case. The blue ribbon panel only gave a lukewarm endorsement to contingent valuations, setting a number of parameters for its future usage. Moreover, the diversity of opinions among consultants led government agencies to settle the *Exxon Valdez* suit out of court, for a compensation of US$1.15 billion (against estimates of total losses averaging nearly US$3 billion).[55] Exxon corporation itself funded several 'counter studies', initially to dismiss the reliability of the valuations commissioned by the plaintiffs and, later on, to influence the methods and techniques used by experts. Ever since, research in the field of contingent valuation methods for ecological damage assessment has been greatly influenced by the oil industry itself.[56]

Needless to say, contingent valuation methods have been controversial not only for their potential politicization, but also for self-evident conceptual problems.[57] If market researchers acknowledge the intrinsic difficulty of estimating WTP for conventional market goods, then it goes without saying that problems are further compounded in surveying unfamiliar goods and concepts, such as the total economic value (TEV) of ecosystem services. By TEV, economists understand the combination of use-value, non-use (or existence) value and option value. Use-value, a classical concept in economics, denotes the utility that people derive from using a specific good (often, but not exclusively, to achieve some other specific objectives). The value of a hammer is commensurate to what I can actually do with it. As an instrumental concept, use-value is fundamental in the valuation of natural resources such as timber, fish, oil, water and the like, which can be converted into building materials, food and energy. However, nature is not only valuable for its specific uses. It also has an intrinsic non-use value. The pleasure (or utility) one derives from gazing into a sunset or admiring a spectacular landscape is not due to the use one can make of it, but rather to its mere existence (which is why non-use value is also known as existence value). Finally, nature is a source of utility with manifold applications, some of which may not be appreciated or known at present. So, its overall value is not only a function of its use and non-use, but also of its potential use. This is what cost–benefit analysts call option value, denoting the utility derived by the preservation of a resource that may be available for use in the future.[58]

These distinct (and complementary) definitions of value are not only relevant from a conceptual perspective. They have important political (and legal) implications too. Take the case of environmental damage litigation. While damage calculated on use-value can only be claimed by those who can demonstrate their direct economic loss from a particular ecosystemic degradation (e.g. farmers for diminishing rainfall, fishermen for water contamination, local residents for poor air quality), in the case of both non-use and option value anybody could – in theory – claim compensation (also known as passive loss). Never mind the evident difficulties in gauging the use-value of ecosystems, which have a fundamental yet largely neglected impact on human life. But the estimation of both non-use and option value is fraught with insurmountable complications due to subjectivity problems and cognitive (and cultural) constraints, which make it almost impossible to produce any meaningful valuation. For instance, a study commissioned by the Exxon Corporation to challenge the acceptability of contingent valuations in court found that respondents gave the same valuation answer in a survey for protecting 2,000, 20,000 or 200,000 birds, thus disproving the alleged capacity of respondents to accurately monetize ecological preservation.[59] Rather, one may argue that respondents were simply using their common sense, which suggested that protecting birds, no matter how many they are, is simply a value in its own right. Perhaps they thought birdlife was something that could not be priced. Or perhaps they just had no idea. As recognized by Costanza and colleagues, respondents 'may be ill-informed' and their preferences 'may not adequately incorporate social fairness, ecological sustainability and other important goals'. In other words,

> if we actually lived in a world that was ecologically sustainable, socially fair and where everyone had perfect knowledge of their connection to ecosystem services, both market prices and surveys of willingness-to-pay would yield very different results than they currently do, and the value of ecosystem services would probably increase.[60]

In a society where short-term utility, self-interest and consumption have been elevated to structural codes of conduct, it is doubtful that the personal preferences of a few experiments' participants or survey respondents (let alone so-called experts' focus groups) can result in a reliable valuation of the world's natural capital. Moreover, all these approaches take for granted an anthropocentric view of valuation (nature is worth what humans can extract from it), entirely disregarding the possibility that the environment may have an intrinsic value, an issue often raised by ethicists as well as natural scientists, and neglecting the broader implications of ecosystem-centric and eco-centric perspectives on nature. As we have discussed in Chapter 3, cost–benefit analysis and economic evaluation are dangerous simplifications, which may easily mislead policy makers. Even those who accept the validity of monetary valuation need to recognize that there are 'simply too many empirical uncertainties about these values', which 'reflect our limited understanding of the physical world.'[61] Indeed, any natural scientist would agree that humans do not know all the ways in which ecosystems provide services and how these change over time. Evaluators, too, change their views on the role of ecosystems as their informational basis shifts and their social context evolves over time and generations.

In many regards, the findings of the 1997 *Nature* article and its 2002 follow up in *Science* can be seen as a 'political manifesto' more than a scientific measurement. Both studies were meant to 'stimulate additional research and debate' and overcome the fact that, for many decades, the valuation of nature had been dominated by a narrow focus on individual utility maximiza-tion.[62] Aware of the contradictions and limitations of their original approach to valuing natural capital, these scholars pledged to investigate new ways to capture two important additional goals, namely ecological sustainability and social distributional fair-ness, as they became aware that 'basing valuation on current individual preferences and utility maximization alone, as is done in conventional analysis, does not necessarily lead to ecological sustainability or social fairness.'[63] A fairness base value requires that individuals choose their preferences as members of the community, not as individuals. This, however, would need a very different process, involving open debate and consultations throughout society in order to reach 'consensus on the values that would be fair to all members of the current and future community (including non-human species)'.[64] As there are always winners and losers in a valuation process, a collective debate would only be fruitful if participants adopt a 'veil of ignorance', as in John Rawls's theory of justice, where everyone votes 'as if they were operating with no knowledge of their own individual status in current or future society'.[65] Finally, a sustainability-based value would require a comprehensive assessment of the way in which ecosystem services are connected to the physical, chemical and biological functioning of the global system. If it is accepted that all species, no matter how seemingly uninteresting or lacking an immediate utility from an anthropocentric perspective, have a fundamental role to play in natural ecosystems, then the valuation of ecosystems should have no direct reference to human preferences. For too long, human beings have operated within ecosystems 'as if they were representatives of the whole system'. By contrast, a true sustainability approach would need to focus on an overall assessment of the 'evolutionary contribution to the survival of the linked ecological economic system' as well as 'the opportunities of choice for future generations'. Needless to say, such objectives would require a totally different methodology. And, because of 'the large uncertainties involved', any model would need to be used in a precautionary way, 'looking for the range of possible values and erring on the side of caution'.[66]

The financialization of nature

But has this been the case? Have new models been treated with the necessary carefulness, trying to incorporate a holistic understanding of value and always erring on the side of caution? Quite the opposite. Just like the burgeoning offset industry in the field of climate change mitigation, natural capital accounting has become a new business for private consultancies, banks and investment groups, mostly aided by new forms of governance at the global level.

In 2006, the United Nations Environment Programme commissioned a study to estimate the value of coral reefs in the Caribbean and the Indian Ocean, where they are among the most important tourist attractions for scuba divers and an important source of fisheries, generating revenues for the local economy. Result: between US$100,000 and 600,000 a year for reefs and between US$200,000 and 900,000 for mangroves. In areas where these ecosystems contributed to maintaining white sandy beaches (another important tourist attraction), the estimated value shot up to US$1 million per year.[67] Another study conducted in the same year argued that various types of insect (in particular the declining population of honeybees) contributed at least US$57 billion per annum to the US economy.[68]

In 2009, *The Economist* ran the story of Iwokrama, a 370,000-hectare rainforest in central Guyana, which had just entered the 'global economy'.[69] Aware that donations would not be enough to maintain the forest, Iwokrama's board of trustees went to the market. First, it introduced moneymaking schemes such as timber extraction, ecotourism programmes, commercialization of forest products such as honey and oils, bio-prospecting and forestry research. Then it decided to sell a licence for the measurement and valuation of the forest's ecosystem services, which was bought by a London-based investment company, Canopy Capital. Ever since, the latter has been marketing 'ecosystem service certificates', which are attached to a 10-year tradable bond, betting on the rising cost of carbon and the financialization of reforestation projects as part of the offset mechanisms REDD (Reducing Emissions from Deforestation and Forest Degradation) and REDD+, two global schemes introduced by the Kyoto Protocol. As declared by Canopy Capital, countries that monetize their natural patrimonies and conserve their forests are likely to see these transformed into global assets worth billions of dollars a year: 'The investment community is beginning to wake up to this opportunity.'[70] The Global Canopy Project, a joint venture between scientists and investors, has been leading the global quest for the monetization of tropical forests and has produced popular publications such as the *Little Book of Forest Finance* and the *Little Book of Biodiversity Finance* which explain the seemingly endless possibilities of financial returns in the field of natural capital. Perhaps not surprisingly, the project's board of trustees is dominated by investment bankers and financiers.[71] In 2011, Canopy Capital ran a workshop titled 'Unlocking Forest Bonds', which was funded and supported by the world's largest investment bank, Goldman Sachs. Participants in the event agreed that 'The issuance of bonds directly addresses the concerns of time and scale, enabling issuers to raise large-scale finance now that will be repaid by existing and anticipated future income.'[72] Nevertheless they highlighted the challenge for bond issuers of convincing investors 'that the cash flows they plan to pay the bond back with are sufficiently secure and predictable', especially now that carbon markets have become less reliable. Thus, as a way to make forests look profitable, they recommended introducing 'ecosystem service markets (e.g. water, biodiversity), sustainable timber and agricultural markets, regulation (e.g. taxes, liability regulation), and forest-friendly lending (e.g. to ecosystem-dependent small- and medium-sized enterprises)', which would need to receive the necessary support from governments 'to ensure that these cash flows materialise, making forest preservation an attractive investment'.

The Green Development Mechanism 2010 Initiative, recently renamed Green Development Initiative, is a public–private partnership to develop 'innovative market-based financial mechanisms' under the UN-backed Convention on Biological Diversity.[73] Its main goal is to guide private investment in the management of biodiversity according to certified standards and independent audits, which require an assessment of the economic value of biodiversity. As argued by the specialized magazine *Ecosystem Marketplace*, certified agricultural and forest products, private land trusts, payments for watersheds and other environmental services, and offsets for biodiversity loss could soon come to rival the billions of dollars generated by offset schemes under the Clean Development Mechanism.[74] In Australia, biodiversity banks (also known as 'biobanks') have been introduced to certify biodiversity credits generated by landowners who commit to enhance and protect biodiversity values, which can then be sold to developers with a view to counterbalancing (or offsetting) the impacts on biodiversity values that are likely to occur as a result of new construction projects.[75] In 2011, a bunch of global businesses, including the two largest consumer goods companies in the world, Nestlé and Unilever, joined a natural capital leadership compact, allegedly with a view to stimulating changes in the business response to nature.[76] At the Rio+20 summit in June 2012, two dozen multinational corporations, including Coca-Cola, Dow Chemical and Nike, vowed to introduce methods to value natural capital in the running of their operations and investments. In their report titled *The New Business Imperative: Valuing Natural Capital* they identified the range of benefits that accrue from such an initiative.[77] During the same summit, some of the world's leading private financial institutions signed a 'natural capital declaration', in which they pledged to integrate environmental accounting into their investment plans and operations.[78] In their words, 'every economic activity can have an impact on natural capital. ... These impacts can lead to material financial risks, but also to relevant business opportunities.'[79]

While these new governance trends are presented as important breakthroughs, the growing involvement of private financial groups and corporate giants in natural capital accounting and the economics of ecosystems should be viewed with suspicion. It also raises important issues as to the integrity of most of these allegedly 'green' programmes. For starters, the involvement of Goldman Sachs in the new business of forest bonds raises serious concerns, given the bank's involvement in triggering the global financial crisis and, more specifically, its dubious role in the Greek sovereign debt crisis, when the bank was hired to help this country's leadership disguise its actual financial status vis-à-vis European authorities.[80] Most of the other commercial and investment banks participating in these new 'deals' have also been deeply involved in the marketization of the very financial products that caused the Euro-crisis. One of the signatories of the natural capital declaration, the Italian banking giant UniCredit, which boasts operations in over twenty countries, has been taken to court by Italian authorities for tax evasion and for having actively passed toxic derivative contracts onto investors and consumers in order to clean up its books.[81] The mastermind behind the TEEB programme was also managing director in the global markets division at Deutsche Bank, an organization that has become the utmost symbol of Europe's banking elite and one of the major drivers of the collateralized debt obligations in this continent, already investigated for fraud, espionage, tax evasion and interest rate fixing in the Libor and Euribor scandals.[82] The same can be said with respect to some of the companies leading corporate involvement in this field. A corporation like Nestlé, for instance, has a rather questionable track record with respect to food production and distribution. Ever since the 1970s, civil society groups around the world have been leading an international boycott of Nestlé's products because of what they claim is the company's aggressive and unethical marketing of breast milk substitutes (infant formula) in African countries, which has allegedly resulted in malnourishment and deaths.[83] The company has also been criticized by health groups for refusing to label genetically modified food, by environmental NGOs for buying palm oil from subsidiaries that trash rain forests, by human rights defenders for doing business with the military junta in Burma/Myanmar, and by trade unions for exploiting farmers and undermining workers' rights.[84] In a 2005 film documentary the then CEO of Nestlé, Peter Brabeck-Letmathe, attacked organic farming, argued in favour of the massive commercialization of genetically modified food and candidly accused NGOs of extremism for defending water as a public right.[85] The Coca-Cola Company, too, cannot boast a shining resumé in environmental protection. Besides having been denounced for union busting in South America, the soft drink giant has built an oligopolistic control of water distribution in countries like India, where its plants have been accused of draining public water resources available to local farmers and have been investigated by federal and local government for massive use of pesticides.[86] Not only was Dow Chemical Company one of the main producers of the infamous Agent Orange used by US troops in Vietnam, but it consistently refused to clean up the contamination caused by the 1984 Bhopal gas tragedy, the world's worst industrial disaster, which was caused by an India-based pesticide plant owned by Union Carbide, a company acquired by Dow in 2001.[87]

The global consultancy company McKinsey, which besides working with some of the largest and most powerful companies in the world (they also pride themselves to be listed in the top 10 on *Fortune* magazine's World's Best Companies for Leaders) is also a leader in advising governments on reforestation and afforestation policies as part of the REDD+ scheme, has been involved in some of the most spectacular financial scandals in recent times. Jeff Skilling, the CEO of energy giant Enron, who is currently serving a fourteen-year prison sentence (reduced in a deal from twenty-four years) for fraud and other federal felonies, used to be a prominent partner at McKinsey. As reported by the *Wall Street Journal*, McKinsey itself was a strategic adviser to Enron during the years that led to the company's collapse (at the time, the largest corporate bankruptcy in America's history), raising questions of consultancy liability, given the finding that Enron's financial condition and operations had been sustained over various years through a systematic accounting fraud.[88] More recently, McKinsey was implicated in the Galleon scandal, the biggest insider-trading case ever.[89] According to prosecutors, the Galleon hedge fund was fed lucrative and illegal tips about McKinsey clients by some of the consultancy's top executives, including Anil Kumar, top senior partner and director, who pleaded guilty to securities fraud and cooperated with the government, revealing the involvement of Rajat Gupta, former CEO of McKinsey, who was sentenced to two years in prison in 2012.[90]

In environmental governance, McKinsey has risen to prominence thanks to the wide adoption of its global greenhouse gas abatement cost curve, a cost–benefit analysis conceived in 2007 outlining different options for a gradual reduction of emissions, in which height represents cost and the width of each segment indicates the relative amount of carbon abatement.[91] The cost curve has become rather popular among policymakers, particularly as it places more emphasis on cost-effective (read low cost for business) measures. According to environmental group Greenpeace, though, McKinsey's approach oversimplifies reality and is flawed by unrealistic assumptions about comparative costs:

> if the true costs of displacing local subsistence farming are underestimated ... by ignoring transaction costs and wider social and environmental impacts, whilst the costs of addressing industrial logging are overestimated (for example by exaggerating the economic value of logging to the economy), and these assumptions are built-in to the cost curve, then every policy decision flowing from the use of the curve will tend to favour logging interests over those of small-scale farmers. The result will not just be socially destructive, but may prove impossible to implement, economically irrational, and ineffective in reducing emissions.[92]

Greenpeace also lamented that, while McKinsey claims to 'rely on facts', it refuses to disclose the data and models on which it bases its calculations, justifying it with the company's application of intellectual property rights: 'the outside world has no way of knowing how McKinsey arrives at the different cost estimates attributed to various abatement measures.'[93]

Against this backdrop, it is not surprising that among the frequently asked questions posted by the UK natural capital committee we find: 'Can we trust accountants and economists to capture the true value of nature?' Although the committee has taken great pains to explain that valuation processes are the result of a multidisciplinary process involving both social and natural scientists, the evident link between financial and corporate powers, on the one hand, and most initiatives aimed at measuring the value of nature, on the other, remains troubling. As journalist Christine MacDonald showed in her book *Green, Inc.: An Environmental Insider Reveals How a Good Cause Has Gone Bad*, most of these policies simply provide green makeovers to companies that are notorious for their negligence and disregard of basic rights.[94]

Against this background, it comes as no surprise that the potential launch of a Green Development Mechanism, which would apply the rationale of Kyoto's Clean Development Mechanism to support biodiversity, has been criticized by environmental movements across the world. Many doubt the genuineness of private investors' motives to support biodiversity, arguing that if a genuine corporate interest in biodiversity existed, 'there would not be a problem with biodiversity loss in the first place'.[95] Fame, wealth and power are viewed as fundamental driving forces behind the new interest in the 'environmental cause'.[96] Others, especially in less industrialized countries, warn that the financialization of biodiversity will ultimately result in a global process of dispossession, displacement and violence against local populations, including indigenous movements, who are the true guardians of biodiversity.[97] Apparently harmless concepts such as eco-tourism have triggered consumptive desires in many local communities and introduced non-local lifestyles and agendas, invariably impacting the traditional equilibria of hitherto pristine ecosystems. Autonomous food production systems which have sustained communities over centuries have also been negatively affected by corporate and financial interests in biodiversity.[98]

In his book *Imperial Nature*, sociologist Michael Goldman noted that,

> In remarkable synchronicity, the sustainability crowd and the neoliberal development crowd have united to remake nature in the South, transforming vast areas of community-managed uncapitalized lands into transnationally regulated zones for commercial logging, pharmaceutical bio-prospecting, export orientated cash cropping, megafauna preservation and elite eco-tourism.[99]

Biodiversity preservation has thus become an excuse for a massive wave of 'green grabbing', in which large tracts of land are acquired for biodiversity conservation, biocarbon sequestration, biofuels, ecosystem services, eco-tourism and emissions offsets.[100] Such a global excitement for environmental preservation is led by an extraordinary new range of actors and unlikely alliances, which include 'pension funds and venture capitalists, commodity traders and consultants, GIS service providers and business entrepreneurs, ecotourism companies and the military, green activists and anxious consumers'.[101] Adding to its legitimacy is the host of international conventions, institutional reforms and governance agreements that purportedly aim to save nature and fight climate change, but may ultimately result in a global 'enclosure' of the commons.[102]

Environmental scholars Bram Büscher, Sian Sullivan and their colleagues have described these trends in both the corporate and the financial world as a case of 'neoliberal biodiversity conservation', by which they mean 'an amalgamation of *ideology and techniques* informed by the premiss that nature can only be "saved" through its submission to capital and its subsequent revaluation in capitalist terms'.[103] In their view, such a hegemonic discourse is essential for current capitalism as it opens investment opportunities and new areas of accumulation, while 'consolidating the *appearance* of general consensus' on what, in fact, are very controversial values and methods. Through numbers, prices, cost curves and other derivatives, this process of financialization is 'able to place itself outside of the realm of contradictions it stimulates, even while appropriating and misrepresenting these contradictions in critical ways'.[104]

Conclusion: Nature Inc.

In 2008, the BBC launched a documentary series titled *Nature Inc.*, which promised to open everybody's eyes 'to just how much we rely on nature to keep our economy going'.[105] Supported in part by the UN Environment Programme, the series featured scientists, investors in the biodiversity business and financial experts. No other title could have better summarized the process of marketization of natural capital that has been unfolding in the past decade, mostly under the radar screen of public scrutiny and civil society debate.[106] The experimentation with new accounting models, contingent valuation methods and other forms of monetization of natural capital has ultimately led to a dangerous collusion between entrenched financial and corporate interests, on the one hand, and entire natural ecosystems, on the other. As in the case of climate change mitigation discussed in the previous chapter, economic reasoning and the use of numerical models have been instrumental in generating an aura of neutrality behind the valuation of nature. Numbers have been used to give tangible authority to abstract concepts such as costs, benefits, values and prices. The very process of monetization of nature has relied on the capacity of numbers to provide objectivity when, in reality, subjective decisions are being made.

Many of these initiatives are probably genuine in their ultimate goal. They may be honestly trying to use economic models for the preservation of social and environmental quality. In their view, pricing would force people into 'a rational decision-making frame of mind' to analyse the 'gains and losses' of a certain type of development trajectory.[107] Sportswear giant Puma is the first company to commit to disclosing 'an environmental profit and loss account', spearheading a coalition of businesses willing to include environmental costs on price tags. According to Puma's boss: 'By showing environmental costs in euros and cents, our new Puma product EP&L visualises the environmental impacts Puma products cause and makes comparing products in terms of sustainability easy for everyone.'[108] In 2014, the data agency Trucost launched the Natural Capital Leaders index to assess business commitment to natural capital preservation. The resistance that oil and mining companies initially displayed to the integration of contingent valuation methods in the calculation of environment damage costs attests to the fact that natural capital 'subjective' valuations can also be detrimental to corporate interests. The tool can cut both ways.

The Global Canopy Programme argues that market schemes can help pool resources to prevent the power of speculation against biodiversity, especially in agricultural commodities: 'We need to demystify and explore innovative finance mechanisms that could help stimulate a new natural-capital-inclusive economy.'[109] If international markets are destroying tropical forests through the support of commodities such as beef, soy and palm oil, then an equally powerful but opposite response can come from within markets themselves. For them, market can be used to fight market. The only way to save nature is to sell it.[110]

There is little doubt that international finance and corporate powers have been able to exploit the environmental crisis to get a new lease from society. By purporting to take in hand the saving of the environment, they have been seeking a new legitimization for themselves, especially in the wake of the 2008 financial crisis. Their approach has been reinforced by 'the politics of environmental discourse', centred on concepts such as rationality, sustainability, managerialism and modernization, and based on the commandments of cost effectiveness and utility maximization.[111] The logic of imbuing conservation strategies with the potential for future economic profit extends to the assumption that human motivation is directed primarily by personal gain, and that the aggregate effect invariably leads to collective wealth and well-being.[112] In this vision of the world, economic models can combine profitability and healthy ecosystem in what looks like the most successful win–win scenario.

Market models (whether to destroy or to repair nature) have been built on a particular anthropological paradigm, which is usually defined as *Homo economicus*. The preferences of *Homo economicus* are given (that is, they are not culturally and socially produced) and cost–benefit calculations govern his self-interested rationality. In the reality of *Homo economicus*, markets are everywhere. If for certain resources or services there are no markets, then 'a pseudo market can be simulated' through experiments and questionnaires.[113] As we have seen, the numerical representations of costs, prices and benefits unduly simplify the complexity of real-life processes. Reducing ecosystems to priceable goods has the powerful consequence of subjecting nature to the artificial rules of economics. More importantly, it flattens distributional issues by hiding the fact that there are always losers and winners in environmental governance (something that *Homo economicus* is not willing to accept). The very concept of cost is misleading. Costs are based on prices, and prices are social artefacts. Prices do not exist in reality. What exists is the willingness to attribute a nominal value to a product based on a variety of factors, which include scarcity and desirability, but also tradition, customs and other types of social influence. All of these factors are transient: by definition, they change over time. To build entire governance systems on such subjective and temporary constructs is, at best, short-sighted.

It is interesting to note how natural scientists, who normally pride themselves on being data-driven, are loath to apply highly abstract models to the field of environmental governance. As remarked by biologist David Ehrenfeld, founding editor of the Society for Conservation Biology's official journal,

> The reduction of all conservation problems to economic terms is counter-productive and dangerous. Trusting to market forces and the laws of supply and demand to correct inequities and restore healthy equilibria does not work in economics and certainly does not work in conservation.[114]

To paraphrase social constructivism, we may say that costs are 'what we want them to be'. Ultimately, we decide what costs are. Or do we? As my discount rate is different from yours, it becomes particularly appropriate to wonder whose discount rates are being used in the valuation of nature. And the answer often is: market rates. This means that the expectations and projections shared by financial markets become parameters to guide the financialization of nature. Never mind whether this is done through the UN-sponsored SEEA, which adopts the GDP framework to measure the contribution of natural capital to economic growth, through the contingent valuations carried out by consultants for the oil industry, or through the marketing models adopted to gauge the WTP for ecosystem services.

As discussed in the previous chapter, what is cheap in terms of cost–benefit analyses, especially in the environmental sector, tends to be more expensive for society at large. All cost-based functions can only measure a limited range of dimensions. The process of pricing is very selective and tends to neglect fundamental elements just because they cannot be valued in market conditions. What cannot be priced has no cost and, as such, does not enter the cost–benefit equation. But whether it has a cost or not, somebody will eventually have to 'pay' for it. And these payers of last resort are, normally, us. In some cases, the *current* us; in others, future generations.

Putting a price on ecosystems may force us to realize the economic contribution of nature. Yet, it may also open up dangerous possibilities for the commodification of natural resources, given that anything that has a price can be bought and sold. As discussed in this chapter, most people do not easily grasp the complex articulations of use, non-use and option value. When we see a price we think of another type of value: exchange value. Prices invariably lead us to think that goods are exchangeable. Indeed, what has a price can be sold, or exchanged for something of the same value. Prices create the illusion that natural goods and services can be exchanged on the market as if they are conventional factors of production. The natural sciences' concept of 'strong sustainability' – that is, the idea that certain resources are scarce and irreplaceable and therefore human activities must be subject to the limitations of the planet's capacity – tends to be replaced by the economic principle of 'weak sustainability', which holds that any type of capital is perfectly substitutable for natural capital as an input to production.[115] The tautological consequence of this logic is that mankind can subjugate and ultimately rescue nature from itself. No surprise then if, in a world in which states are running out of cash (because of, among other factors, continuous financial bailouts to private banks), the investment fund Climate Change Capital maintains that what the world needs is a 'habitat banking system': 'we need a paradigm shift in the way we raise capital for nature conservation and that progress will require us to rapidly increase the money available from the private sector.' We need a new 'currency', with established equivalences or 'exchange rates', for biodiversity credits, which 'will be essential for attracting investment by creating a deeper and more liquid market'.[116] In a word, the only solution to environmental problems is to bring nature under the control, language and jurisdiction of private investment markets.

Biologists are taught that ecosystems are the result of complex, multifaceted equilibria and continuous evolutions, in which all parts hang together. For natural scientists, the web of interconnections making up the Earth is a kaleidoscope of mutual dependencies, in which each segment is fundamental to the resilience of the whole. There is no mankind without nature. By contrast, the financialization of nature splits, separates, fragments and ultimately alienates ecosystems in various 'sellable' packages, which are measured, valued and exchanged.[117] Just as in the financial industry, the market of 'nature derivatives' must be sliced and diced to suit the demand of investors and their expectations in terms of financial returns.

This reasoning has generated evident paradoxes. In 2000, the UN secretary general called for a 'millennium ecosystem assessment' to provide a state-of-the-art analysis of natural capital and its relationship with humanity. The results of this survey were released in 2005, after more than 1,300 scientists compiled reports and estimates. The conclusion was that human activities had taken 'the planet to the edge of a massive wave of species extinctions' and that the 'pressures on ecosystems will increase globally in coming decades unless human attitudes and actions change'.[118] Yet the report also found that human well-being had increased despite such a collapse in ecosystem services. This finding ran counter to decades of environmental campaigns arguing that ecological degradation would ultimately lead to declines in the

well-being of people.[119] What came to be known as the environmentalist's paradox appeared to confirm that both technology
and modernity had finally decoupled human well-being from
the course of nature: the paradox suggested that more well-being
could be successfully exchanged for natural losses.

Reacting against the growing excitement surrounding the monetization of ecosystem services, the environmental advocacy group
Greenpeace pointed out that giving numerical values to 'deeply
interconnected natural systems is inherently speculative and not
always sensible'.[120] The reduction of nature to crude numbers can
be dangerously misleading as it ignores 'the interconnectedness
of natural systems' and the 'possibility of tipping points and
abrupt changes'. Moreover, it gives the impression that mankind
can control nature as 'assets' so as to have a possibility to 'bail
out' Earth systems when they break down. But the Earth is not a
financial market and if we ignore planetary boundaries 'a bailout
may be too late, and no money in the world will be able to help
us'.[121]

As this chapter has shown, a good cause can easily turn into
an extremely dangerous business, given that statistics can be used
and abused to serve different interests. Saving our ecosystems
is a laudable mission and, in a world obsessed with numbers,
some form of measurement may be inevitable to gauge the size
and scope of conservation policies. But when these measurements turn into prices, as they systematically do in the field of
natural capital and ecosystem services accounting, then markets
crowd out other forms of governance. Through a set of apparently
neutral methodologies, the invaluable is valued, priced and then
turned into a commodity. The translation of the complexity of
nature into the simplicity of numbers thus paves the way for a
narrow economic approach that sees nature as an investment
which must yield financial returns. For nature to count, it must be
owned and made 'productive'. In a world in crisis, where financial

markets need to expand into new areas to generate profits, the financialization of nature may very well open up new possibilities for capital accumulation and speculation, to the utmost detriment of our ecosystems and societies.

As famously remarked by John Maynard Keynes in his 'National Self-Sufficiency' address at the University College Dublin in 1933,

> We destroy the beauty of the countryside because the unappropriated splendours of nature have non-economic value. We are capable of shutting off the sun and stars because they pay no dividend. ... But once we allow ourselves to be disobedient to the test of an accountant's profit, we have begun to change our civilization.[122]

CHAPTER 5

Numbers for good?
The quest for aid effectiveness
and social impact

Not everything that counts can be counted. And not everything that can be counted counts.

Albert Einstein

The strength of 'development' discourse comes of its power
to seduce, in every sense of the term: to charm, to please, to
fascinate, to set dreaming, but also to abuse, to turn away
from the truth, to deceive.

Gilbert Rist, *The History of Development: From
Western Origins to Global Faith*, 1997

Measurements help us gauge if and to what extent we are achieving intended results. Doctors rely on numbers to monitor the
effects of medical treatments on patients, engineers develop
numbers to assess the stability of buildings, and mechanics use
them to measure the amounts of water, oil and fuel that go into
a vehicle. As we have seen, while numbers do not possess any
intrinsic normative value, their power is derived from the capacity to reduce complexity to a few observable facts. This is why,
when numerical reasoning is systematically applied to the world

of human interactions, it can lead to all sorts of aberrations. In no field is this as evident as in the policies of development cooperation and social change, where statistical measurements have become the cornerstones to design and evaluate programmes and projects across the world. The international debate on aid effectiveness is fundamentally trapped in a global quest to produce quantitative indicators of all sorts to show that development policies work. In the field of social change, impact evaluations are largely dominated by econometric models, in which the complexity of social relations is lost through the cracks of mathematical algorithms. As is the case with climate change and natural capital accounting, these new measurements of success have paved the way to a transfer of technical tools from the business sector to the world of philanthropy and the nonprofit. Concepts such as social investment ratings, social return on investment, cost-effectiveness and standardized assessments have become particularly popular in a sector traditionally characterized by qualitative analyses, long-term horizons and social engagement.

As a young and inexperienced academic, I lived through this change myself. In the mid-2000s I got invited to advise one of the largest development organizations in Europe, whose name (for obvious reasons) shall not be mentioned. At that time I was consulting for NGOs and governments on how to construct social indicators and develop participatory evaluation tools. I remember that it was a beautiful day in September and my client boasted an impressive multi-storey office, whose main entrance opened onto a touristy street, right in the middle of town, in an area where most international development agencies had their headquarters. With pictures of needy African children, natural disasters and melting ice caps on the wall, the building's hall really made one feel as if that was the place where all the problems of the world were coming together to be tackled at once. It was a powerful albeit depressing vision.

They had invited me to help them improve their impact assessment tools. I have always been sceptical of impact assessments, as I recognize – just like any reasonable person with a little bit of common sense – that tracing causal processes in real-life social phenomena is a very daunting task, marred by conceptual and methodological complexities, more often than not impossible to solve. At the same time, I have been equally aware that simply averting the 'impact' question by refusing to introduce assessment tools would be just as naive. Experience indeed shows that when no methodologies are used to measure impact, then space is left for all sorts of rhetorical arguments. It is a troubling dilemma: measuring impact is difficult and often impossible, but not doing it means that marketing strategies (e.g. PR campaigns, moving pictures and other forms of unsubstantiated claims) will fill the gap, trying to capture the public eye in the absence of clear evidence of success. This is why I had accepted the job. I was sincerely committed to helping move the impact agenda forward by finding new and promising tools.

This was a time when most traditional donors, such as OECD governments and traditional philanthropic foundations, were suffering from a generalized development 'fatigue'. After decades of work in the so-called developing world, there was little evidence (if anything) to argue for a continuation of development aid flows. Injustices, inequalities and endemic poverty had remained rampant. Recipient countries seemed trapped in a vicious circle of corruption and social imbalances, with timid progress invariably followed by new breakdowns. Moreover, the electoral success of right-wing parties across Europe had led to a generalized 'aid bashing' public debate. More and more people were questioning whether it made sense to continue investing in overseas development aid when money was running out at home. Public budgets were being cut, spending reviews were trimming welfare systems, while unemployment and xenophobia were becoming daily issues.

If the development industry were to survive, it needed to show convincingly that it was worth it.

Although aware of the challenges, I was up to the task and wanted my clients to think out of the box. This is why I delivered a presentation focused on the need for multi-sectoral analysis and bottom-up participation. I emphasized the importance of participatory methods, which could then be scaled up through the adoption of online tools such as 'wikis', with a view to harnessing the potential of mass collaboration in areas where top-down traditional evaluations could never have succeeded. I wanted them to realize that information exchange and open participatory processes would have helped reduce the costs of impact assessment while tracing a multitude of direct and indirect effects of projects funded across the world. Moreover, I made the argument that an integrated participatory process of impact assessment should not be seen as an add-on, an additional burden on already tight budgets and overworked development professionals. Rather, an integrated system of assessment should be seen as part and parcel of development work. A good participatory and ongoing process of impact assessment could indeed reinforce the projects themselves, or even prove to be the most effective way to exert sustainable impact, as empowerment of participants is the precondition for any type of social and economic development. When I concluded, they looked at me in disbelief. They were evidently unimpressed by my participatory, bottom-up approach and did not seem to grasp the alleged wonders of mass collaboration. Silence reigned in the room for a few long seconds. Then the CEO, a charismatic lady in her late fifties, grabbed the microphone and told me without hesitation: 'Dr Fioramonti, there must have been a misunderstanding. We don't want any wiki and we are not interested in any participatory integrated assessment. We want you to develop one number which can tell us if what we do works or doesn't. As simple as that.'

The politics of aid effectiveness: a brief historical overview

We live in a world in which the so-called 'rich' countries spend billions on development aid to low-income nations every year. This is just a fraction of the estimated minimum of $1.7 trillion of international flows targeting what we conventionally (and, I believe, erroneously) call the developing world. These various forms of development financing include official development assistance (also known as ODA, which is the development aid disbursed by governments), public and private borrowing, programmes run by foundations and non-governmental organizations (NGOs), remittances by migrant workers and other types of aid schemes funded by countries outside of the OECD, which has a dedicated Development Assistance Committee. Although this total aid amounts to only 2.5 per cent of the global economic output (global GDP was about $69 trillion in 2012), it is nevertheless a huge industry by any measure.

The international aid system was born out of the ruins of the Second World War, with the Bretton Woods conference and the effort to rebuild post-war Europe through the International Bank for Reconstruction and Development, now incorporated into the World Bank group, and the International Monetary Fund (IMF). The European Recovery Program, commonly known as the Marshall Plan, was established in 1948 and ran until 1952, leading to the creation of the Economic Cooperation Administration, the precursor of the United States Agency for International Development (USAID). In 1949, President Harry Truman gave an inaugural speech that would go down in history as the beginning of the 'development age'. Besides reiterating the US government's commitment to the UN and to the reconstruction of Europe via financing and military cooperation (an element that would be sealed after a few months with the creation of the North Atlantic

Treaty Organization, NATO), Truman also mentioned a 'fourth'
point:

> Fourth, we must embark on a bold new program for making the
> benefits of our scientific advances and industrial progress avail-
> able for the improvement and growth of underdeveloped areas.
> ... Their economic life is primitive and stagnant. ... For the first
> time in history, humanity possesses the knowledge and skill to
> relieve the suffering of these people.[1]

Truman and his advisers were disciples of the New Deal and
had personally witnessed how the invention of GDP accounts
had helped America not only win the war, but also build a mass
consumption society which was unparalleled in the world. For
them, development was the result of economic technology. This is
why, in his speech, the president made it plain that such development efforts for 'underdeveloped areas' would not just translate
into funding, but would serve mainly as a form of 'technical
assistance'. He explained that 'The material resources which we
can afford to use for assistance to other peoples are limited. But
our imponderable resources in technical knowledge are constantly
growing and are inexhaustible.'[2] Truman's fourth point connected,
in a few paragraphs, to the essence of the development paradigm:
transferring economic knowledge and market-based governance
from the 'developed' countries to the 'underdeveloped' world.
Not only did this view profoundly influence our understanding
of what it means to be developed by fundamentally labelling non-
market less formalized economies as backward, but it also framed
the quest for development as nothing more than a technology: the
transposition of key economic (read market-based) principles and
institutions to the developing world.

Following Truman's fourth point, the UN General Assembly
approved the creation of an 'Expanded Programme of Technical
Assistance', which focused on sending technical experts to developing countries to train managerial personnel; this would later

become the United Nations Development Programme (UNDP). In 1951, the UN issued a report titled 'Measures for the Economic Development of Under-Developed Countries' (also known as the Lewis Report), which proposed the creation of an International Finance Corporation, mainly designed to make investments in the equity market and lend to private companies, which was then established by the World Bank in 1956. In the USA, a national system of development aid was instituted in the early 1950s, with the adoption of the 'Mutual Security Act', which provided for major technical assistance programmes targeting countries in Asia. As its very name suggests, the Act was conceived to build a security wall against the spread of Communism in the Far East. Unsurprisingly, the first countries to become recipients of US aid were South Korea (against North Korea), Taiwan (against China), the Shah's Iran (to exercise control in the Middle East) and Pakistan (against India and China). In 1957, the then European Community followed a rather similar approach with the establishment of the European Development Fund, a joint 'pot' of money seconded by France to support ex-European colonies around the world, especially in Africa. During this period, the international aid system was fully integrated into the security framework of the Cold War and used as leverage to support the foreign policy agenda of donor countries, especially vis-à-vis allied nations and client states in Africa, Asia and Latin America.

In the 1960s, the aid system grew more complex both institutionally and financially. In 1958, the World Council of Churches tabled a proposal to the leading countries represented at the UN Assembly which, for the first time, called for a minimum ratio between development aid and national GDP: they identified a 1 per cent target, but in the following decades the goal would be revised downward to 0.7 per cent. In 1960, the then Organisation for European Economic Co-operation (OEEC) became the Organisation for Economic Co-operation and Development (OECD) and the leading donor countries formed the Development Assistance Group (DAG, currently DAC), a forum for consultation initially including only European countries (Belgium, France, Germany, Italy, Portugal and the UK), their North American counterparts (Canada and the USA) and Japan. The 1970s saw the growth of multilateral assistance, which came to complement bilateral forms of cooperation. With the growing support of the Bretton Woods institutions, international development assistance shifted from a loose focus on poverty alleviation to economic growth, which was increasingly viewed as the best way to 'develop' societies. Aid policies became intertwined with multilateral loan schemes administered by the World Bank and the IMF, which were fundamentally designed to promote (free) market reforms in low-income countries.

As Gilbert Rist documents in his detailed history of how development went from being a 'Western invention to a global faith', economic evolutionist theories profoundly influenced this phase of development policy. In particular, Walt Rostow's *The Stages of Economic Growth: A Non-Communist Manifesto* became a classical blueprint for the emancipation of the 'underdeveloped' world, as it powerfully resonated with the USA's emphasis on market supremacy and its approach to development as a social technology. Rostow's model identified five successive categories of economic development: the traditional society, the preconditions for take-off, the take-off, the drive to maturity, and the age of high mass consumption.[3] By depicting developing societies as an airplane speeding along the runway and then through the sky, Rostow intentionally conveyed the idea of economic development as an aerodynamic trajectory, in which the flight is made possible by an optimal market performance. In his book, Rostow celebrated 'the powerful arithmetic of compound interest', which made growth the essential prerequisite of economic stability in a world in which money was based on credit.[4] In this theorization, growth is sustained by an almost divine force, which ensures that 'the age of high-mass consumption becomes universal'.[5] Of little use was Rostow's disclaimer that such 'stages-of-growth are an arbitrary and limited way of looking at the sequence of modern history; and they are, in no absolute sense, a correct way.'[6] His model became the law.

Throughout the years, as economic growth could be achieved more quickly through the sale of raw materials (e.g. under-soil resources such as minerals and fossil fuels), developing countries were largely re-engineered as export-oriented economies and loans were granted to their (often authoritarian) regimes to carry out social and economic structural adjustments. As recipient countries defaulted on their debt obligations throughout the 1980s, more money was lent to minimize the role of the state, privatize national industries and liberalize trade. With the end of the Cold War, the common policy of turning a blind eye to issues of democratic accountability in client states began to fade away. The aid industry started to pay attention (or perhaps lip service) to 'softer' issues, such as human rights, corruption and civil society. While the emphasis on growth remained central to donors' agendas, elements of good governance became important too. Yet, despite the reorientation of the industry, success stories were lacking. Most developing countries, especially in Africa, appeared trapped in a vicious circle of instabilities and political and economic crises, while endemic poverty and other forms of destitution remained prevalent.

It is against this background that the aid-effectiveness debate began to take shape in the late 1990s. Institutional donors, aid agencies and private foundations started cooperating with one another, and with receiving countries, in a desperate bid to prove that aid works. In 2000, the United Nations promulgated the so-called Millennium Development Goals, a list of eight global objectives to attain by 2015, which included specific targets such as the eradication of extreme poverty by halving the number of people living on less than $1.25 a day, a reduction in child mortality rates by two-thirds, decreasing maternal mortality by three-quarters, as well as vague commitments to building a global partnership for development. While the MDGs have been heralded as a progressive turn in the politics of international development, there is little doubt that they have also contributed to reinforcing the supremacy of numbers in the development industry. One reason why they have gained widespread attention is because of their measurability and their declination in terms of numerical targets. At the same time, however, voices within the UN itself have lamented that the MDGs have been largely taken out of context and, because of their numerical structure, they have used a 'one-size-fits-all' approach to development, which has misguided aid allocation policies and condemned 'more than half of the countries to the category of 'poor' performers – thereby undermining the support for the global targets among politicians and the public at large'.[7] Within the UNDP, which was tasked with leading the MDG agenda, new departments were created to implement the results-based management of aid policies. Indicators proliferated at all levels, often diluting the UNDP's traditional focus on capacity development as a gradual process of nurturing local skills, institutions and relationships. As some have argued, such a focus on numbers represented 'a divergence within the UNDP between advocacy in achieving qualitative outcomes and the trend towards seeking 'simplicity and measurability' through quantitative results', albeit in line with the agency's new focus on credit rating, as discussed in Chapter 2.

The MDGs also reiterated the call for international donors to give more aid and the 0.7 per cent of GDP target was reaffirmed (as of 2013, however, only five countries – Norway, Sweden, Denmark, Luxembourg and the Netherlands – had reached this target). The quest for effectiveness gained momentum in 2002, with the International Conference on Financing for Development held in Monterrey, Mexico. A new jargon of partnership replaced the more traditional (patron–client or donor–recipient) relationship and, in 2005, the aid community endorsed the Paris Declaration on Aid Effectiveness, which committed donors to focus systematically on measurable results and tangible outcomes.

In parallel with the redefinition of the aid system, the effectiveness debate also entered academic circles, triggering heated confrontations between proponents and detractors of the development cooperation industry. According to former World Bank economist William Easterly, who has made a name for himself as a leading critic of the aid industry, the problem with aid is aid itself. In his 2006 book *The Elusive Quest for Growth: Economists' Adventures and Misadventures in the Tropics*, Easterly reviews decades of development programmes and concludes that the aid industry has generated a parasitic attitude in low-GDP economies, further exacerbated by the 'benevolence' with which aid has been offered to corrupt governments.[8] A firm believer in free markets, Easterly maintains that the nature of aid does not take into account how humans react to economic incentives. Because of the continuous inflow of development funding, governments have had no serious incentives to promote systemic reforms, liberalizations were delayed and true competition (both at the political and economic level) was stifled. For Easterly aid has only been a 'carrot', never a 'stick' with which to coerce countries into supporting long-term and deep economic reforms. Moreover, the tendency to cancel debt has produced moral hazards. For Easterly, the aid industry is founded on poor economic thinking and does not recognize that 'true' development can only happen when genuine market forces are unleashed, good performance is rewarded and competition is encouraged. In 2007, Easterly reiterated the critique in his book *The White Man's Burden: Why the West's Efforts to Aid the Rest Have Done So Much Ill and So Little Good.*

A similar argument has been put forward by former Goldman Sachs economist and bestselling author Dambisa Moyo, who argues that 'by encouraging corruption, creating dependency, fueling inflation, creating debt burdens and disenfranchising Africans (to name a few), an aid-based strategy hurts more that it helps.'[9] Moyo recognizes that interventions such as the Marshall Plan in Europe 'played vital roles in economic (re)construction.' However, she remarks that the 'key and (often ignored) difference' between such interventions and those carried out throughout the world today 'is that the former were short, sharp and finite, whereas the latter are open-ended commitments with no end in sight'. Following Easterly's argument, she is adamant that such open-ended systems provide governments with 'no incentive to look for other, better, ways of financing their development'. Along the same lines, the British economist Paul Collier has been referring to the 'diminishing returns' of aid, whereby the transfer of more money towards recipient countries (as indicated by the 0.7 per cent goal) does not necessarily add value. By citing a series of examples, Collier shows that just a small fraction (roughly 1–2 per cent) of all the funding given to the aid industry actually ever reaches the intended targets.[10]

Such negative views on aid have been rejected by more optimistic commentators. The best-known 'defence' was made in 2005 by the director of the Earth Institute at Columbia University Jeffrey Sachs, with his book *The End of Poverty: Economic Possibilities for Our Time*, in which he argues that 'aid is fundamental and, when used efficiently, it can achieve durable and sustainable goals'.[11] Sachs got involved in a personal spat with both Easterly and Moyo and accused them of 'peddling their simplistic concoction of free markets and self-help'. By pointing out that both critics had actually benefited from the aid industry (Easterly was at the World Bank and his research was funded by philanthropic institutions, while Moyo studied at Harvard thanks to an aid-funded scholarship for young Africans), Sachs emphasizes 'the realities of life, in which all of us need help at some time or other and in countless ways, and even more importantly we should think about the life-and-death consequences for impoverished people who are denied that help'.

Despite their differences and vested interests (e.g. Easterly was himself involved in Ghana's structural adjustment programme during his stint at the World Bank, and Sachs advises development organizations, big charities and international philanthropists), the protagonists of the aid effectiveness dispute agree on one issue: the aid industry needs more sophisticated approaches based on statistical evidence, which can inform meaningful generalizations and show which approaches work and which do not. For most of them, the sector can only achieve effectiveness (that is, promote durable results) by adopting sophisticated methods of measurement to inform better funding allocation. Without this type of clarity, criticism and praise will continue to be based on anecdotal evidence and personal preferences.

The quest for evidence

Most critics of the aid industry point to a number of methodological solutions, including the application of experimental tools to assess the effectiveness of interventions. The centrality of experiments in scientific knowledge is not a new topic. The founder of modern science, the Italian Galileo Galilei, championed the use of experiments and redefined the scientific method of investigation as based on inductive enquiry rather than deductive reasoning. In 1849, the physicist Michael Faraday wrote that 'Nothing is too wonderful to be true, if it be consistent with laws of nature and, in such things as these, experiment is the best test of such consistency.'[12] Also Charles Darwin emphasized the use of experimental techniques in agriculture and biology.[13] In the biomedical field, too, the use of experimental methods has become routine to assess the effectiveness of drugs, protocols and treatments. The most common approach in this field is represented by the randomized controlled trial (RCT). RCT is an evaluation method designed to isolate potential causal relations through the random selection of participants in the intervention group, which includes only individuals having received the 'treatment', and in the so-called control group, which – by contrast – has not been subject to the intervention. As aid providers and their consultants are interested in establishing 'causal' inferences using various types of economic technique, randomized experiments have become extremely popular in the development field and, more generally, in economic and social research.[14]

Although nowadays there is a vast array of RCT specialists operating in the international development sector, a leading role is played by a group of economists based at the Massachusetts Institute of Technology (MIT), where the Abdul Latif Jameel Poverty Action Lab (J-PAL) was established in 2003. J-PAL is a 'global network of researchers who use randomized evaluations to answer critical policy questions in the fight against poverty'. The lab is headed by Abhijit Vinayak Banerjee and Esther Duflo, two development economists who have dedicated their careers to the incorporation of randomized trials into development impact assessments. Their 2011 book *Poor Economics*, recipient of the *Financial Times*/Goldman Sachs Business Book of the Year award, has become the most cited resource in the field. It provides an overview of over fifteen years of evidence generated through the implementation of RCTs across the world. The book emphasizes the need to develop 'theories that help us make sense of both what the poor are able to achieve, and where and for what they need a push'.[15] Indeed, J-PAL researchers believe that 'all too often development policy is based on fads, and randomized evaluations could allow it to be based on evidence'.[16] With a view to 'fighting global poverty with hard numbers', they encourage a systematic application of RCTs to 'produce unbiased estimates of the true impact of a program or policy in the field', thus overcoming the paradox that while enormous resources are spent every day on development programmes, there is 'surprisingly little hard evidence on what are the most effective ways to reduce poverty'.[17] For the J-PAL researchers, poverty is the outcome of irrational behaviour, the consequence of suboptimal economic decisions; *Poor Economics* shows 'how the stress of living on less than 99 cents per day encourages the poor to make questionable decisions that feed – not fight – poverty'. In this regard, the role of researchers is to study how the poor behave, what mistakes they make and how aid can be used to correct them.

J-PAL works closely with the think-tank Innovations for Poverty Action (IPA), which also leads the field through a systematic use of randomized evaluations 'to determine the actual impact and cost effectiveness of different programmes'.[18] Unlike J-PAL, which retains a more academic profile, IPA has a clear hands-on approach to technical assistance and purports 'to disseminate the lessons to policymakers, practitioners, investors and donors around the world'. Their language is also bold. In their reports, they speak about 'funding what works', identifying 'cost-effective' solutions and undertaking 'rigorous evaluations'. Interestingly, they single out microcredit as the 'perfect example of an idea that generated tremendous enthusiasm and support long before there was evidence on its impact', even though it was 'predicated on a double standard about the useful role of high-interest debt'.[19] Basing their focus on evidence, they set out to scientifically scrutinize unconventional options, with a view to checking whether or not they confirm our preconceived notions and expectations.

Of particular interest is their Proven Impact initiative, the organization's flagship selection of what approaches to development have produced intended results. In order for an intervention to be selected as part of the initiative, it must be tested 'at least in one context', must be assessed 'using scientifically rigorous methods (randomized controlled trials)' and must pass 'cost-effectiveness tests'. A selection committee is in charge of the scientific review and selection process: ideas designated as 'proven' are deemed ready for scale-up with some or no additional operational research; those designated as 'promising' will need to meet additional criteria before being declared fit for replication. The Proven Impact initiative even has a dedicated fund, which showcases good practices and encourages investors to target their donations accordingly. In his recent book, *More than Good Intentions: How a New Economics is Helping Solve Global Problems*, IPA's funder Dean Karlan recalls the main camps in the aid-effectiveness debate and their apparently irreconcilable support/criticism of development aid: 'My hunch is that, at the end of the day, even Sachs and Easterly could agree on the following: Sometimes aid works, and sometimes it does not.'[20] For Karlan, the critical question is: *which* aid works? Instead of getting hung up on the extremes, answers can be found on the ground. Look at a specific challenge, propose a potential solution, and then measure it to see if it works: this is the only 'real, measurable, and meaningful progress toward eradicating [poverty]'.[21]

Despite their bold approach, however, IPA's 'proven' impact areas are far from being unconventional. Their list includes: chlorine dispensers, school-based deworming, incentives for vaccines, investment vouchers and reminders to save. The 'promising' ideas are remedial education and free bed nets. In spite of the assertiveness with which they are presented, these ideas do not really strike the reader as the most radical. This is not to argue that chlorine is useless or that deworming school children is not effective. Common sense suggests that both are important for sanitation and health purposes. Also one cannot dispute that bed nets protect people from mosquitoes. Similarly, providing incentives for families to vaccinate their children or to save money seems like a reasonable suggestion. But is this the new economics that 'is helping solve global problems', as the subtitle of Karlan's book suggests? Are these the solutions to the world's most enduring social injustices?

Echoing J-PAL's approach combining traditional and behavioural economics, Karlan and his colleagues argue that, just like everyone else, 'poor people make mistakes that end up making them poorer, sicker, and less happy'. And then they add, jokingly: 'If they didn't, they could quickly escape poverty by selling self-help classes to the rest of us.' Together with J-PAL, IPA's job is to use hard data and scientific reasoning to correct these mistakes. Take the case of agriculture, for instance. If fertilizers and 'improved' seeds (that is, genetically modified seeds) can improve crop yields, 'shouldn't more farmers be investing in them?' ask IPA researchers on their website.[22] Yes, is their answer, but only if the right incentives are provided at the right time. By relying on models of procrastination in psychology and economics, these economists '*know* that many people value present over future consumption, leading them to delay a profitable investment even if they are certain they would like to make it' (emphasis added). As farmers procrastinate, they risk missing 'the point in the season when investing in fertilizers or other agricultural investments will be profitable'. This inherent inability to understand the real value of investment is 'why marketing fertilizers door-to-door, right after the last season's harvest (when farmers are more likely to have cash on hand) and including time-limited discounts, like free delivery for pre-paid fertilizer, can counteract some of these behavioural tendencies'. Following the same reasoning, IPA encourages the use of voucher systems and smart subsidies 'to help individuals budget for the coming season, such as the planting season, or, in an educational context, the back-to-school season'.

The language adopted by Karlan and his colleagues is not particularly different from that utilized by the most conservative proponents of cost–benefit analyses. According to this approach, the only way to make individuals behave rationally is to present them with vouchers, time-bound subsidies and other forms of financial persuasion. It is interesting to note that most of these claims run counter to studies conducted by another proponent of hard data, the consultancy Bridgespan, which has showcased the nonprofit Give Directly as a best practice. Give Directly, which in 2012 was one of the recipients of the Global Impact Awards, Google's programme to support entrepreneurial nonprofits, has used randomized controlled trials to show that the best way to help people is through direct cash transfers. Their 'rigorous approach' leads them to disagree with both J-PAL and IPA in so far as Give Directly maintains that no-strings-attached cash transfers improve health and downstream financial gains, as poor people invest in everything from food for starving children to long-term assets, including land, livestock and housing.[23] For them, poor people are rational enough to know what they need and how to get it. They do not require development consultants to make them behave rationally. Who's right? Can the same data produce opposing results?

It is interesting to note that, although IPA affirms to reject simplistic economic approaches to development, its solutions are not particularly different from those advanced by the free-market Copenhagen Consensus Centre (CCC), an acquaintance of ours from Chapter 3, whose researchers have become the global champions of 'techno-fixes' for the world's problems. In 2008, the CCC's 'dream team' of Nobel laureate economists found that micronutrient interventions – fortification and supplements designed to increase nutrient intake – were the most effective investment against malnutrition in developing countries, 'with massive benefits for a tiny price-tag', echoing some of the proposals put forward by IPA. In 2012, the

Consensus researchers maintained that for less than $700 million per year, 'the problem of hunger can be solved' (*sic*). Similar to IPA, their recipe was a list of technical solutions: 'bundling nutrition interventions; increasing global food production; and improving market functioning through better communications and increased competition in fertilizer markets'.[24] Obviously they conceded that 'increasing global food production might seem a strange proposal given that globally, food production exceeds food needs.' However, they maintained that 'lower prices are necessary to make food more affordable' and 'to provide a buffer against some of the negative consequences of climate change'. No surprise, then, that their conclusions were essentially in line with the key corporate interests in the food industry: ensure higher yields through extensive breeding; increase tolerance to drought, heat and salt; identify and disseminate the best varieties of crops; and ensure the optimal use of fertilizers. They also recommended introducing programmes that send market information via SMS to farmers (for a monthly fee) and reducing barriers to fertilizer access, for instance by marketing them door to door. According to the CCC economists, these 'innovations' would yield 'up to 8.35 in return for every dollar spent'.

Fertilizers, genetically modified seeds, SMS reminders, door-to-door marketing: thanks to its hard data approach, the CCC's macroeconomic analysis comes to conclusions that are very similar to those reached by the IPA at the micro-level of individual behaviour. Of course the CCC researchers acknowledge that 'there have been mixed results from policies designed to stimulate sustainable fertilizer use', given that 'a small number of countries control most of the production capacity for the main nitrogen, phosphate, and potash fertilizers' and 'the top four firms control more than half of each country's production capacity'. Yet, to address this problem they would discourage policymakers from considering 'the forcible break-up of this concentrated industry', as this would cause 'disruption' and would lead to 'a loss of economies of scale'. They would also discourage regulation, as this would lead to 'unproductive rent-seeking'. Instead, the researchers propose public investment 'in the construction of new production capacity [to] be turned over to the private sector'. The goal would be to build two major conglomerates, one in Asia and one in Africa, for an overall cost (taxpayers' money) of roughly US$ 1.3 billion. These Asian and African equivalents of Monsanto would then distribute fertilizers and genetically modified seeds to their countries, with a net return of $12.5 billion.

Busy as they are to calculate cost–benefit ratios, both the IPA and the CCC forget to mention something that a wide range of research has demonstrated over the past few decades, that the market-driven destruction of localized farming is perhaps the most important reason why much of the world has become food 'insecure'.[25] India is the perfect example in this regard. In the past, Indian peasants used to rely on natural processes to grow their crops. Good seasons would result in better yields and whatever surplus in production and seeds would be used to mitigate the negative impact of bad years. Men and women followed the rhythm of nature, which meant that food production remained a subsistence activity. Peasants were not enriching themselves. They were officially 'poor' but, unless some major natural disaster occurred, their villages would have enough locally produced food to feed themselves. Then, starting in the 1980s, the Indian government began to listen to aid experts, development economists and food corporations, who recommended harnessing the pro-poor potential of new technologies. As a consequence, the state introduced genetically modified (GM) seeds to help peasants move out of subsistence farming with a view to achieving large-scale production. Ever since, these 'improved' seeds have been marketed door to door, with the first batches made available for free or sold with a discount at the end of each season, when farmers have more cash on their hands, just like the IPA experts recommend. Massive advertising campaigns have led thousands of peasants to believe that there is an easy way to produce more with less effort. Thus, over the course of a few decades, entire districts in India have switched from natural seeds to genetically modified ones, which are patented and commercialized by one of the world's leading multinational corporations, Monsanto. These new seeds hold the promise of resisting attacks from a variety of parasites, including the much-dreaded mealybug. As they are not freely available in nature, the GM seeds must be bought on the commercial market, which often requires peasants to take out a loan to front-load enough capital for the investment.[26] In a society in which banks are loath to lend to the poor, this means that many small farmers have to accept the conditions imposed by loan sharks, which generally involve a property transfer of the land in case of non-repayment. And that is when things spiral out of control. As the power of GM seeds falls short of expectations and yields are only moderately better than those achieved through natural (cost-free) techniques, peasants end up worse off. They realize that their income is no longer enough to repay their debt, feed their families and, at the same time, save enough capital to buy a new set of seeds for next year's crops. In the short run, costs invariably outweigh benefits. No surprise, then, that an agrarian country like India, where more than half the population depends on agriculture, has become notorious for the huge increase in the rate of suicides among peasants. Most estimates put the number of farmers' suicides at around 17,000 every year.[27] According to a survey conducted by India's National Crime Records Bureau, the number of suicides between 1997 and 2008 totalled 199,132.[28] Yet these figures may significantly underestimate the scale of the tragedy. For starters, only individuals with an explicit title to land are 'counted' as farmers, which by default excludes women and tenant farmers. Moreover, the definition of farmers includes both full-time peasants and individuals who farm more sporadically. As a result, 'we are saddled with figures that undercount farm suicides but overcount the number of "farmers".'[29]

These peasants are not killing themselves because of weather patterns, stronger parasites or effects of climate change. Their suicides are an extreme reaction against the loss of dignity that indebtedness causes, especially when this is coupled with the loss of their only source of social status and income: land. And peasants are not simply dying. Many of them, deprived of an income, are abandoning rural areas to move to urban settlements. They turn into squatters, servants and beggars, filling the ranks of the swelling slums of India's metropolitan areas. In the end, farmers' suicides, land dispossession and commercialization of seeds are simply components of a fundamental process of privatization of the commons, which is often touted as a precondition for India's shift from underdevelopment to global powerhouse.

In 2013, the Institution of Mechanical Engineers, the largest professional engineering association in the UK, reported that over a third of all food produced globally (roughly 2 billion tonnes) 'never reaches a human stomach'. It simply goes to waste due to a combination of 'market and consumer wastage'.[30] While this problem is particularly widespread in less industrialized nations, where land ownership and commercial agriculture have generally deprived local communities of access to land and food, market-based food wastage is also a widespread phenomenon in the so-called developed world. Major supermarkets routinely reject entire crops of perfectly edible fruit and vegetables 'because they do not meet exacting marketing standards for their physical characteristics, such as size and appearance'. In Great Britain, for example, up to 30 per cent of the vegetable crop is never harvested 'as a result of such practices'. At the global level, the largest retailers 'generate 1.6 million tonnes of food waste annually in this way'. Moreover, marketing strategies and sales promotions encourage customers to purchase more than they actually need, which inevitably generates wastage at home: 'between 30 per cent and 50 per cent of what has been bought in developed countries is thrown away by the purchaser'. As the professional association of engineers concludes, the capacity to control and reduce the level of wastage is 'beyond the capability of the individual farmer, distributor or consumer, since it depends on market philosophies'.[31]

Inevitably the question, then, is: how much of this is captured in the randomized trials? To what extent can experimental methods and cost–benefit analyses grasp the profound dynamics leading to poverty and destitution? If it is true that a new economic revolution is helping solve global problems, shouldn't it start from the re-embedding of the subjects of research within a social context dominated by power dynamics and institutional failures? Much to the contrary, the focus on evidence is pushing the aid industry towards an even greater reliance on technocratic solutions and short-term returns. As argued by Morten Jerven, author of *Poor Numbers*, a book focusing on how statistics in developing countries can mislead policies, randomized trials reveal no understanding of 'the political dimensions' of social life: 'studying these issues in laboratory-like experiments may misguide scholars and policymakers; arguably, it is the differences, not the similarities, between the political economy and the laboratories that are most important.'[32]

The rise of philanthrocapitalism

The focus on hard data and its declination in terms of both efficiency and effectiveness (which are concepts largely drawn from the business jargon) have driven a new trend in the aid industry, quite aptly captured by the term 'philanthrocapitalism'. This idea was launched in 2006 by Matthew Bishop, US business editor of *The Economist*, and then turned into a bestselling book in 2008, *Philanthrocapitalism: How the Rich Can Save the World*. Ironically, the book was launched in New York just a few months before the fall of Lehman Brothers and the collapse of global capital finance, when the rich appeared intent on sinking rather than saving the world. The idea behind philanthrocapitalism is simple: in order to succeed at fighting poverty, we must let the champions (and the principles) of market success take over the aid industry. While decades of traditional aid policies have not generated tangible results, global markets and their business leaders have multiplied wealth to unprecedented levels. This stark contrast alone – as the philanthrocapitalist creed has it – would justify the role of business in solving the world's most pressing problems. How? By reinventing methods to assess what works and what does not, just like the randomized revolution.

As the book's synopsis reads, 'Proceeding from interviews with some of the most powerful people on the planet ... [the authors] show how a web of motivated givers has set out to change the world.'[33] Also known as the Good Club, arguably the most elite and powerful group in the world, the network of philanthrocapitalists includes billionaires such as Bill Gates, Warren Buffet, Richard Branson and former US president Bill Clinton.[34] According to City University of New York sociologist Robin Rogers, 'if you want to understand philanthrocapitalism, start with the three M's: Money, Markets, and Measurement':

> The first M, money, is the idea that the wealthy, particularly the super wealthy, should take greater responsibility for using their wealth for the common good. ... The second M, markets, is the idea that market forces should sort effective social programs from ineffective social programs. The third M, measurement, is the idea that resources should be used in a targeted and rational way based on data in order to identify and scale successful social programs.[35]

A core element of the philanthrocapitalists' approach to development is problem-solving: as they see poverty as a discrete problem – that is, something separate from complex social and economic structures – they look for innovative methods to 'fix it'. By adopting the very business frameworks in which they have excelled as entrepreneurs, philanthrocapitalists are convinced that they can find better, quicker and more efficient ways to resolve deep-seated social predicaments. For instance, the Bill and Melinda Gates Foundation has been leading the development sector in the field of health care and related issues, such as nutrition, water, sanitation and agricultural development. With an asset trust endowment of over $36 billion (and annual donations to the health sector equivalent to the budget of the World Health Organization), the Gates Foundation has become the world's largest and most influential private philanthropy. In their 'letter to the foundation', Bill and Melinda Gates explain that their focus is on identifying 'new techniques to help farmers in developing countries grow more food and earn more money; new tools to prevent and treat deadly diseases; new methods to help students and teachers in the classroom'.[36] In the agricultural sector, for instance, they emphasize the importance of 'improved' seeds and access to better soil, water and livestock solutions. They also intend to 'help farmers hone their business management skills, gain greater purchasing power and marketing leverage, and improve their crop and resource management skills'. In January 2003, the Foundation launched an initiative called Grand Challenges in Global Health, which aimed to stimulate scientific research into 'solutions to critical scientific and technological problems that, if solved, could lead to important advances against diseases in the developing world'.[37] The grand challenges included the attainment of a series of technical objectives, ranging from creating effective single-dose vaccines to be used right after birth to developing technologies to quantitatively assess a population's health status. Indeed, one aspect the Foundation is insisting on is the importance of evidence-based results. In an op-ed titled 'My Plan to Fix the World's Biggest Problems' and published by the *Wall Street Journal* in January 2013, Bill Gates emphasized how important 'measurement' is to improving the human condition: 'You can achieve incredible progress if you set a clear goal and find a measure that will drive progress toward that goal.'[38] After reviewing the many fields in which his philanthropy has been active, Gates maintained that the lives of the poorest have improved more rapidly in the past decade because of new measurements and business-like approaches. And he concluded that, 'thanks to measurement, progress isn't doomed to be rare and erratic. We can, in fact, make it commonplace.'

According to Mike Edwards, former director of the 'traditional' Ford Foundation, arguably the most vocal critic of this new trend in the aid industry, the Good Club leaders present themselves as venture philanthropists, emphasizing the fact that their social missions are founded on market methods. In their jargon, they make continuous reference to 'new', 'engaged', 'strategic', 'effective' or 'impact' philanthropy, 'but these terms are not very useful as definitions because they are so inclusive – unless there are foundations who deliberately seek to be distant and ineffective'.[39] As a matter of fact, the very concept of venture philanthropy is somewhat confusing. The etymology of the word 'venture' implies a high degree of uncertainty, as well as the willingness to support causes in the face of risk. By contrast, the rhetoric of these new donors is permeated by references to 'high-performance', 'results-based' and 'data-driven' and they champion cost–benefit analyses as tools to decide in what fields to intervene and how, which makes them decisively risk-adverse and less prone to embark on the more 'political' terrain. Adam Waldman, founder and president of the Endeavor Group, a Washington-based philanthropic consultancy, believes that the hallmarks of the new philanthropy are 'an entrepreneurial results-oriented framework, leverage, personal engagement, and impatience'.[40] According to Kavita Ramdas, former president of the Global Fund for Women, these new philanthropic practices are animated by the very same 'fix-the-problem' mentality that has made their leaders successful as hedge-fund managers, financial mavericks, ICT entrepreneurs and software developers.[41] Their approach to international development is designed 'to yield measurable and fairly quick solutions', which is so evidently reflected in the professional profiles their 'mega-philanthropies' are looking for: 'managers, consultants, engineers, business practitioners, former industry leaders or lobbyists'. Their focus is exclusively on efficiency and sectoral technical expertise, while 'the realization that development has to do with people, with human and social complexity, with cultural and traditional realities ... [has] no cachet in this metrics-driven, efficiency-seeking, technology-focused approach to social change.'[42] Such a view is echoed by Melanie Schnoll Begun, managing director and head of philanthropy management at Morgan Stanley Private Wealth Management, for whom 'the generation we are dealing with today has an unending thirst and desire for sudden impact, they want results. ... Is it fair? No. Is it right? No. Organisations need to take a step back and educate donors about how difficult it is to measure results.'[43]

As sustainable development is a long-term process aimed at designing and reinforcing cultural ties and economic and political institutions, rather than a set of successful aid-funded projects, the data-driven 'impatience' of philanthrocapitalists can profoundly undermine the capacity of countries around the world to achieve durable and equitable objectives. In many regards, the current debate on aid-effectiveness and its results-based approach is likely to generate counterproductive tendencies, as the focus of the debate shifts from what is needed to what is measurable. This trend also influences the operations and priorities of publicly

funded development agencies, which – similarly to my experience
with the European aid organization mentioned above – feel the
pressure of domestic constituencies to make 'the results of aid programs visible, quantifiable, and directly attributable to the donor's
activities – even when doing so reduces the developmental impact
of aid'.[44] This is why proponents of the 'measuring what works'
philosophy have gone so far as to argue that development funding
should exclusively be channelled to interventions that pass 'hard'
evidence tests based on statistical experimental methods.[45] As
the beneficiaries of development projects are largely voiceless,
the capacity to produce numbers to please either taxpayers or
investors becomes more important than listening to the needs of
those on the ground. The increasing importance of results-based
development work has turned numerical models into a key factor to
decide what gets funded and what does not. In the case of RCTs,
for instance, not all types of development interventions can be
randomized. Macro-level projects that deal with economic reform,
institutional development, community empowerment and the like
are often impossible to assess with standardized models. Generally, the bigger and more complex the intervention, the harder it is
to design a model to evaluate it. In this regard, advocates of standardization have fiercely criticized new trends in the development
sector, such as national budget support. It is useful to remember,
however, that national budget support (the process of channelling
aid through the recipient governments' policy priorities) was
designed precisely as a response to the fragmentation and the
lack of coordination within the development industry. Moreover,
the focus on partnership and local ownership in the development
sector inherently calls for an alignment between the national priorities set out by recipient nations and those supported by donor
countries, hence the growing stress on funding national budgets
rather than individual projects. However, proponents of evidence-
based methods such as Banerjee and Duflo regard national budget

support as 'disastrous', in so far as it pools various resources together, thus making it impossible to disentangle clear causal relations between aid and expected results.[46] This criticism is also having an impact on donors. In particular the new philanthropic foundations (but also the World Bank) have become unwilling to finance projects that cannot be evaluated using experimental tests based on 'hard' data.[47] 'In the end', as some analysts warn, 'the methodology may end up determining what questions to ask, rather than letting an analysis of our knowledge gaps determine where to look for the answers.'[48] Moreover, as hard data tends to focus on those variables that can be more easily observed and quantified, thus neglecting larger and more influential dynamics, the application of standardized models is likely to produce 'clear answers to the wrong question'.[49] Things that really matter, such as cultural learning, social trust and institutional development, may very well become secondary factors (or even be treated as externalities) when they cannot be counted in the same way as the number of children being vaccinated, the number of start-up businesses made possible by micro-finance projects, the sets of malaria bed nets distributed to local villages or students' scores in elementary school tests.

It thus becomes clear that there is a trade-off between focusing on tangible results in the short term (the much-heralded 'impatience' of philanthrocapitalists, which has become a mantra of the whole development industry in the age of aid effectiveness) and the uncertainty and risks of promoting grassroots empowerment in the long run. Self-interested aid agencies, whether because of pressure from their own constituencies (taxpayers) or to improve their public image (as is often the case with the new megaphilanthropies), are more likely to opt for short project cycles and verifiable results. The quest for accountability, a welcome principle in public debate, has paradoxically triggered undesired effects by privileging results-driven short-termism. Through the lens of the technocratic data-driven philosophy, development becomes the outcome of technical operations within the existing economic, political and social frameworks, thus neglecting the possibility of deeper and more radical social change.

One may very well wonder how it is possible that amid the largest bailouts and public takeovers of private companies in history, the argument that business techniques are inherently superior to government and charity may still find a (growing) audience. Indeed, one may even cheekily point out the 'inauspicious timing' of the philanthrocapitalist manifesto, starting with its 2008 release, just a few weeks before the collapse of Wall Street. However, with the worsening of the crisis, the lack of resources available to conventional aid projects has generated a greater opportunity to bring business and market approaches into the aid industry. With the global recession, many development organizations, NGOs and nonprofits have been scrambling to stay afloat. And, of course, in a world in which public budgets are shrinking and governments are increasingly unable to meet the demands of their own citizens (let alone worry about overseas development goals), there is growing room for private action by the global billionaires. As the authors of *Philanthrocapitalism* argue,

> the fiscal fallout of the financial crisis of 2008 also means that public budgets and government ambitions are going to have to be scaled back for at least a generation. ... The philanthrocapitalism revolution will have huge implications. As governments cut back their spending on social causes, giving may be the greatest force for societal change in our world.[50]

The focus on results and data is already changing the way in which global philanthropy operates. As philanthropists behave more and more like investors, gauging the feasibility of development projects by staring at a set of statistics, there is an increasing need for catchy assessments of 'worthiness'. This new market requires an infrastructure, which includes the philanthropic equivalent of stock markets, investment banks, research houses and management consultants, based no more on principles, missions and value judgements, but on factual ratings. And in the age of spending reviews and public austerity, the reach of the three Ms (money, markets and measurement) is no longer confined to aid policies in low-income countries, but has made its powerful entry also into more affluent societies.

Numbers strike back home: the politics of impact assessment in the social field

In 1957, the sociologist Donald Campbell published a book that would have a lasting impact in the social sciences. In *Factors Relevant to the Validity of Experiments in Social Settings*, Campbell introduced concepts that have nowadays become common jargon in the methodology of social research, including internal/external validity and (quasi-)experimental design. He preferred the use of randomization techniques, but – as a practical man – was aware that quasi-experiments would need to suffice in most cases, due to resource constraints and real-life limitations. His writings on the 'experimenting society' became a blueprint for a world 'committed to identifying effective reforms suitable for broad implementation'.[51] His focus on 'hard' evaluation techniques was entirely based on the conviction that scientific enquiry could always identify a clear link between cause and effect. In the academic community, Campbell has become the icon of experimental methods and positivistic approaches to evaluation in the social field. The Campbell Collaborative, an initiative named in his honour, was established in 2000 to produce systematic reviews of the effects of social interventions, including education, crime and justice, and social welfare. Just like J-PAL has been advocating the adoption of randomized control trials in foreign aid projects, the Campbell Collaborative has become one of the most vocal proponents of these experimental techniques to assess social work in the USA.

Besides being an integral component of the social sciences' methodological debate, the practice of impact assessment goes back to the first systematic attempts by government to understand the effects of public service programmes. For instance, in 1964 the US administration launched the 'War on Poverty' initiative, which led to the establishment of the Office of Economic Opportunity, with a dedicated research and evaluation team. In 1968, the Office carried out a field experiment in New Jersey to test the real-world feasibility of a negative income tax, which would go down in history as the first large-scale social science experiment to use randomized controlled trials. Also in the field of environmental impact assessment, various forms of assessment of costs and benefits as well as social impacts were introduced by the National Environmental Policy Act and endorsed by the Council of the American Sociological Association. The term 'social impact assessment' was first used by the Department of the Interior while preparing an Environmental Impact Statement in 1973, and in 1974 the Ford Foundation along with a number of federal agencies established the Manpower Demonstration Research Corporation (MDRC), a nonprofit research organization that pioneered the use of randomization 'to shape legislation, program design, and operational practices across the country'.[52] As declared on the MDRC's website, they work 'in fields where emotion and ideology often dominate public debates' and strive to be 'a source of objective, unbiased evidence about cost-effective solutions that can be replicated and expanded to scale'. In the 1980s, social impact assessments began to be integrated into the development work of the World Bank, and in the 1990s the US government constituted the Interorganizational Committee on Guidelines and Principles for Social Impact Assessment, which developed standards and requirements for federal agencies' evaluation methods.

Since then, foundations, non-profits, venture philanthropists and social investors have entered the assessment field, experimenting with a range of models, approaches and formulas for hard-core impact evaluation. A leading role in this regard has been played by the San Francisco-based Roberts Enterprise Development Foundation (REDF). REDF was founded in 1997 by former Bear Stearns financier George Roberts, who had made himself known to the world for having led the largest leveraged buyout in the history of global finance: the $25 billion takeover of the tobacco company RJR Nabisco in 1989. A leveraged buyout is the acquisition of a company using a significant amount of borrowed money (usually a ratio of 90 per cent debt to 10 per cent equity, but there have been cases of 100 per cent debt operations), through the issuance of bonds by 'friendly' banks (in some instances, these bonds are non-investment grade and are referred to as 'junk bonds'). As the target company's current success (or expected projection) can be used as collateral by a hostile bidder, leveraged buyouts have tended to become ruthless and predatory tactics, particularly to acquire and/or destroy competitors, as the more successful a company is the more likely it is to be 'attacked'. According to G.A. Jarrell, former chief economist at the US Securities and Exchange Commission (SEC), the vulnerability of leveraged buyouts stems from the 'value gap' – that is, the difference between a company's current value and the expected higher value of the stock, which often results in the overindebtedness of the target firm in the case of successful takeover or in trying to protect itself against it.[53] Critics of leveraged buyouts, which include the former chairmen of the Fed and the SEC, Paul Volcker and John Shad, have traditionally pointed to the high risks that these debt-fuelled takeovers impose on shareholders, bondholders, employees, customers, suppliers, local communities and taxpayers, thus increasing the likelihood of a financial crash, destroying assets and jobs.[54] The Nabisco episode marked the history of hostile financial takeovers, with the magazine *Time* dedicating a full cover page to it in 1988 (aptly titled 'A Game of Greed') and the movie industry producing a television film in 1993, *Barbarians at the Gate*, which criticized the excess of the up-and-coming financial tycoons and their connections with Wall Street investment banks.[55]

Against this backdrop it probably comes as no surprise that it was precisely Roberts's nonprofit creation, the REDF, that pioneered the use of financial models to assess the success of social projects. In particular, the REDF was instrumental in introducing the idea of social return on investment (SROI) among philanthropists and non-profits. SROI follows the same rationale as cost–benefit analysis by measuring the value of social benefits generated by a social intervention (or the activities of a whole organization) as compared to the relative scale of the investment needed to achieve those benefits.[56] By assigning monetary values to social (and also environmental) returns, SROI aims to use 'hard' economic data to demonstrate value creation in the social field.[57]

The SROI can be generically described like this:

$$\frac{\text{Net present value of benefits}}{\text{Net present value of investment}^{58}}$$

The result is a simple ratio of monetized value. For example, an SROI ratio of 4:1 indicates that an investment of $1 delivers $4 of social value. It is impressively simple and, of course, powerfully convincing for social investors the world over. Nowadays there are endless types of SROI analyses being implemented by academics, evaluators, consultants and social workers. Some of them have a clearly evaluative nature – that is, they are used to assess past interventions. Some, by contrast, are prospective; that is, they are used to forecast the potential social value of new interventions and are mainly targeted at philanthropists and social investors interested in getting good 'social' bangs for their bucks.[59] In some cases, SROI is also used as a feasibility methodology (in this case it is also referred to as 'break-even' analysis), designed to indicate how successful a given intervention would need to be in order for the social value of its results to outweigh the costs.

As we already know from the previous chapters, the 'net present value' is an extremely controversial concept. It is calculated through a discount rate applied to future returns, which postulates that 'people prefer to receive money today rather than tomorrow because there is a risk (e.g., that the money will not be paid) or because there is an opportunity cost (e.g., potential gains from investing the money elsewhere)'.[60] The 2012 *Guide to SROI* acknowledges that this approach 'encourages short-termism by discounting the future' and 'betrays the extent to which people actually value their future and their children's future'.[61] Yet discount rates are officially applied everywhere in the implementation of SROI analyses. In the UK, for instance, the basic rate recommended by the Treasury's *Green Book*, which sets out the framework for the appraisal and evaluation of all policies, programmes and projects, is 3.5 per cent.

In the European context, the UK-based New Philanthropy Capital (NPC) has become a recognized leader in the SROI field. For them, one way of thinking about SROI 'is to ask whether the stakeholders would rather receive money directly or receive whatever service it is that the charity offers':

> For example, giving £100 to a lonely pensioner might improve their life in the very short term; they could use the money to pay for services or buy goods or might just appreciate the extra financial security it gives them. But giving £100 to a charity that runs social activities for pensioners might help that person to form and maintain lasting friendships. Many of the older people

the charity works with feel that the 'social value' that they receive is far in excess of £100. The goal of SROI is to *quantify* this value – to say by *how much* it exceeds the financial inputs (if, indeed, it *does* exceed them). ... By putting outcomes in financial terms we see whether particular activities are worth the money that we spend on them.[62]

Measuring costs and benefits is paramount for the NPC's approach to philanthropy. They argue that, although 'we all know that the environment is important', 'it was not until environmental economists managed to value the environment, and compared this value to the costs of protecting it, that governments were motivated to act to combat global warming.'[63] It is peculiar for the NPC to draw a comparison between SROI and the use of cost–benefit analyses in the field of environmental governance. As Chapters 3 and 4 in this book have shown, things went the other way around: governments were pushed to introduce environmental regulations by the mounting pressure of social movements and civil society, until economists decided to use cost–benefit analyses to assess pros and cons of regulations, which paved the way for the introduction of market-based mechanisms such as emissions trading. Ever since, progress on a number of crucial environmental fronts has stalled.

SROI analyses generally follow a set of predetermined steps. First of all, researchers identify the target community (that is, the stakeholders) and map both inputs and outputs. Among the first we find rather conventional factors such as salaries of staff, volunteers' time, rental costs and other forms of investment that go into the specific intervention. Among the outputs we find the number of people targeted by the project, the quantity of services provided to them and other elements directly associated with the type of intervention being assessed (e.g. school performance if we are analysing an educational project). In order to gather such information, questionnaires need to be administered to stakeholders and additional 'hard' data must be collected (e.g. health reports on the target population in the case of health-care projects). Ideally, an SROI should also be able to trace the link between direct outputs (which are the immediate results of the intervention) and 'indirect' outcomes, which describe the wider range of effects the intervention may have on the community at large. In a literacy project, outputs would include the amount of teaching hours provided, the number of students enrolled and the results of their exam tests, while outcomes would include the overall socio-economic, cultural and physical well-being of the learners. Yet 'outcomes are trickier' to assess, let alone trace back directly to the intervention that is being evaluated. Then, of course, all of these (inputs, outputs and outcomes) must be monetized. In this regard, the NPC suggests adopting 'robust' willingness-to-pay studies, as these can better incorporate a 'stakeholder perspective', which is considered one of the key goals of SROI.[64] It is not clear, however, what they mean by robust, as the problems associated with willingness-to-pay surveys remain critical, as we have seen in Chapter 4.

SROI proponents are aware that it is 'not easy to assess directly the value various stakeholders place on outcomes', which is why they often use financial proxies.[65] These are estimates of value based on service costs (e.g. how much the reduction of crimes saves the police service or the total costs of hospital bed spaces saved due to better health) or market values (e.g. the cost of accommodation averted by a housing project). In the UK, both the Cabinet Office and the Scottish government have been working to develop a database of indicators and financial proxies to standardize the valuation process of SROI analyses and improve their reliability. As two of the key principles of SROI are to 'value the things that matter' and 'only include what is material', preference goes to inputting financial costs 'in order that value of the outcomes can be recognised'.[66] Yet, using financial proxies inevitably reduces the capacity of SROI evaluations to capture the 'stakeholder' perspective. This is why some evaluators (a minority, it is true) prefer to carry out SROI analyses without attributing specific financial value to results (in this case, experts speak of a cost-effectiveness approach rather than cost–benefit analysis). The Global Reporting Initiative has produced a wide range of guidelines to strengthen monitoring and assessment tools to measure value other than financial. The Centre for Social Investment at the University of Heidelberg in Germany, where I worked between 2010 and 2012 (and where I'm still a fellow), has devised a number of methods to employ the SROI framework without turning everything into monetary values.[67]

Evidently, conventional SROI approaches pose significant methodological problems. While finding the financial value of a housing project may be relatively uncontroversial (even though one could easily argue that the value of having a 'home' cannot be reduced to its market price), it is impossible to attribute a figure to 'soft' outcomes such as empowerment, emancipation or human rights education, which involve a number of qualitative and nuanced non-market considerations.[68] Inevitably, here we find the same degree of selectivity encountered in the analysis of other evidence-based tools, such as the randomized trials. Furthermore, SROI requires some idea of 'what would have happened anyway', but this counterfactual evidence is obviously not available, and whatever approximation/estimation one comes up with may easily result in calculation errors.[69] All these methodological constraints and the high risk of producing inconsistent data mean that it is impossible to compare SROI ratios across different organizations, thus limiting the capacity to learn from each other and assess what works best.[70] At the same time, measuring returns on investment is a resource-intensive effort. Most non-profits and social enterprises are likely to see this type of measurement as a burden, rather than a source of competitive advantage or a useful activity.[71] SROI requires an organization to have a systematic data collection mechanism, which is likely to drain resources (e.g. people, time and money) away from the social intervention. In turn, this poses an unavoidable moral question: should social work be more about helping people or about studying them?

Despite all its evident limitations, SROI has been growing in popularity because it is attractive to donors and investors, who are keen to adapt the analytical framework of financial markets to the charity world. When considering this, it may perhaps come as no surprise that a leading role in this field is played by the Goldman Sachs Foundation, the nonprofit grant-making arm of investment bank Goldman Sachs. In 2003, the Foundation hosted a meeting among grant-makers at its New York headquarters to discuss the future of impact assessment. All participants, most of whom were venture philanthropists and investment bankers, agreed that the era of traditional nonprofit work was over and a new impulse to social causes could be given by adopting best practices and modi operandi from the financial sector. As the meeting's report highlighted,

> The past decade has witnessed a marked shift from project-related grantmaking toward venture-type philanthropic investment characterized by ... heightened emphasis on measurement and results. Investors are now insisting on greater transparency and accountability. They want to understand the impact that their dollars are having on the world.[72]

Although there is a learning component to SROI, it is clear that the fundamental goal of some SROI supporters is to create an investment market for social goals which is designed along the lines of conventional financial markets. Gavyin Davies and Peter Wheeler, the founders of NPC, were partners at Goldman Sachs and the idea of founding a service company for philanthropists came during a conversation they had at the bank's cafeteria in London. Reflecting on their decision to found NPC, Davies says:

In financial markets in the late 1990s there was an enormous industry dedicated to putting capital to use where it gets the highest returns. So why couldn't the same be true of philanthropy? We found there wasn't enough information produced in a hardheaded, independent, high-quality way.[73]

In Europe, the UK has been at the forefront of the 'social' market revolution. Although enthusiasm for 'hard' measurement had already begun during the New Labour tenure, the Tory-led government of David Cameron has further insisted on adopting tools that can help the growth of social enterprises and private investment, as this resonates well with its concept of a Big Society.[74] In this field, the government has launched, among other initiatives, Big Society Capital, a £600 million fund to support the creation of a fully fledged social investment market.[75] There has also been increasing interest in so-called social impact bonds (SIBs), a form of outcomes-based contracting which enables philanthropic investors to lend their money to projects aimed at tackling social problems while guaranteeing a financial return if the expected social outcomes are achieved. SIBs are being tested in programmes aimed at, for example, reducing reoffending rates among short-term prisoners, decreasing the number of children sent to correctional services, diverting persistent women offenders from prison, and developing more effective drug rehabilitation projects.

Following the NPC's approach, the German-based Phineo has developed a rating methodology for non-profits, which they use to guide social investors and cater for their philanthropic plans. Similar to the analytical work of credit rating agencies, Phineo and its associates conduct quality assessments of nonprofit organizations and award the highest rating (what they call the 'impact label') to those likely to bring the highest returns on investment.[76] Some opinion leaders in the social investment arena, such as Howard Husock of the Manhattan Institute, have been working to establish nonprofit 'stock markets'.[77] Steven Goldberg, author of *Billions of Drops in Millions of Buckets*, has proposed the adoption of an 'impact index', following the model of prediction markets and stock-picking websites that have proliferated on the Internet, through which millions of people every day bet on the results of football games, political elections, stock prices and even the death of celebrities.[78] By noting that these forms of collective prediction have been rather accurate at forecasting events, Goldberg advocates using the same approach to measure the worthiness of charitable causes. In the words of philanthrocapitalist guru Matthew Bishop and his co-author Michael Green, who support Goldberg's idea, 'IMPEX [the impact index] is about harnessing the wisdom of crowds to assess and rank nonprofit performance, flooding the market with new information about where donors think they will get the most bangs for their bucks.'[79]

The marketization of 'doing good'

We are faced with an apparent paradox. The quest for aid-effectiveness and impact assessment, two noble goals in their own right, has ended up subordinating social change to the imperatives of market efficiency. Tools and methods designed to increase transparency and accountability, two other worthy principles by any means, have become Trojan Horses in a strategy aimed at marketizing charity, whether at the international or the domestic level.[80] Perhaps this is not so new. I personally am among those who have always been sceptical of the very essence of philanthropy. As an admirer of the novelist John Steinbeck, I agree with him that 'perhaps the most overrated virtue in our list of shoddy virtues is that of giving.'

> Giving builds the ego of the giver, makes him superior and higher and larger than the receiver. Nearly always, giving is a selfish pleasure, and in many cases is a downright destructive

and evil thing. One has only to remember some of our wolfish financiers who spend two-thirds of their lives clawing fortunes out of the guts of society and the latter third pushing it back.[81]

Regardless of how we feel about philanthropy per se, there is little doubt that, as the global economic crisis worsens and governments struggle to find revenues to sustain their welfare systems, market forces have become more assertive. They aim to reinvent development cooperation and revolutionize social work through business frameworks, which in turn deeply affects the type of society in which we all live. The new 'do-gooders' scrutinize social causes as they would do for any other type of financial investment. This is why they need metrics to assess potential, scalability and likelihood of short-term returns. They are impatient. They have no time for step-by-step development. They want it all and quickly, 'consistent with their own results-oriented values and their own patterns of behavior'.[82] Their understanding of venture philanthropy has nothing to do with the inevitable risk of promoting social and political change: it is founded on the certainty of business success. Where most of us see persistent injustices, they simply see a lack of efficient methods. Where we see power imbalances that keep people in poverty and destitution, they see the need to promote entrepreneurial opportunities. While we stress the importance of social and political empowerment, they believe in a technocratic approach to problem-solving based on 'hard' data and economic models: 'They want a ROI (return on investment), a SROI (social return on investment), FROI (financial return on investment), and an EROI (emotional return on investment).'[83]

These new philanthropists are doers, not social scientists. For them, things are easy. They have managed to build successful corporations (some of which are wealthier than most of the countries their benevolent projects are targeting); why should they not also aspire to fix the world's biggest problems, as Bill Gates would put it? 'Just do it', as the notorious slogan by shoemaking company Nike has it (incidentally, both the Nike Foundation and Nike's founder, Phil Knight, are leading venture philanthropists). They love technical problems because they are clear, identifiable and measurable. Take vaccinations, for instance, one of the campaigns championed by the Gates Foundation. There is a problem (a disease), with a clear cause (a virus) that can be prevented through a specific intervention (a vaccine). But is this the root cause of poor health conditions in low-income countries around the world? An article published in 2005 in the medical review *The Lancet* takes a critical position vis-à-vis the Gates Foundation's involvement in the health-care sector. The article argues that 'the Gates Foundation has turned to a narrowly conceived understanding of health as the product of technical interventions divorced from economic, social, and political contexts.'[84] Looking at the historical evolution of medical technologies and health-care reforms, *The Lancet* argues that longer life expectancy and well-being have always been the outcome of a functioning and universally accessible public health system, rather than the availability of medical technologies (without, of course, disputing the complementary importance of the latter). But a public health-care infrastructure requires patience, long-term commitment and political will. Moreover, it necessitates a significant dose of risk-taking to oppose those interests (especially among private health-care providers) that militate against a universal public health-care system. The magnitude of the challenges and vested interests involved are well exemplified by how hard it has been for the Obama administration to establish a public health-care programme in the USA. Vaccinations are simpler, quicker and do not require a fundamental rethinking of our political and economic systems. At the same time, though, vaccinations (especially when imposed on populations without their consent) continue to be a subject of debate among medical experts. For instance, the development of single-dose or needle-free vaccines, while certainly cost-effective, might decrease the number of well-baby visits, 'which are essential to monitoring healthy growth and development'. In some cases, effective vaccines against conditions such as diarrhoea could make the problem of extending clean water and sanitation seem 'far less pressing' to governments facing budget constraints.[85]

The controversy is further amplified by the Gates Foundation's insistence that vaccinating children is the best way to reduce global population growth and thus mitigate climate change (both problems are considered the most important challenges of our time by the Good Club). Vaccines are expected to slow global population growth and climate change: how could Gates substantiate such a counterintuitive claim? Hard data is the answer. His foundation has built models demonstrating that increased life expectancy in children is positively correlated with fewer births.[86] Fair enough. Common sense and historical evidence tell us that better living conditions are very likely to lead to lower birth rates (although countries like France and Germany have been able to marry high living standards with a resurgence of natality). But, regardless of whether we agree or not with the finding, can we concur with the claim that this is a response to climate change? The answer is a resounding no. Last time I checked, large African families were not at all responsible for the greenhouse gas emissions engulfing our atmosphere: the demographically shrinking old West is to be blamed for them. It is the consumption model in most low-birth-rate countries that is incompatible with the planet, not the way in which (large) African families behave. This is not to dispute the importance of vaccinations, of course. But simplistically linking them to demographic control and then associating this very delicate issue with climate change mitigation is just incorrect. Much to the contrary, exporting our unequal and unsustainable development model to these countries can easily worsen climate change, as we would end up generating billions of new hyper-consumers.

Contradictions, of course, abounds at all levels. The Gates Foundation has been criticized for all sorts of reasons, including the fact that its mother company, Microsoft, has always championed strict regulation in the field of intellectual property rights, which is the primary reason why generic pharmaceuticals are difficult to access in the poorest countries of the world. Moreover, Microsoft's aggressive policies and de facto monopoly in the field of software has limited the capacity of new social enterprises to produce the very innovations Gates is fond of. As we know, most innovations in this field (from new web browsers to applets) have been developed by open-source mass collaborations among programmers, which have been fiercely opposed by Microsoft and its founder. Quite interestingly, one of Gates's best friends and a leading benefactor, the billionaire Warren Buffet, has opposed the introduction of the very rating systems he favours in the nonprofit world for the assessment of corporate conduct. When accused by consumers' groups of having allowed his company Berkshire Hathaway to invest in businesses that violate environmental and human rights standards, he considered 'efforts to rate the performance of companies on social, human rights or environmental measures to be of dubious merit and would not consider such factors when selecting investments'.[87] So much for the consistency and coherence of the philanthrocapitalists' creed in results and measurement.

Edwards has argued that the hard-data technical evaluations (often reinforced by graphics and statistical calculations) promoted by Gates and his colleagues in the social field 'show a high degree of failure in terms of the quality, quantity and sustainability of their results'.[88] Moreover, through rating systems and investment models based on 'objective numbers', these new forms of social engagement are supporting a culture of 'junk food participation', whereby one can simply follow nonprofit stock markets on a computer screen, shift social investments accordingly and then 'write it off to tax'. He contrasts the approach of philanthrocapitalists to that of civic groups and social movements, which are characterized by looser objectives and longer time horizons, and maintains that 'business metrics and measures of success privilege size, growth and market share, as opposed to the quality of interactions between people in civil society and the capacities and institutions they help to create'.[89] 'The reason the nonprofit sector exists at all is because it can fund and invest in social issues that the for-profit market can't touch because they can't be measured', remarks Paul Shoemaker, executive director of the Seattle affiliate of Social Venture Partners International: 'The nonprofit "market" is not designed to be efficient in that way. Yet we're applying the same efficiency metrics to both sectors.'[90] What happens is that when the focus is switched from social change to results-based accounting, the long-term effectiveness is traded for short-term efficiency. As a consequence, externally funded non-profits and non-governmental organizations are gradually discouraged from focusing on political advocacy or working for social change, which require 'deep resources and the ability to change tactics overnight if the situation demands it'.[91]

As some have underlined, the process of turning social work into a series of statistics and abstract models is particularly insidious because it creates 'the false impression that marketized philanthropy leads to systemic change rather than stabilization'.[92] Much to the contrary, by establishing net returns, cost–benefit ratios and causal relations based on randomized trials, the new aid industry is building a 'veiled discourse of stabilization that freezes the world falsely into ontological permanence'.[93] With its emphasis on numbers and outcomes, it appears to reinforce 'the very system that results in poverty, disease, and environmental destruction'.[94] It is interesting to note that most of the new mega-philanthropists are blurring the boundaries between the market and civil society also through the way in which they provide funding, as most of their donations are not made in cash but in stocks. While this makes beneficiaries able to benefit further from the 'gift' in times of financial bonanza, it also exposes them to serious risks during economic slumps. But, more critically, this type of donation turns recipients into involuntary stakeholders of the financial markets. As reported in 2013 by the magazine *Chronicle of Philanthropy*, the donations of America's wealthiest individuals have been falling in the past few years due to the turmoil in the financial world, thus creating further volatility and pro-cyclical tendencies also in the social field.[95]

The new global givers have no interest in asking deeper questions. Their technocratic lens does not allow for exploring systemic issues, including the obvious elephant in the room of whether we can accept a global economic paradigm that appears designed to produce endemic inequalities and concentrate wealth (and resources) in the hands of a few individuals. Moreover, as argued by Ramdas, while the downsides of so-called 'development' in the global North become more evident by the day (among them we can include growing inequality, unsustainable consumption patterns, financial systems that systematically favour elites, and widespread lifestyle-related health problems), philanthrocapitalism 'seeks to invest in efforts and initiatives that can bring the wonders of this model of development to people and communities around the globe'.[96] The more the so-called West learns about the food insecurity produced by commercial agriculture, the environmental and social consequences of an over-reliance on fossil fuels, the instabilities produced by an economic model built on the systematic exploitation of natural resources and the political bankruptcy of democratic systems regularly captured by the interests of corporate power, 'the more it seems determined to share its successful development strategies with the so-called "developing" world'.

As statistics tend to separate complex phenomena in measurable units, they hide the interconnectedness between systemic poverty, economic imbalances and uneven access to resources. As social measurements inevitably simplify what is being measured, the risk is to end up with results that distort reality and mislead policies. Because of their own nature, these metrics reward easy fixes and just-do-it approaches, which can be better captured by numbers and tested through standardized experiments. They focus our attention on technical solutions, although history has often shown that sustainable and long-term social change can only be achieved through participation, confrontation and political action. While numbers tend to emphasize the importance of business and its capacity to find 'solutions', the reality is much more complex. Most of the injustices we face today are the outcome of deep-seated power structures. 'It's politics, stupid!' one may say paraphrasing president Clinton's famous electoral slogan. But numbers do not reveal that. They highlight the tip of the iceberg, thereby hiding the rotten political and economic structures that entrench and perpetuate inequalities.

Rethinking numbers, rethinking governance

If numbers are a mysterious aspect of the universe put there by God, we tend to become subject to control and manipulation by accountant priests. If they are a method by which humanity can control chaos, they become part of the tools of a technocratic scientific elite.

D. Boyle, *The Tyranny of Numbers*, 2001

How can one argue with numbers? As this book has shown, the very nature of statistics is to convey the essence of facts. Never mind whether they *actually* do so. We know that statistics are partial representations of social phenomena and are often scientifically or politically manipulated. Yet, their appearance and design are structured around the notion of evidence – neutral evidence. When we see a number, we perceive certainty – factual information. Numbers are not like words, which require interpretation. Numbers are a source of authority in so far as they reveal truth. And truth cannot be disputed.

This is not to say, of course, that statistical studies are never contested. In academic circles, we often argue about numbers. We discuss methodologies and strive to guarantee full disclosure. Our students know this very well. When presenting their research work, they fear the inevitable question: 'Where did you get this number from?' In our publications, it is usual practice to include disclaimers, especially when statistical models constitute the backbone of our analysis. We, as academics, are fond of warning readers that our data may be incomplete and that the critical assumptions upon which we base our models may be oversimplifying real life. Usually we deal with such weaknesses through footnotes, endnotes, asterisks and appendices, perhaps because we know that those are the sections very few people read. It is a bit like in advertising, when after publicizing all the incredible features of a new product companies add the sentence 'Terms and conditions apply', in minuscule font, at the bottom of the advert, where it is hard to see.

Having some numbers to substantiate academic analyses is now, by and large, a precondition to publishing. The best-known journals in the social sciences have become reluctant to publish any research that does not have at least an equation, a couple of re-gressions or a factor analysis. These are hard times for 'qualitative' researchers. Unfortunately, the scramble for numbers inevitably reduces the analytical depth of our work. As we desperately look for correlations and statistical significance across our data sets, we seldom wonder about the real quality of our numbers. And reviewing the quality does not mean ensuring that averages are correct or that missing data do not influence the results. It means questioning the ultimate validity of numbers as good descriptors of the social phenomena we are investigating. Do these numbers really tell us anything valuable about society? Are we not forcing complexity into claustrophobic metrics which deprive reality of any meaning? Do numbers simply describe social reality or have they become normative tools through which we shape society? And, importantly, are we teaching our students to view numbers with a critical eye? Unfortunately, intellectual complacency is pervasive in academia, with detrimental effects on the originality of our thinking and the capacity to deviate from preconceived notions. And disclaimers, no matter how sincere, may not be enough to 'deliver us from evil'.

There is no doubt that numbers have come to dominate not only academic thinking, but also our own understanding of the role of academia. For starters, we are continually subject to standardized performance assessments. Such a trend originated in North America and the UK in the 1970s, and then spread to Europe and most emerging countries in Asia, South America and Africa. Our existence revolves around a critical number, the so-called H-Index, which is a sophisticated way of calculating how regularly citations of our work pop up in the academic literature. Google Scholar, which is a formidable resource in the age of the digital revolution, has also become a curse for many of us, as most indexes are based on the automatic calculations made by Google. And when Google does not pick up on one of our papers, then we are in trouble. 'Publish or perish' has become our mantra. 'Cite and be cited' is our new iron law. Another fundamental number in academic life is the so-called 'impact factor', which is calculated by the information agency Thomson Reuters and indicates the average number of article citations of a given journal. If you want to survive in the academic jungle of numbers, you need to elbow your way into high-impact journals. The rest is irrelevant. But do these statistics really tell us anything about the quality of research? Perhaps. At the same time, though, they generate perverse incentives. As quantity becomes paramount, academics feel the pressure of meeting standardized requirements. When numbers drop, entire faculties fret. Special meetings are called and jobs are on the line. Name and shame has become routine. It is not unusual to find colleagues who agree to cite one another in their respective work. Self-citations abound. Reviewers often subject the acceptance of a paper for publication to the citation of one or more of their works. All these statistics have become the most critical asset for those seeking promotion, a salary raise or a job at an Ivy League university. They have a fundamental 'impact' not only on our reputation, but also on our bank account. And amid this numbers-led frenzy, it is not surprising that many academics are caught plagiarizing, replicating publications and forging data, as a desperate attempt to keep up with the performance treadmill.

In defence of numbers

This book does not intend to dispute the importance of numbers for the advancement of knowledge and for the betterment of society. Nor does it deny the critical role that numbers play in supporting decisions and policies. I am fully aware that public decision-making without statistics would be dominated by gut feelings and shallow rhetorical arguments, which is one of the reasons why authoritarian governments have an excellent track record of not releasing regular statistics or of withholding data altogether. Just as the scientific revolution questioned the religious explanation of the universe, thereby weakening the secular power of the churches and ushering in the modern era, numbers have had (and can have) an emancipatory potential: they can empower people and weaken dictators. Numbers can empower young students who use them to challenge professors and their 'bogus' data. Numbers can help environmental organizations take polluting corporations to court for ecological damage. Numbers can help citizens understand whom to vote for and what policies to support. In academia, too, numbers are critical. No matter how much one can criticize inventions such as the H-index and the impact factor, the pursuit of excellence requires some form of assessment of academic quality. Nobody wants a lethargic academia, where professors have no incentives, be it reputational or economic, to generate good research and outstanding teaching.

Public policy, too, needs numbers to function. As the physicist Lord Kelvin once said, 'if you cannot measure it, you cannot improve it.' And, as an oft-quoted aphorism by business guru W.E. Deming goes, 'you cannot manage what you can't measure.' Measuring is a fundamental component of human life. We measure things every day and we base our decisions on that. Rejecting measurement per se would not only be naive, but impossible for society. It would take away a significant part of what defines human nature. Measurements are also fundamental to communicate. Without scales, there would be no local markets. Without thermometers, there would be no doctors. Without meters, there would be no carpenters. Our education, health care and housing depend on measurements. And we appreciate that as a sign of progress.

At the same time, though, there are many things that we refuse to measure, and we have very good reasons for that. For instance, we consider it awkward to measure art. We believe that the value of art cannot be translated into crude numbers. Of course, we often put a price on art crafts, but we would find it odd to measure the beauty of the Statue of Liberty or the Pyramids and then assess which one is stronger, better or more valuable. We also reject quantitative measures of friendship. Some people may very well consider themselves lucky for having more Facebook friends than others, but nobody would seriously believe that the number of friends (whether in person or on line) is a proxy of the quality of friendship. Much to the contrary, we feel that if we were to measure friendship according to some numerical parameter, we would somehow offend the very nature of it. By measuring it, we would turn friendship into something else: a numerical unit, deprived of that human feeling that makes it so important in the first place. Similarly, we refuse to measure love. We do not use scales to quantify the goodness of parents or the harmony of a couple. Although some economists and psychologists may adopt metrics to measure these 'soft' elements of social life, we – as a society – recoil at the idea of introducing standardized assessments of parenting or married life.

In the natural sciences, numbers are used to describe physical phenomena. And there are good and bad numbers there too. As historians have shown, hard sciences are not immune to over-simplifications and paradigmatic shifts. Quite to the contrary, the historical evolution of sciences has been that of questioning dominant models (and their numbers) with a view to replacing them with better theories, which in turn have been challenged again in a continuous process of scientific revolution.[1] Good or bad, however, the numbers of physics can hardly affect the behaviour of the atom. This is not true when numbers are applied to human phenomena. As measurements enter social life, they contribute to shaping reality. Standardized assessments, for instance, are not just tools to analyse performance. They are tools to guide it. If what counts is quantity, then academics will strive to publish every little piece of research they have, not matter how dubious its quality may be. If what counts is to have more friends on Facebook, then users will try their best to accumulate new connections rather than strengthen the intimacy of those they already have. If the quantity of love becomes the explanatory criterion to measure a good family structure, then parents may decide to pay more attention to what can be measured, such as the number of outings, toys and time they spend with their children, rather than the quality of such interactions. The risk is not just that of being misled in how we define our priorities. There is also a clear risk of losing the capacity to appreciate the value of what is intangible. Paraphrasing the German political theorist Hannah Arendt, we may say that the problem with systematic application of numbers to social life 'is not that they are wrong, but that they could become true'.[2]

Beyond good and bad numbers

From a governance perspective, there is a double problem with the influence of numbers in policymaking. As we have seen throughout the book, some numbers are simply 'bad'. The quality of statistical surveys, such as those forming the national income accounts on which the calculation of GDP is based, varies dramatically across the world. In many African countries, income statistics are incomplete and largely rely on imputations made by local statisticians, which generate all sorts of inconsistencies. Yet, policymakers and international donors use these 'poor numbers' every day to gauge the effectiveness of structural reforms, development aid and macro-economic policies.[3] The Bureau of Economic Analysis, too, has admitted that GDP statistics in the USA are not always of good quality, especially during economic crises.[4] Moreover, numbers are continually revised, adjusted and recalculated in different ways by each statistical agency, which makes international comparisons harder than we are made to believe. For instance, in mid-2013 the Bureau introduced a reform to the GDP accounts for the calculation of expenditures in research and development, entertainment, literary and other artistic originals.[5] Traditionally treated as business costs, they are now dealt with as fixed investments, thus adding fully to national income. This spurred criticism that the US government was desperately trying to inflate its estimate of economic growth with a view to downplaying the increase in national debt as a percentage of GDP.[6]

We also know that many data sets have been manipulated or completely fabricated. Rating agencies, for instance, have admitted adapting credit ratings to suit their clients, and investment banks have manipulated sovereign debt statistics. Academics have been caught out using fake data, and in some cases bestselling books and entire careers have been based on bogus evidence. We also know that the peer review system leaves much to be desired, as many journals, including those with the highest impact factor, have fallen into the numbers trap, taking as uncontested evidence what is in fact man-made fabrication. The phrase 'garbage in, garbage out', which has become a common expression in computer science, indicates that statistical models unquestioningly reproduce whatever 'garbage' one feeds them with. If nonsensical information is inputted, the models will produce nonsensical results, which will however look evidence-based to all of us.

Numbers can also be twisted to serve particular political agendas. Environmental sceptics have used data to prove that a Hummer is more energy efficient than a Prius, while contrarian scientists have employed randomized trials to show that tobacco smoking does not cause cancer. In 1954, the American writer Darrell Huff published a little book, *How to Lie with Statistics*, which has become a classic read for all students sceptical of numbers. Through a lively and captivating narrative, Huff pointed out all sorts of manipulations that can occur when data is misrepresented (for instance, by truncating graphs to overemphasize minor differences) or when it is poorly interpreted.[7] As we have learned, 'Proofiness is the raw material that arms partisans to fight off the assault of knowledge, to clothe irrationality in the garb of the rational and the scientific.'[8]

However, if the quality of data were the only problem with numbers, then it could be easily resolved through stricter observation, transparency and regulation. Unfortunately, numbers can mislead decisionmaking even when they are not overtly manipulated. As numbers focus attention only on what can be measured, this inevitably influences our priorities, given that what is not measurable is left out. To use Descartes's classical distinction between *res extensa* (the measured reality) and *res cogitans* (the spiritual reality), what is measured becomes the only reality that matters. The rest is useless and valueless. Take, once again, the case of GDP. Even if we were able to improve its statistical quality (and several attempts are being made), GDP would still be a measure of market output, which is by no means a complete picture of the overall economy. As we know, what is not exchanged through the mediation of the market is not included in the national income accounts. As a consequence, by using GDP as a measure of economic performance, our governments pursue policies that strengthen the market at the expense of informal economic areas, such as household services, the care economy and the gift economy. Moreover, as GDP is based on market prices, what is not priced becomes valueless. As this book has shown, such an emphasis on prices generates perverse incentives. On the one hand, our governance systems tend to privilege a model of development that disregards what is free, such as natural resources. On the other hand, policymakers are encouraged to privatize and marketize common resources in order to make them productive in GDP terms. Within the GDP framework of governance, only what is monetized counts. Therefore, for the environment to be taken seriously, it needs to be measured and monetized. Many economists will tell you that it is possible to price anything. Even when there are no markets, prices can be simply simulated. Basically, for many of them, refining GDP is just a matter of technical adjustments and more accurate models. But this monetization 'trap' reveals all sorts of inconsistencies, as we have seen throughout the book. In fact, the very idea of accuracy becomes a metaphysical concept. How can we accurately measure the value of nature? Who measures nature? According to which standards? Do we choose an anthropocentric approach, whereby nature is worth how much human beings decide? Or do we adopt a holistic ecosystemic approach, which takes into account the interconnectedness of the natural world? We have analysed all conceptual shortcomings affecting available methodologies, from willingness-to-pay surveys to the calculation of replacement costs or the identification of proxy markets. All these valuation methods rest on weak assumptions and reveal basic conceptual flaws. When they are applied to governance models, even in the absence of intentional manipulations and conflicts of interest (which systematically occur), they become dangerous policy tools.

In the business community, too, there have been fervent debates as to whether numbers help build financial success or kill innovation. Two well-known academics, Robert Kaplan of Harvard Business School and Thomas Johnson of Portland State University, have personally embodied such a battle of ideas. In the late 1980s, Kaplan and Johnson co-authored the bestseller *Relevance Lost: The Rise and Fall of Management Accounting*, which maintained that while cost accounting had been the key feature driving the expansion of the new corporations in the nineteenth century, these metrics had become fundamentally 'toxic' for business in the globalized age, as they separated managers from the productive components of their companies, thus making them even more dependent on abstract calculations for the estimate of costs, prices and returns on investment. Ever since, however, their intellectual paths have grown further apart, with Kaplan supporting the adoption of all sorts of econometric models to run successful businesses and Johnson arguing for hands-on management and human judgement. Through a series of successful management books, Kaplan has been advocating the systematic use of activity-based costing and balanced scorecards, which help managers 'draw forth from a mass of numerical data those few statistics and results that genuinely matter'. For Johnson, by contrast, these economics-dominated metrics force managers to lead companies through quantitative data, rather than through detailed knowledge of how business works. In turn, this has contributed 'to the modern obsession in business with "looking good" by the numbers ... no matter what damage [it] does to the underlying system of relationships that sustain any human organization'.[9]

The problem with numbers is therefore more philosophical than the simplistic distinction between good and bad numbers. In a sense it is an issue that goes back to the battle of ideas between Plato and Aristotle. For the first, numbers are symbols of truth. For the second, numbers are tools to advance knowledge. Following Pythagoras, Plato believed in numbers as revealing the essence of the world. By contrast, Aristotle saw the world as a messy object of study, in which mathematical reasoning could guide knowledge, but never represent a higher truth. For him, numbers do not reveal 'forms', as opposed to the more mundane 'substance'. They are heuristic devices to dissect the intricacy of nature. They are not more perfect than the substance they attempt to describe.

Such a classical distinction between numbers as essences and numbers as tools is still influencing our contemporary societies. And, by and large, Plato has been victorious. Indeed, despite their imperfections and partiality, numbers tend to acquire a life of their own. They abstract themselves from the real world and generate a fictitious 'hyperuranium'. They embody evidence. They cease to represent a phenomenon; they become the phenomenon itself. Since the very idea of representation is by definition imperfect, numbers cannot represent; they must signify reality.

This inherent power of numbers, which is founded on our innate search for truth, explains why all sorts of data, good or bad, can become a potent weapon to shape complacency and subservience in society. Although they are presented as tools that advance knowledge, in so far as they remove our collective capacity to exercise our critical mind, they run the risk of fostering stupidity. A society based on numbers 'endangers itself because it invests too heavily in shallow rituals of verification at the expense of other forms of organizational intelligence', argues LSE accounting professor Michael Power. Through numerical-based auditing systems, it becomes 'a form of learned ignorance'.[10] These standardized approaches 'support abstract managerial values at the expense of other cultures of performance evaluation' and 'tend to prioritize that which can be measured and audited in economic terms'.[11]

Governance, numbers and the public sphere

In political studies, it has become rather common to talk about decision-making processes in terms of governance. The word indicates the fragmentation of authority in contemporary societies, where national governments have become facilitators rather than monopolists of policymaking power, in closer cooperation with global institutions and private entities, from corporations to NGOs.[12] In studying governance, one can identify three distinct but connected sectors: the state, the market and civil society. Obviously, this is by no means an accurate description. The boundaries between these three areas of collective action are not so well defined as we may believe. For instance, the public (state) and the private (market) sectors have significant areas of overlap, especially when public–private partnerships proliferate in the design, execution and management of a number of policies.[13] Similarly, the distinction between for-profit (market) and nonprofit (state and civil society) functions is increasingly challenged by 'hybrid' organizations which merge solidarity-based features with profit functions (e.g. social enterprises), or public utility companies which are controlled by government but follow market principles.

As boundaries become increasingly blurred, the three sectors not only cooperate but also compete for power. As governance mechanisms open new opportunities to exert influence in decision-making, the state, the market and civil society enter a dynamic relationship of mutual balancing, where the risk of unidimensional takeover is, however, always present. Governance can therefore be seen as the new terrain of political confrontation, in which different (albeit often complementary) principles and values clash or cooperate to arrive at collective decisions. In short, governance is the process whereby cultural, social, economic and political hegemony is constructed.

Arguably, the most complex of the three sectors is what we generally (and perhaps too simplistically) call civil society. What is civil society? This question has been part and parcel of philosophical debates since time immemorial. In the history of political thought we can distinguish several complementary (and at times opposing) ways in which civil society has been conceptualized.[14] In classical Greek political thought, the term 'civil society' described the 'good' society: that is, the set of manners, rules and forms of participation that characterized the polis vis-à-vis other forms of government. For Aristotle, civil society was society organized through self-government as opposed to the savage world of the 'barbarians'. It was civil because of 'civility'. In Rome's republican tradition, civil society was the ensemble of active citizens, who regularly contributed to the various social, cultural, economic and political splendour of the republic. It was civil because of the *civis*, the Latin word for citizen. The concept of *vita activa*, which fundamentally identified the roles and responsibilities of citizens in the Roman tradition, was later popularized by Machiavelli in the 1500s and by Hannah Arendt in the mid-1900s. In modern political philosophy, the idea of civil society resurfaced with the development of personal liberties and rights. For John Locke and Adam Ferguson, two forefathers of modern liberalism, civil society was the expression of the modern proprietary class, which created spaces of autonomy and self-determination within a state characterized by inherent oppressive tendencies. For these thinkers civil society was a fundamentally political concept, a bastion against the tendency of the state to override individual rights.[15]

Similarly, Alexis de Tocqueville treated civil society as the locus of self-organization as opposed to government, which was by contrast viewed as the source of coercion. This self-organized world is characterized by associations and networks that cut across and transcend traditional social relationships founded on patron–client ties. In this conception, civil society provides a breeding ground for democratic values and a formidable curb against oppression. Moreover, as Harvard political scientist Robert Putnam demonstrated, such horizontal interaction contributes deeply to the diffusion and production of social capital.[16] Another tradition of thought, tracing its origins to Hegel, sees civil society as the ensemble of all those groups and entities that exist between the state and the family. This view portrays organizations and groups as vehicles of cultural permeation throughout society according to the order imposed by the state, and deeply influenced Marx's notion of civil society as the core of the capitalist system (the bourgeoisie).[17] Re-elaborating on Marx, the Italian intellectual Antonio Gramsci understood civil society as the realm of hegemony, constructed around the notion of consent, as opposed to the realm of force that pertains to the domination exerted by the state.[18] He saw greater potential in civil society than Marx, noting that it could also provide the space needed for people to rebel against capitalist dominant structures. For the social anthropologist Ernest Gellner, civil society has been the defining character of Western liberalism vis-à-vis other forms of political ideology.[19]

According to the German philosopher Jürgen Habermas, civil society should be seen as the locus of communicative action, the so-called 'public sphere', in which ideas and values are discussed and processed. In this view, civil society becomes the foundation of a dialogic society.[20] This sphere lies between the state and the private realm: it is the space where public debate takes place and information is exchanged and where groups and individuals can express their views and interests, discuss common objectives as well as confront their biases and prejudices. In this regard, civil society is the arena where discursive interaction – that is, a continuous process of confrontation, argumentation and deliberation – sustains the very essence of democracy. The public sphere is not static. It is an ever-evolving dynamic, in which confrontation leads to change; in turn, this affects the identity and values of participants, thus redesigning the contours of the civil society arena itself. The idea of civil society as the public sphere inherently presupposes conflicting ideas and goals. Communication, confrontation and debate cannot take place where uniformity reigns. As Gramsci suggested in his analysis of hegemony, civil society is a social sphere characterized by an inherent potential transformative power.

Whether one agrees with classical theorists who underlined the opposition of civil society to the state and the market, or with those who see civil society as the locus of participation and deliberation, it is clear that in the world of numbers the very political nature of civil society as the locus of change is increasingly challenged. By virtue of their own nature, numbers reduce debate. They are not dynamic entities. To the contrary, their essence is static. As we have discussed in Chapter 1, statistics were designed to eliminate discretion and avoid political contestation in modern bureaucracies. They were invented to control, albeit without giving the impression of control. They were designed to rule, without coercion. In Foucault's terms, they were instruments of governmentality. The subtlety of numbers is that they do not eliminate power; they hide it. And it is precisely this cloaking capacity that makes them so influential in politics and dangerous for public debate.

Statistics, ratings, results, measurements and all the other forms that numbers can assume in public policy have had the effect of 'depoliticizing governance', thereby stripping civil society of its truly transformative potential. By reducing different values, principles and ideas to measurements, numbers have fundamentally altered the political interaction between the state, the market and civil society. The continual confrontation of ideas that should characterize the public sphere has become a unidimensional quest for efficiency in decision-making. The political nature of public debate has been replaced by the efficiency of numbers as cognitive devices to identify the best solutions to the world's problems. On the one hand, this has grossly centralized policymaking, by affording increasing power to the masters of numbers – that is, the so-called experts and technocrats. On the other hand, as markets are considered the ideal locus of numerical reasoning, such a trend has propelled a new form of market supremacy, characterized by the narrow form of economic thinking dominating contemporary societies. As I have discussed at length in *Gross Domestic Problem*, the invention of GDP has been instrumental in generating the most powerful narrative of all times: that is, that markets are the only producers of wealth and that endless market production is the ultimate objective of politics. GDP has also provided a critical face-lift to all polluting industries, which have seen all their 'bads' disappear, while subjugating trade unions in a state of subservience and undermining the capacity of environmental movements to stimulate a meaningful debate on the desirability and feasibility of economic growth. Governance institutions, whether locally or nationally, have been crafted around the prestige bestowed by this almighty number, while alternative economic thinking has been sidelined and non-market, less formalized economies have been destroyed. Moreover, GDP has afforded immense power to central bankers, economic advisers, development consultants, IMF specialists, World Bank-ers and the like, as these technocrats know best how to propel economic growth and manage the business cycle. The power of technocracy has become all the more evident in the industry of credit rating, where a few private companies

largely rule the planet. Their numbers dictate policies throughout
the world and force entire nations into austerity programmes to
the detriment of social justice and collective well-being. Here
again, numbers have been used to strengthen the grip of markets
over other sectors of social life, while affording immense power
to a few gatekeepers.

Nowadays, there is virtually no social or environmental policy
that is not vetted through cost–benefit analyses. At first sight,
these methodologies appear rational. It makes sense to measure
the costs and benefits of a policy before adopting it. But, when
looking more closely, we notice unreasonable assumptions and
biased conceptualizations. Discount rates systematically assign
a higher value to the present at the expense of the future, thus
producing a clear bias towards short-term approaches. Moreover, the conflation of costs and benefits into one number hides
a fundamental question: whose costs and whose benefits? In
society, costs and benefits are not shared equally by all members.
When it comes to regulation (especially in the environmental
field), costs are generally borne by companies and benefits shared
by society at large. But cost–benefit analyses unduly present
their costs and *our* benefits as if they were on the same level,
with the consequence that allegedly cost-effective solutions are
systematically preferred to those based on principles such as
social justice and environmental sustainability. This has been the
case with all major environmental regulations of the past decades,
best exemplified by the triumph of markets in the governance of
climate-change mitigation. Behind this approach is the idea that
climate change can be fixed through the right formulas, by identifying critical equilibria and optimal pricing mechanisms. But as
numerous analysts have observed, 'climate change is not amenable
to an elegant solution because it is not a discrete problem. It is
better understood as a symptom of a particular development
path', which forms 'a complex nexus of mutually reinforcing,

intertwined patterns of human behaviour, physical materials and the resulting technology. It is impossible to change such complex systems in desired ways by focusing on just one thing.'[21]

As this book has shown, no matter how many times markets fail (e.g. with credit ratings and carbon trading), the power of numbers seems to resuscitate ideas and approaches that should be viewed as bankrupt beyond any reasonable doubt. The growing power of 'philanthrocapitalists' is a clear example of a field in which a metric-driven business mentality is virtually hegemonic, in terms of both resources and modus operandi. According to Edwards, civil society 'works best when its ecosystems are healthy and diverse'. But because of the metric-driven ideology endorsed by philanthrocapitalists, 'distance is increasing between inter-mediary advocacy groups and NGOs, and the constituencies on whose behalf they are supposed to work', and 'older associations that used to bring citizens together across the lines of class, geography and (less so) race are disappearing'.[22] A report published by the Kellogg Foundation in 2003 maintained that the emphasis on 'efficiency and market share has the potential to endanger the most basic value of the nonprofit sector – the availability of "free space" within society for people to invent solutions to social problems and serve the public good'.[23]

We have seen how the proliferation of markets is also evident in the governance of biodiversity conservation. New measurement tools, audits and other quantitative methodologies are being continually developed by financial firms to put a price on nature, as measuring natural capital has become a lucrative business. But behind these numbers lies a world of conflicts of interest, speculative deals and other hazardous tendencies, which are cloaked under the apparent neutrality of numerical models. Through a system of governance by numbers, we deal with nature as if it were a counterpart in a financial transaction. We allow so-called experts to set thresholds and assess risk. Then, based on these statistics, we play a dangerous game with Mother Earth, in which we gauge our moves based on estimates of ecological damage, environmental risk and climate change. Instead of encouraging an open debate on what the developmental path of mankind should be in order to marry social, economic and environmental well-being, we use a variety of dubious models to 'gamble' with nature in order to achieve the maximum results with the least effort.

What now? Governance of complexity

By obscuring the politics of numbers, the current model of governance is stifling a rational public debate on some of the most profound injustices marring our societies. As some have argued, governance by numbers 'can rob us of our democratic right to think for ourselves'.[24] The systematic application of measurements, ratings, cost–benefit analyses, standardized assessments, returns on investment and pricing models has resulted in what one could call 'the inevitability of the market'. As our conceptual tools are so deeply influenced by numerical reasoning, we cannot think outside of the market 'box'. Paraphrasing Yale economist Charles Lindblom, we may say that markets have become 'conceptual prisons'.[25] No matter how many times they fail, no matter how many times we realize the inherent short-termism of the market philosophy, we seem bound to acquiesce to its almighty dominance not only of our governance systems but also of our intellect.

Our ideas are imprisoned by numbers. This is why we respond to their failures with even more trust. In an article published in 1987, sociologist Susan Shapiro analysed what she called 'the social control of impersonal trust'. She reflected on the classical question 'who guards the guardians?' and noted that society assumes that guardians will 'tell the truth, fulfil their obligations competently, follow established procedures, and act like disinterested fiduciaries'.[26] But when they fail us, instead of re-thinking political and social mechanisms, we 'throw 'good' money after bad'; that is, we 'protect trust and respond to its failures by conferring even more trust'.[27] In the words of David Boyle, it is 'one of the paradoxes of the modern world that the failure of auditors is expected to be solved by employing more auditors.'[28] Why do we do that? Perhaps it is because, as social animals, we have no choice but to trust. Society is, in the end, based on interpersonal trust. However, I find this answer unsatisfactory. As a matter of fact, we live in a world in which social distrust is rampant. We protect our homes with security gates. We seldom interact with our neighbours. We expect contracts to include li-ability provisions. We hold on to our wallets when we walk down the street. But then, almost magically, all this distrust evaporates when it comes to market governance models. In this case, we consciously or unconsciously commit to believe in the wonders of ratings, carbon markets, offset mechanisms and biodiversity credits. Although we would carefully check if the street vendor has given us the correct change, we unquestioningly assume that the cost-benefit analyses run by a team of economists or the social return on investment carried out by some experts are truthful.

This book's answer to such a paradox is that numbers turn the governance field into a technical process, which projects an image of expertise and professionalism. Moreover, numbers transform the governance process into something that can be managed with the appropriate technology. To be sure, this idea is quite comforting. It simplifies the world. It indicates that there are discrete solutions to discrete problems. Most importantly, it shows that, through the right formulas, we can make decisions in which everybody wins: you and I, the poor and the rich, polluters and Mother Nature. In a world in which every day looks more arduous, I suppose many people find it reassuring to hear that there are easy solutions to our overarching problems, from the financial crisis to climate change and global poverty. By delegating the task of fixing the world to the masters of numbers, our ultimate objective seems to be that of enjoying the lightness of our daily disempowerment.

As comforting as this sense of delegation may be, the reality is that we live in a complex world. Numbers, albeit critical to human progress, are double-edged swords, which can surreptitiously reduce the complexity of social phenomena and ultimately lead us in the wrong direction. Just like a conscientious mother would never reduce her role to that summarized in an algorithm, we should not expect governance systems to be automatically driven by econometric models. Governance is a public good: the most important public good. Not only our future as human beings but that of the whole planet depends on our commitment to governance, in all its ramifications, from the global to the local level. The more the public sphere retracts under the increasing pressure of market rationalism, the more we lose the capacity to regain control over our democratic institutions. More dangerously, as market mechanisms crowd out other forms of social interaction, we extirpate alternative forms of socialization. As they cannot be measured in conventional terms, gift economies, community-based reciprocity schemes and other types of informal dynamics tend to disappear under the pressure of formal market structures. In this process we are losing not only entire communities and ecosystems, but also millennia of knowledge.

By subscribing to a metrics-based 'learned ignorance', we unlearn other ways of life. We become unidimensional human beings: utility maximers, who increasingly fit the numerical models applied to them. In 2009, Elinor Ostrom won the Nobel Prize in Economics for her work on the governance of the commons. A woman trained as a political scientist, she had the courage to oppose centuries of conventional wisdom in economics by arguing that there was another way. She believed that privatization and commodification, on the one hand, or top-down regulation, on the other hand, were not the only ways in which human beings could govern their common resources.[29] She travelled across the world, from Japan to Switzerland, from California to the Philippines, from Canada to Turkey to demonstrate that bottom-up systems of collective governance, in which citizens build shared institutions and collective cooperative mechanisms, not only achieve better governance results, but are also resilient, balanced and long-lasting. This is why the public sphere is so important. All those soft elements of social life, from mutual respect to solidarity, which systematically escape our obsession with measurement, are ultimately much more important than what is integrated into the numerical models driving contemporary governance. True, participation can be a painful experience. The process of interacting, debating, compromising and deliberating can be tedious and frustrating. Yet, we have no other way. We are social animals and live in a profoundly interconnected world. As remarked by Raj Patel, the solution will not come from market society but 'from the liberty of living together and engaging in the democratic politics that will help us value our common future'.[30] Numbers will not save us. We will need to do it ourselves.

Notes

INTRODUCTION

1. R.A. Fisher, 'The Expansion of Statistics', *American Scientist* 42 (1954): 276.
2. H.K. Hansen and A. Muhlen-Schulte, 'The Power of Numbers in Global Governance', *Journal of International Relations and Development*, 15 (4) (2012): 455–65.
3. A.C. Cutler, V. Haufler and T. Porter (eds), *Private Authority and International Affairs* (Albany, NY: State University of New York Press, 1999); R.B. Hall and T. J. Biersteker (eds), *The Emergence of Private Authority in Global Governance* (Cambridge: Cambridge University Press, 2002); J.C. Graz and A. Nolke (eds), *Transnational Private Governance and its Limits* (London and New York: Routledge, 2008).
4. Quoted in G. Gigerenzer et al., *The Empire of Chance: How Probability Changed Science and Everyday Life* (Cambridge: Cambridge University Press, 1989), p. 238.
5. M.J. Sandel, *What Money Can't Buy: The Moral Limits of Markets* (New York: Farrar, Straus & Giroux, 2012), p. 177.
6. Ibid., p. 179.

CHAPTER 1

1. R.M. Hare, *Plato* (Oxford: Oxford University Press, 1996 [1982]), p. 10.
2. B. Russell, *A History of Western Philosophy* (New York: Simon & Schuster, 1967).
3. Hare, *Plato*, p. 11.
4. Ibid.

5. N. Canny, *From Reformation to Resistance: Ireland, 1534-1660* (Dublin: Helicon, 1987).

6. A. Roncaglia, *Petty: The Origins of Political Economy* (Armonk, NY: M.E. Sharpe, 1985), p. 5.

7. Lavoisier's study of the wealth of France was published with the title *De la richesse territoriale du royaume de France*.

8. T. Fougner, 'Neoliberal Governance of States: The Role of Competitiveness Indexing and Benchmarking', *Millennium: Journal of International Studies*, 37(2) (2008): 303-26.

9. T.J. Sinclair, *The New Masters of Capital: American Bond Rating Agencies and the Politics of Creditworthiness* (Ithaca, NY: Cornell University Press, 2005).

10. O. Lowenheim, 'Examining the State: A Foucauldian Perspective on International "Governance Indicators"', *Third World Quarterly*, 29 (2) (2008): 255-74. See also J.C. Sharman, 'The Bark Is the Bite: International Organizations and Blacklisting', *Review of International Political Economy*, 16 (4) (2009): 573-96.

11. Cited by T.M. Porter, *Trust in Numbers: The Pursuit of Objectivity in Science and Public Life* (Princeton, NJ: Princeton University Press, 1995), p. 37.

12. 'Democrats Optimistic about Census', *New York Times*, 21 December 2010, http://thecaucus.blogs.nytimes.com/2010/12/21/democrats-optimistic-about-census (accessed 30 June 2013).

13. A. Hamilton, J. Jay and J. Madison, *The Federalist Papers* (New York: Cosimo Books, 2006 [1787]), p. 359.

14. M.J. Cullen, *The Statistical Movement in Early Victorian Britain: The Foundations of Empirical Social Research* (Hassocks: Harvester Press, 1975); T.M. Porter, *The Rise of Statistical Thinking, 1820-1900* (Princeton, NJ: Princeton University Press, 1986).

15. Porter, *Trust in Numbers*, p. 21

16. K. Pearson, *The Grammar of Science* (New York: Cosimo Books, 2007 [1911]), p. 12.

17. Porter, *Trust in Numbers*, p. 49.

18. Ibid., p. 49 (emphasis added).

19. J. Best, *Damned Lies and Statistics: Untangling Numbers from the Media, Politicians and Activists* (Berkeley and Los Angeles: University of California Press, 2001), p. 7.

20. M. Blastland and A. Dilnot, *The Numbers Game: The Commonsense Guide to Understanding Numbers in the News, in Politics, and in Life* (New York: Gotham Books, 2009), p. 79.

21. 'You Can Count Me Out', *Observer*, 14 January 2001, www.guardian.co.uk/theobserver/2001/jan/14/featuresreview.review (accessed 30 June 2013).

22. P. Starr, 'The Sociology of Official Statistics', in W. Alonso and P. Starr

(eds), *The Politics of Numbers* (New York: Russell Sage Foundation, 1987), p. 52.

23. Blastland and Dilnot, *The Numbers Game*, p. 80.
24. Ibid., p. 85.
25. D. Meier et al., *Many Children Left Behind* (Boston, MA: Beacon Press, 2004).
26. 'TNLI Survey: No Child Left Behind Highlight', *Teachers Network*, http://teachersnetwork.org/tnli/survey_highlights.htm (accessed 30 June 2013).
27. 'What's Wrong With Standardized Tests?', *The National Center for Fair and Open Testing*, 22 May 2012, www.fairtest.org/facts/whatwron.htm (accessed 30 June 2013).
28. 'You Can Count Me Out'.
29. The citation is from P. Miller, 'Accounting and Objectivity: The Invention of Calculating Selves and Calculable Spaces', in A. Megill (ed.), *Rethinking Objectivity* (Durham, NC: Duke University Press, 1994).
30. M. Foucault, 'Governmentality', in G. Burchell, C. Gordon and P.Miller (eds), *The Foucault Effect: Studies in Governmentality* (Chicago: University of Chicago Press, 1991), p. 95.
31. P. Becker and W. Clark (eds), *Little Tools of Knowledge: Historical Essays on Academic and Bureaucratic Practices* (Ann Arbor: University of Michigan Press, 2001).
32. K. Asdal, 'The Office: Weakness of Numbers and the Production of Non-authority', *Accounting, Organizations and Society*, 36 (1) (2011): 1–9, p. 1.
33. Porter, *Trust in Numbers*, p. 152.
34. Gigerenzer et al., *The Empire of Chance*, pp. 236–7.
35. Porter, *Trust in Numbers*, p. 157.
36. Ibid., p. 148.
37. Ibid., p. 149.
38. Ibid., p. 27.
39. M. Power, *The Audit Society. Rituals of Verification* (Oxford and New York: Oxford University Press, 1997), p. 3.
40. Ibid., pp. 8, 10.
41. Gigerenzer et al., *Empire of Chance*, pp. 235–6.
42. Ibid., p. 236.
43. J. Van Maanen and B. Pentland, 'Cops and Auditors: The Rhetoric of Records', in S.B. Sitkin and R.J Bies (eds), *The Legalistic Organization* (Thousand Oaks, CA: Sage, 1994), p. 54.
44. P. Day ad R. Klein, *Accountabilities: Five Public Services* (London: Tavistock, 1987), p. 244.
45. Power, *The Audit Society*, p. 127.
46. Day and Klein, *Accountabilities*, p. 171.
47. Power, *The Audit Society*, p. 128.
48. S.P. Shapiro, 'The Social Control of Impersonal Trust', *American*

Journal of Sociology, 93 (3) 1987: 623–58; quotations from pp. 649, 651.

49. D.J. Kevles, *The Baltimore Case: A Trial of Politics, Science and Character* (New York: W.W. Norton, 2000).

50. 'Just Another Piece of Furniture', *The Economist*, 7 March 2002, www.economist.com/node/1021660 (accessed 30 June 2013).

51. C.M. Reinhart and K.S. Rogoff, 'Growth in a Time of Debt', National Bureau of Economic Research, Working Paper 15639, January 2010, p. 3, www.nber.org/papers/w15639 (accessed 30 June 2013).

52. 'Reinhart, Rogoff … and Herndon: The Student Who Caught Out the Profs', *BBC News*, 19 April 2013, www.bbc.co.uk/news/magazine-22223190 (accessed 30 June 2013). See also T. Herndon, M. Ash and R. Pollin, 'Does High Public Debt Consistently Stifle Economic Growth? A Critique of Reinhart and Rogoff', Political Economy Research Institute Working Paper No. 322, April 2013.

53. 'Rogoff and Reinhart Defend Their Numbers', *Guardian*, 17 April 2013, www.guardian.co.uk/business/economics-blog/2013/apr/17/rogoff-reinhart-defend-debt-study (accessed 30 June 2013).

54. 'Reinhart, Rogoff … and Herndon: The Student Who Caught Out the Profs'.

55. D. Stape, *Ontsporing* (Amsterdam: Prometheus, 2012), p. 167. The quotation is taken from the book review published by *Observer* 26 (1) (January 2013), the magazine of the Association for Psychological Science.

56. Gigerenzer et al., *Empire of Chance*, p. 236.

57. J. Ellul, *Propaganda: The Formation of Men's Attitudes* (New York: Knopf, 1965), p. 84.

58. Best, *Damned Lies and Statistics*, p. 13.

59. Cited by C. Seife, *Proofiness: The Dark Arts of Mathematical Deception* (Viking: New York, 2010), p. 226.

60. Ibid., pp. 226–7.

61. Best, *Damned Lies and Statistics*, p. 35.

62. Ibid., p. 35.

63. N. Oreskes and E.M Conway, *Merchants of Doubt: How a Handful of Scientists Obscured the Truth on Issues from Tobacco Smoke to Global Warming* (New York: Bloomsbury, 2010).

64. Seife, *Proofiness*, p. 229.

65. M. Weber, *General Economic History* (New Brunswick, NJ: Transaction Books 1981 [1927]), p. 275. See also B.S. Yamey, 'Scientific Bookkeeping and the Rise of Capitalism', *Economic History Review*, 1 (2/3) (1949): 99–113.

66. Cited in R. Palan, *The Offshore World: Sovereign Markets, Virtual Places, and Nomad Millionaires* (Ithaca, NJ: Cornell University Press, 2006), p. 171.

67. Ibid., p. 174.

68. B. Bridgman et al., 'Accounting for Household Production in the National

Accounts, 1965–2010', *Survey of Current Business*, 92 (5) (2012): 23–36.

69. See www.oecdobserver.org/news/archivestory.php/aid/1518/Is_GDP_a_satisfactory_measure_of_growth_.html (accessed 30 June 2013).

70. Cited by Porter, *Trust in Numbers*, p. 63.

71. F.H. Hayek, 'The Use of Knowledge in Society', *American Economic Review*, 35 (4) (1945): 525ff.

72. 'Greenspan Testimony on Sources of Financial Crisis', *Wall Street Journal*, 23 October 2008, http://blogs.wsj.com/economics/2008/10/23/greenspan-testimony-on-sources-of-financial-crisis (accessed 30 June 2013).

73. R. Patel, *The Value of Nothing: How to Reshape Market Society and Redefine Democracy* (London: Portobello Books, 2009).

74. Palan, *The Offshore World*.

75. L.H. Summers, Fourth Annual Marshall J. Seidman Lecture on Health Policy, 27 April 2004, www.hcp.med.harvard.edu/files/SummersLecture.pdf (accessed 30 June 2013).

76. Asdal, 'The Office', p. 8.

CHAPTER 2

1. Cited by R. Sylla, 'An Historical Primer on the Business of Credit Rating', in R.M. Levich, G. Majnoni and C. Reinhart (eds), *Ratings, Rating Agencies and the Global Financial System* (Boston, MA: Kluwer Academic, 2002), p. 35; emphasis added.

2. 'Moody's Blues, Poor Standards, and the Debt', *New York Times*, 24 July 2011, http://krugman.blogs.nytimes.com/2011/07/24/moodys-blues-poor-standards-and-the-debt (accessed 30 June 2013; emphasis added).

3. C.A. Hill, 'Why Did Rating Agencies Do Such a Bad Job Rating Subprime Securities?', *Minnesota Legal Studies Research Paper* 10–18 (2010), p. 14.

4. L.J. White, 'Markets: The Credit Rating Agencies', *Journal of Economic Perspectives*, 24 (2) (2010): 211–26.

5. 'Credit Rating Agencies Triggered Financial Crisis, U.S. Congressional Report Finds', *Huffington Post*, 13 April 2011.

6. Financial Crisis Inquiry Commission, *Final Report of the National Commission on the Causes of the Financial Crisis in the United States* (Washington, DC: Financial Crisis Inquiry Commission, 2011), p. xxv.

7. This disclaimer is available on S&P's website: www.structuredfinanceinterface.com/CdoOnlineWeb/Help/disclaimer_popup.html (accessed 30 June 2013).

8. M.C. Rom, 'The Credit Rating Agencies and the Subprime Mess: Greedy, Ignorant, and Stressed?', *Public Administration Review*, 69 (4) (2009): 641.

9. J.M. Whitehead and H.S. Mathis, 'Finding a Way Out of the Rating

Agency Morass', statement submitted to the US House Financial Services
Committee. Subcommittee on Capital Markets, Insurance, and Government Sponsored Enterprises, 27 September 2007.

10. D. Kerwer, 'Holding Global Regulators Accountable: The Case of Credit
Rating Agencies', *Governance: An International Journal of Policy, Administration, and Institutions*, 18 (3) (2005): 453–75.

11. C. Crouch, 'The Global Firm: The Problem of the Giant Firm in Demo-
cratic Capitalism', in D. Coen, W. Grant and G. Wilson (eds), *Oxford
Handbook of Business and Government* (Oxford: Oxford University
Press, 2010).

12. Rom, 'The Credit Rating Agencies and the Subprime Mess', p. 641.

13. P. Pattberg, 'The Institutionalization of Private Governance: How
Business and Nonprofit Organizations Agree on Transnational Rules',
*Governance: An International Journal of Policy, Administration, and
Institutions*, 18 (4) (2005): 589–610. See also B. Cashore, 'Legitimacy and
the Privatization of Environmental Governance: How Non-State Market-
Driven (NSMD) Governance Systems Gain Rule-Making Authority',
*Governance: An International Journal of Policy, Administration, and
Institutions*, 15 (4) (2002): 503–29.

14. S. Strange, *The Retreat of the State: The Diffusion of Power in the World
Economy* (Cambridge: Cambridge University Press, 1996).

15. J.R. Macey, 'Testimony before the U.S. Senate Committee on Govern-
mental Affairs', 20 March 2002, in *Rating the Raters: Enron and the Credit
Rating Agencies, Hearings Before the Senate Committee on Governmental
Affairs* (Washington, DC: Government Printing Office, 2002), p. 1.

16. T.J. Sinclair, 'Passing Judgment: Credit Rating Processes as Regulatory
Mechanisms of Governance in the Emerging World Order', *Review of
International Political Economy*, 1 (1) (1994): 133–59.

17. T.J. Sinclair, 'Private Makers of Public Policy: Bond Rating Agencies
and the New Global Finance', in A. Héritier (ed.), *Common Goods and
Governance* (Oxford: Rowman & Littlefield, 2002), p. 279.

18. T.J. Sinclair, 'The Infrastructure of Global Governance: Quasi-Regulatory Mechanisms and the New Global Finance', *Global Governance*, 7(4)
(2001): 441–51.

19. Sylla, 'An Historical Primer on the Business of Credit Rating'.

20. T.J. Sinclair, 'Global Monitor. Bond Rating Agencies', *New Political
Economy*, 8 (1) (2003): 147–61.

21. H.V. Poor, *Manual of the Railroads of the United States* (New York: H.V.
& H.W. Poor, 1868), cited by B. Paudyn, 'The Analytics of Ratings:
European Union Attempts to Regulate Credit Rating Agencies', paper
presented at the International Studies Association annual convention,
Montreal, 16–20 March 2010.

22. 'Moody's History: A Century of Market Leadership, Moody's, www.
moodys.com/Pages/atc001.aspx (accessed 30 June 2013).

23. M. Taylor and S. Singleton, 'The Communal Resource: Transaction Costs and the Solution of Collective Action Problems', *Politics and Society*, 21 (2) (1993): 204.

24. T.J. Sinclair, *The New Masters of Capital: American Bond Rating Agencies and the Politics of Creditworthiness* (New York: Cornell University Press, 2005).

25. L.J. White, 'The Credit-Rating Agencies and the Subprime Debacle', *Critical Review*, 21 (2–3) (2009): 391.

26. The Security and Exchange Commission is a public oversight body established by the US Congress in 1934 as an independent, quasi-judicial regulatory agency to regulate the stock market and prevent corporate abuses relating to the offering and sale of securities and corporate reporting. The SEC was given the power to license and regulate stock exchanges, the companies whose securities traded on them, and the brokers and dealers who conducted the trading.

27. Sinclair, *The New Masters of Capital*.

28. White, 'The Credit-Rating Agencies and the Subprime Debacle', p. 391.

29. D. Kerwer, 'Standardising as Governance: The Case of Credit Rating Agencies', in A. Heritier (ed.), *Common Goods: Reinventing European and International Governance* (Lanham, MD: Rowman & Littlefield, 2002).

30. J.W. Pratt and R.J. Zeckhauser (eds), *Principals and Agents: The Structure of Business* (Cambridge, MA: Harvard University Press, 1985).

31. See www.sifma.org/issues/regulatory-reform/credit-rating-agencies/overview (accessed 30 June 2013).

32. Hill, 'Why Did Rating Agencies Do Such a Bad Job Rating Subprime Securities?', Minnesota Legal Studies Research Paper no. 10–18.

33. 'Insight. When Rating Agencies Judge the World', Reuters, 2 August 2011, www.reuters.com/article/2011/08/02/us-ratings-insight-idUSTRE7714 TI20110802 (accessed 30 June 2013).

34. US Senate, *Wall Street and the Financial Crisis: Anatomy of a Financial Collapse*, Majority and Minority Staff Report of the Permanent Subcommittee on Investigations for the Committee on Homeland Security and Governmental Affairs, 14 April 2011 (Washington, DC: US Senate), p. 267.

35. Sinclair, *The New Masters of Capital*.

36. Rom, 'The Credit Rating Agencies and the Subprime Mess', p. 642.

37. A.V. Cutler, V. Haufler, V. and T. Porter, 'The Contours and Significance of Private Authority in International Affairs', in A.C. Cutler, V. Haufler, V. and T. Porter (eds), *Private Authority and International Affairs* (New York: State University of New York Press, 1999), p. 334.

38. B. Becker and T. Milbourn, 'How Did Increased Competition Affect Credit Ratings?' Working Paper 09–051 (2010), Harvard Business School, p. 6.

39. The first quotation is from 'Moody's, S&P Defer Cuts on AAA Sub-prime, Hiding Loss', Bloomberg, 11 March 2011, www.bloomberg.com/apps/news?pid=newsarchive&sid=aRLWzHsFi6lY (accessed 30 June 2013). The second quotation is from 'Why a Rating Agency Should Be Concerned about the Survival of the Company It's Assessing', MIT Sloan Experts, 21 June 2011, http://mitsloanexperts.com/2011/06/13/why-a-rating-agency-should-be-concerned-about-the-survival-of-the-company-it%E2%80%99s-assessing (accessed 30 June 2013).

40. J. Mathis, J. McAndrews and J.-C. Rochet, 'Rating the Raters: Are Reputation Concerns Powerful Enough to Discipline Rating Agencies?', Journal of Monetary Economics, 56 (5) (2009): 657.

41. N. Véron, 'Rate Expectations: What Can and Cannot be Done about Rating Agencies', Bruegel Policy Contribution, issue 2011/14 (2011).

42. N. Véron, 'Rating Agencies: An Information Privilege Whose Time Has Passed', Bruegel Policy Contribution, issue 2009/01 (2009), p. 2.

43. T. Strulik, 'Rating Agencies and Systemic Risk: Paradoxes of Governance', in A. Héritier (ed.), Common Goods and Governance (Oxford: Rowman & Littlefield, 2002).

44. H. White, 'Agency as Control', in J.W. Pratt and R.J. Zeckhauser (eds), Principals and Agents: The Structure of Business (Cambridge, MA: Harvard University Press, 1985), p. 205.

45. Ibid., p. 204.

46. M. Tyrell and C. Bannier, 'Modeling the Role of Credit Rating Agencies: Do They Spark Off a Virtuous Circle?', Working Papers Series in Finance and Accounting, Paper no. 160 (Frankfurt: Johann Wolfgang Goethe Universität, 2005).

47. J. Stiglitz, G. Ferri and G. Liu, 'The Procyclical Role of Rating Agencies: Evidence from the East Asian Crisis', Economic Notes, 28 (3) (1999): 335–55.

48. S&P used the First Amendment defence in 1996 when it was sued for professional negligence by Orange County, California. S&P had given the county an AA rating before the county filed for the largest-ever municipal bankruptcy. The US District Court in Santa Ana, California, found that the credit agency could not be held liable for mere negligence, agreeing with S&P that it was shielded by the First Amendment. See Kerwer, 'Holding Global Regulators Accountable'; D. Muegge, 'From Pragmatism to Dogmatism: EU Governance, Policy Paradigms and Financial Meltdown', Journal of New Political Economy, 16 (2) (2011): 185–206.

49. F. Partnoy, 'How and Why Credit Rating Agencies Are Not Like Other Gatekeepers', Legal Studies Research Paper Series, Research Paper No. 07-46, May 2006, University of San Diego, California.

50. J. Katz, E. Salinas and C. Stephanou, 'Credit Rating Agencies: No Easy Regulatory Solutions', Crisis Response, Note No. 8, October 2009.

51. M. Elkhoury, 'Credit Rating Agencies and Their Potential Impact on

Developing Countries', *UNCTAD Discussion Paper* 186 (2008), p. 4.

52. Katz, Salinas and Stephanou, 'Credit Rating Agencies', p. 2.

53. CESR, *Technical Advice to the European Commission on Possible Measures Concerning Credit Rating Agencies* (Paris: Committee of European Security Regulators, 2005), p. 51.

54. One exception is the agency Egan–Jones. See C. Bruner and R. Abdelal, 'To Judge Leviathan: Sovereign Credit Ratings, National Law and the World Economy', *Journal of Public Policy*, 25 (2) (2005): 191–217.

55. Katz, Salinas and Stephanou, 'Credit Rating Agencies', p. 4.

56. 'Ex-Moody's Analyst: "By 2006 It Was Toxic Everywhere"', *Guardian*, 17 December 2012.

57. 'Investors Cite Rating Agencies' Conflicts of Interest', *Financial Week*, 8 July 2008, www.financialweek.com/apps/pbcs.dll/article?AID=/20080708/REG/689125144/-1/FWDailyAlert01 (accessed 30 June 2013).

58. 'Debt Ranking Finally Fizzled, but the Deal Fizzled First', *New York Times*, 29 November 2001.

59. Several of the world's largest financial firms were implicated in this multifaceted fraud, including Bank of America, Citigroup, Deutsche Bank, J.P. Morgan and ABN.

60. 'If You Try to Control Everything It Would Probably Kill Capitalism', *Guardian*, 3 October 2007.

61. Paudyn, 'The Analytics of Ratings'.

62. 'Flawed Credit Ratings Reap Profits as Regulators Fail', Bloomberg, 29 April 2009, www.bloomberg.com/apps/news?sid=au4oIx.judz4&pid=newsarchive (accessed 30 June 2013).

63. J.B. Taylor, 'The Financial Crisis and the Policy Responses: An Empirical Analysis of What Went Wrong', NBER Working Paper no. 14631 (2009), www.nber.org/papers/w14631 (accessed 30 June 2013).

64. US Senate, *Wall Street and the Financial Crisis: Anatomy of a Financial Collapse*, p. 245.

65. Sinclair, 'Global Monitor. Bond Rating Agencies'.

66. 'Flawed Credit Ratings Reap Profits as Regulators Fail', Bloomberg, 29 April 2009, www.bloomberg.com/apps/news?sid=au4oIx.judz4&pid=newsarchive (accessed 30 June 2013).

67. Hill, 'Why Did Rating Agencies Do Such a Bad Job Rating Subprime Securities?'

68. A clear example of this trend was the introduction of so-called Brady bonds (after the US treasury secretary Nicholas Brady, who proposed them), which were dollar-nominated obligations allowing banks to trade their claims on developing countries and thus spread the risk and get debt off their balance sheets. After that most of these states defaulted on their repayment promises.

69. A. Mühlen-Schulte, 'Full Faith in Credit? The Power of Numbers in Rating Frontier Sovereigns and the Global Governance of Development

by the UNDP', *Journal of International Relations and Development*, 15 (4) (2012): 471.

70. Mühlen-Schulte, 'Full Faith in Credit? See also J. Vandemoortele, 'Credit Quality Moves Center Stage as African Countries Seek to Improve their Economic Performance', in Standard & Poor's, *Sovereign Ratings in Africa* (New York: Standard & Poor's, 2004).

71. Bruner and Abdelal, 'To Judge Leviathan', p. 195.

72. Véron, 'Rating Agencies, p. 2.

73. P. Gavras, 'Regulatory Abdication as Public Policy: Government Failure and the Real Conflicts of Interest of Credit Rating Agencies', *Journal of Southeast European and Black Sea Studies*, 10 (4) (2010): 475–88.

74. Katz, Salinas and Stephanou, 'Credit Rating Agencies; Hill, 'Why Did Rating Agencies Do Such a Bad Job Rating Subprime Securities?'

75. Kerwer, 'Standardising as Governance'.

76. Council Directive 93/6/EEC of 15 March 1993 on the capital adequacy of investments firms and credit institutions.

77. A. Kruck, *Private Ratings, Public Regulations: Credit Rating Agencies and Global Financial Governance* (Basingstoke: Palgrave Macmillan, 2011). See also L.J. White, 'Markets: The Credit Rating Agencies', *Journal of Economic Perspectives*, 24 (2) (2010): 211–26.

78. 'Flawed Credit Ratings Reap Profits as Regulators Fail'.

79. Katz, Salinas and Stephanou, 'Credit Rating Agencies', p. 3. See also Partnoy, 'How and Why Credit Rating Agencies Are Not Like Other Gatekeepers'.

80. Rom, 'The Credit Rating Agencies and the Subprime Mess'.

81. Directive 2006/49/EC of the European Parliament and of the Council of 14 June 2006 on the Capital Adequacy of Investment Firms and Credit Institutions (Recast), L 177/201.

82. IOSCO, *Code of Conduct Fundamentals for Credit Rating Agencies* (Madrid: International Organization of Securities Commission, 2004).

83. Véron, 'Rating Agencies', p. 2.

84. 'S.& P. Downgrades Debt Rating of U.S. for the First Time', *New York Times*, 5 August 2011.

85. 'Standard & Poor's', *New York Times*, 11 November 2011.

86. 'Flawed Credit Ratings Reap Profits as Regulators Fail'.

87. 'US Accuses S&P of Fraud in Suit on Loan Bundles', *New York Times*, 4 February 2013.

88. 'US Loses AAA Credit Rating as S&P Slams Debt Levels, Political Process', Bloomberg, 6 August 2011.

89. 'EU to Curb Power of Rating Agencies in Rule Shake-up', *Independent*, 16 November 2011, www.independent.ie/business/european/eu-to-curb-power-of-rating-agencies-in-rule-shakeup-2935623.html (accessed 30 June 2013).

90. 'Rede von Helmut Schmidt im Wortlaut', *Bild*, 4 December 2011.

91. 'EU to Curb Power of Rating Agencies in Rule Shake-up'.
92. 'The Credit Rating Controversy', Council on Foreign Relations, 19 January 2012, www.cfr.org/united-states/credit-rating-controversy/p22328 (accessed 30 June 2013). See also 'EU Steps Up Attack on Major Credit Rating Agencies', *Guardian*, 11 November 2011.
93. 'Barroso to Rating Agencies: We Know Better', *EU Observer*, 6 July 2011, http://euobserver.com/19/32597 (accessed 30 June 2013).
94. 'Moody's Downgrades Italy's Government Bond Ratings to A2 with a Negative Outlook', *Moody's*, 4 October 2011, www.moodys.com/research/Moodys-downgrades-Italys-government-bond-ratings-to-A2–with-a-- PR_227333 (accessed 30 June 2013). See also 'Moody's Downgrades Italy for First Time in Two Decades', *Telegraph*, 4 October 2011.
95. 'S&P Downgrades Nine Euro Zone Countries', Reuters, 14 January 2012, www.reuters.com/article/2012/01/14/us-eurozone-sp-idUSTRE80C1 BC20120114 (accessed 30 June 2013).
96. 'S&P: 'Nel report sull'Italia c'é un errore'. Una mail dell'inchiesta inchioda l'agenzia', *La Repubblica*, 29 June 2012, www.repubblica.it/economia/2012/06/29/news/s_p_sull_italia_abbiamo_sbagliato-38221657/ ?ref=HREA-1 (accessed 30 June 2013).
97. 'Germany's AAA Credit Rating on "Negative Outlook"'', *BBC News*, 24 July 2012, www.bbc.co.uk/news/business-18963810 (accessed 30 June 2013).
98. Sinclair, 'Private Makers of Public Policy', p. 279.
99. A. Hersh, 'The Folly of S&P', Center for American Progress, 12 August 2011.
100. Katz, Salinas and Stephanou, 'Credit Rating Agencies'.
101. The first quotation is from P. Seabright, *The Company of Strangers: A Natural History of Economic Life*, rev. edn (Princeton, NJ: Princeton University Press, 2010), p. 20. The second quotation is from Strulik, 'Rating Agencies and Systemic Risk, p. 318.
102. W.H. Buiter, 'Lessons from the 2007 Financial Crisis', CEPR, Policy Insight No. 18 (December 2007).
103. Sinclair, 'Passing Judgment'.
104. J.A.C. Santos, 'Why Firm Access to the Bond Market Differs over the Business Cycle: A Theory and Some Evidence', *Journal of Banking and Finance*, 30 (10) (2003): 2715-36; P. Bolton, X. Freixas and J. Shapiro, 'The Credit Ratings Game', National Bureau for Economic Research, Working Paper No. 14712, 2009, www.nber.org/papers/w14712 (accessed 30 June 2013).
105. Sinclair, 'Passing Judgment'; Sinclair, 'The Infrastructure of Global Governance'.
106. Sinclair, *The New Masters of Capital*.
107. T. Sinclair, 'Round Up the Usual Suspects: Blame and the Subprime Crisis', *Journal of New Political Economy*, 15 (1) (2010): 91-107.

108. Ibid.
109. J.M. Keynes, *The General Theory of Employment, Interest and Money* (Buffalo: Prometheus Books, 1997 [1936]).
110. 'Appeasing the Bond Gods', *New York Times*, 19 August 2010.
111. 'Flawed Credit Ratings Reap Profits as Regulators Fail'. See also F. Partnoy, *Infectious Greed: How Deceit and Risk Corrupted the Financial Markets* (New York: Times Books, 2003).
112. E. McClintock Ekins and M.A. Calabria, 'Regulation, Market Structure, and the Role of Credit Rating Agencies', *Policy Analysis* 704, 1 August 2012, p. 2.
113. Elkhoury, 'Credit Rating Agencies and their Potential Impact on Developing Countries', p. 16.
114. Ibid.
115. H. Reisen and J. von Maltzan, 'Sovereign Credit Ratings, Emerging Market Risk and Financial Market Volatility', *Intereconomics*, March/April 1998; 73–82.
116. US Senate, *Wall Street and the Financial Crisis: Anatomy of a Financial Collapse*, p. 244.
117. Rom, 'The Credit Rating Agencies and the Subprime Mess'; White, 'Markets: The Credit Rating Agencies'.
118. 'Credit Rating Agencies Triggered Financial Crisis, U.S. Congressional Report Finds'.
119. 'Dalla Ue Guerra alle Agenzie di Rating ... Americane', *Business People*, 7 July 2011, http://businesspeople.it/Business/Finanza/Dall-Ue-guerra-alle-agenzie-di-rating-americane_21987 (accessed 30 June 2013).
120. 'Flawed Credit Ratings Reap Profits as Regulators Fail'.
121. European Parliament and Council, 'CRA Regulation (EC) No. 1060/2009', 16 September 2009.
122. 'Flawed Credit Ratings Reap Profits as Regulators Fail', Bloomberg, 29 April 2009.
123. Ibid.
124. F. Knight, *Risk, Uncertainty and Profit* (New York: A.M. Kelley, 1964 [1921]).
125. J.M. Keynes, *Treatise on Probability* (London: Macmillan, 1921; AMS Press Reprint, 1979).
126. S. Reddy, 'Claims to Expert Knowledge and the Subversion of Democracy: The Triumph of Risk over Uncertainty', *Economy and Society*, 25 (2) (1996): 222–54.
127. 'Ratings and Policy Approach', Moody's, www.moodys.com/Pages/amr002003.aspx (accessed 30 June 2013).
128. 'Flawed Credit Ratings Reap Profits as Regulators Fail'.
129. Sinclair, *The New Masters of Capital*, p. 34.
130. Ibid.

CHAPTER 3

1. World Commission on Environment and Development, *Our Common Future* (Oxford: Oxford University Press, 1987), ch. 2.
2. N. Oreskes and E.M Conway, *Merchants of Doubt: How a Handful of Scientists Obscured the Truth on Issues from Tobacco Smoke to Global Warming* (New York: Bloomsbury, 2010), p. 5.
3. Ibid.
4. 'Cato's Michales Admits 40% of Funding Comes from Big Oil', *Think Progress*, 16 August 2010, http://thinkprogress.org/politics/2010/08/16/113717/oil-fueled-pat-michaels/?mobile=nc (accessed 30 June 2013). The interview with CNN is also viewable at the same link. For the US Congress inquiry, see 'Rep. Waxman Presses for Inquiry on Global Warming Denier Pat Michaels', *Huffington Post*, 25 January 2011, www.huffingtonpost.com/kert-davies/rep-waxman-presses-for-in_b_813251.html (accessed 30 June 2013).
5. Oreskes and Conway, *Merchants of Doubt*.
6. R.E. Dunlap and A.M. McCright, 'Organized Climate Change Denial', in J.S. Dryzek, R.B. Noorgard and D. Schlosberg (eds), *Oxford Handbook of Climate Change and Society* (Oxford and New York: Oxford University Press, 2011), p. 147.
7. S.F. Singer, *Cost–Benefit Analysis as an Aid to Environmental Decision-Making*, Report M77–106 (McLean, VA: Metrek Division, Mitre Corporation, 1979), p. 3.
8. W.D. Nordhaus and J. Boyer, *Warming the World: Economic Models for Global Warming* (Cambridge, MA: MIT Press, 2003). See also W.D. Nordhaus, 'The *Stern Review* on the Economics of Climate Change', National Bureau of Economic Research Working Paper No. 12741 (Cambridge, MA: National Bureau of Economic Research, 2006).
9. 'Global Warming Costs and Benefits', *Cato at Liberty*, 3 November 2006, www.cato.org/blog/global-warming-costs-benefits (accessed 30 June 2013).
10. R. Mendelsohn, 'Comments on Simon Dietz and Nicholas Stern's *Why Economic Analysis Supports Strong Action on Climate Change: A Response to the Stern Review's Critics*', *Review of Environmental Economics and Policy*, 2 (2) (2008): 309, 310.
11. S. Dietz and N. Stern, 'Why Economic Analysis Supports Strong Action on Climate Change: A Response to the Stern Review's Critics', *Review of Environmental Economics and Policy*, 2 (1) (2008): 95.
12. 'Stern Takes Bleaker View on Warming', *Financial Times*, 16 April 2008.
13. H.R. Varian, 'Recalculating the Costs of Climate Change', *New York Times*, 14 December 2006.
14. J. Quiggin, 'Stern and His Critics on Discounting and Climate Change: An Editorial Essay', *Climatic Change*, 89 (3–4) (2008): 195–205.

15. This quotation is from Delong's personal blog, http://delong.typepad. com/sdj/2006/12/do_unto_others.html (accessed 30 June 2013).
16. Oreskes and Conway, *Merchants of Doubt*, p. 92.
17. S.F. Singer, *Report of the Acid Rain Peer Review Panel. Final Report*, July 1984, Office of Science and Technology Policy (Washington, DC: US Government Printing Office), Appendix 5, A5–8.
18. Jones was one of the authors of Chapter 12, 'Detection of Climate Change and Attribution of Causes' in the *Third Report* and the lead author of Chapter 3, 'Observations: Surface and Atmospheric Climate Change' in the *Fourth Report*.
19. F. Pearce, *The Climate Files: The Battle for the Truth about Global Warming* (London: Guardian Books, 2010).
20. 'Climate Scientists Shut Out Critics by Turning Down Data Requests', *Guardian*, 3 February 2010.
21. For the transcripts of most emails and other documents, see US Senate, *United States Senate Report 'Consensus Exposed': The CRU Controversy*, US Senate Committee on Environment and Public Works, Minority Staff, Washington, DC; http1//epw.senate.gov/public/index. cfm?FuseAction=Files.View&FileStore_id=7db3fbd8–f1b4–4fdf-bd15– 12b7df1a0b63 (accessed 30 June 2013).
22. Ibid., p. 21.
23. Ibid., p. 23.
24. The text of this email was reported by the climate sceptic Antony Watts in his blog, Watts Up With That, on 19 November 2009. See http:// wattsupwiththat.com/2009/11/19/breaking-news-story-hadley-cru-has-apparently-been-hacked-hundreds-of-files-released (accessed 30 June 2013). See also www.nature.com/news/2010/101115/full/468362a.html (accessed 30 June 2013).
25. 'Hacked E-mails Is New Fodder for Climate Dispute', *New York Times*, 20 November 2009, www.nytimes.com/2009/11/21/science/earth/21climate. html?_r=1 (accessed 30 June 2013).
26. M.E. Mann, R.S. Bradley and M.K. Hughes, 'Global Scale Temperature Patterns and Climate Forcing over the Past Six Centuries', *Nature* 392 (1998): 779–87.
27. Quoted in Pearce, *The Climate Files*, p. 107.
28. 'Scientists Behaving Badly: A Corrupt Cabal of Global Warming Alarmists Are Exposed by a Massive Document Leak', *Weekly Standard*, 14 December 2009, www.weeklystandard.com/Content/Public/Articles/ 000/000/017/300ubchn.asp (accessed 30 June 2013).
29. S. McIntyre and R. McKitrick, 'Corrections to the Mann et. al. (1998) Proxy Data Base and Northern Hemispheric Average Temperature Series', *Energy and Environment*, 14 (6) (2003): 751–71. A similar critique was raised by Harvard scientists Sallie Balunias and Willie Soon; see '20th Century Climate Not So Hot', press release, Harvard–Smithsonian

Center for Astrophysics, 31 March 2003.

30. 'I Thought Of Killing Myself, Says Scandal Professor Phil Jones', *Sunday Times*, 9 February 2010.

31. 'Climate Researchers "Secrecy" Criticised – but MPs Say Science Remains Intact', *Guardian*, 31 March 2010, www.guardian.co.uk/environment/2010/mar/31/climate-mails-inquiry-jones-cleared (accessed 30 June 2013).

32. 'Conspiracy Theories Finally Laid to Rest by Report on Leaked Climate Change Emails', *Independent*, 8 July 2010, www.independent.co.uk/environment/climate-change/conspiracy-theories-finally-laid-to-rest-by-report-on-leaked-climate-change-emails-2021222.html (accessed 30 June 2013).

33. 'RA-10 Inquiry Report: Concerning the Allegations of Research Misconduct Against Dr. Michael E. Mann, Department of Meteorology, College of Earth and Mineral Sciences', Penn State University, p. 6; www.research.psu.edu/orp/documents/Findings_Mann_Inquiry.pdf.

34. 'Scientists to Review Climate Body', *BBC News*, 10 March 2010; http://news.bbc.co.uk/2/hi/8561004.stm.

35. US Senate, *United States Senate Report 'Consensus Exposed'*, p. 34.

36. 'Climate: The Hottest Year', *Nature* 468: 362–4.

37. C. Monckton, *Caught Green-Handed: Cold Facts About the Hot Topic of Global Temperature Change After the Climategate Scandal* (Haymarket, VA: Science and Public Policy Institute, 2009), pp. 38–9.

38. C. Monckton, 'AIDS: A British View', *American Spectator*, 20 (1) (1987): 29.

39. For more info, see: http://scienceandpublicpolicy.org and www.co2science.org.

40. A.A. Leiserowitz et al., 'Climategate, Public Opinion and the Loss of Trust', Working Paper of the Yale Project on Climate Change Communication, 2010, http://environment.yale.edu/climate/publications/climategate-public-opinion-and-the-loss-of-trust (accessed 30 June 2013).

41. Prof. Dr Richard S.J. Tol, 'An Analysis of Mitigation as a Response to Climate Change', Copenhagen Consensus Center, 14 August 2009.

42. B. Lomborg, 'An Economic Approach to the Environment', *Wall Street Journal*, 24 April 2012.

43. Ibid.

44. Monckton, *Caught Green-Handed*, p. 40.

45. Point Carbon, *Carbon 2012: A Market Waiting for Godot* (Oslo: Point Carbon, 2012).

46. For a review of the regulatory aspects of emission trading schemes, see R. Baldwin, 'Regulation Lite: The Rise of Emissions Trading', *Regulation and Governance* 2 (2008): 193–215.

47. D. Ellerman, R. Schmalensee, F. Bailey, P. Joskow and J.-P. Montero, *Markets for Clean Air: The US Acid Rain Program* (Cambridge: Cambridge

University Press, 2000). See also D. Burtraw, 'Cost Savings Sans Allowance Trades? Evaluating the SO2 Emission Trading Program to Date', Resources For the Future Discussion Paper 95-30-REV (1996), www.rff. org/Publications/Pages/PublicationDetails.aspx?PublicationID=17551 (accessed 30 June 2013).

48. Baldwin, 'Regulation Lite', p. 195.

49. T. Tietenberg, *Environmental and Natural Resource Economics* (New York: HarperCollins, 1996).

50. R. Baldwin, M. Cave and M. Lodge, *Understanding Regulation: Theory, Strategy and Practice* (Oxford: Oxford University Press, 2012).

51. For more information, see: http://ec.europa.eu/clima/policies/transport/aviation/index_en.htm (accessed 30 June 2013).

52. S. Butzengeiger and A. Michaelowa, 'The EU Emissions Trading Scheme – Issues and Challenges', *Intereconomics*, May/June 2004: 116-18

53. G. Svendsen, 'Lobbying and CO2 Trade in the EU', in B. Hansjurgens (ed.), *Emission Trading for Climate Policy* (New York: Cambridge University Press, 2005).

54. Open Europe, *The High Cost of Hot Air: Why the EU Emissions Trading Scheme Is an Environmental and Economic Failure* (London: Open Europe, 2006).

55. 'A Permit to Print Money', *Guardian*, 12 September 2008.

56. 'Power Tool', *Guardian*, 17 May 2006, www.guardian.co.uk/environment/2006/may/17/europeanunion.climatechange (accessed 30 June 2013).

57. Greenpeace's citation is from Baldwin, Cave and Lodge, *Understanding Regulation*, p. 203.

58. Committee on Climate Change, *Building a Low-Carbon Economy: The UK's Contribution to Tackling Climate Change* (London: CCC, 2008), p. 150.

59. 'UK Above Quota, Germany Within', *Telegraph*, 16 May 2006.

60. 'EU to Sell 300 Million CO2 Permits by End-12 for Aid', Bloomberg, 9 November 2012.

61. 'Breathing Difficulties: A Market in Need of a Miracle', *The Economist*, 3 March 2012.

62. 'The Role of Carbon Markets in Preventing Dangerous Climate Change', Environmental Audit Committee. Memorandum submitted by David Newbery, Research Director, Electric Policy Research Group, University of Cambridge, www.publications.parliament.uk/pa/cm200910/cmselect/cmenvaud/290/290we33.htm (accessed 30 June 2013).

63. Cited in Open Europe, *The High Cost of Hot Air*, p. 6.

64. 'EU auctions 5.58 mln phase 3 EUAs at 6.45 euros: traders', *Point Carbon*, 18 December 2012.

65. See Point Carbon, *Carbon 2012*, p. 3.

66. Ibid., p. 4.

67. 'Low Price Saps Carbon Market's Effectiveness', *New York Times*, 22 April 2013.

68. 'EU Emissions Trading an "Open Door" for Crime, Europol says', *EU Observer*, 10 December 2009, http://euobserver.com/environment/29132 (accessed 30 June 2013).

69. 'Further Investigations into VAT Fraud Linked to the Carbon Emission Trading Scheme', Europol press release, 28 December 2010, https://www.europol.europa.eu/content/press/further-investigations-vat-fraud-linked-carbon-emissions-trading-system-641 (accessed 30 June 2013).

70. 'Carbon Trading: Into Thin Air', *Financial Times*, 14 February 2011.

71. 'Real Emission Cuts in Europe Preferable to Dubious Offsets Elsewhere', *WWF Global*, press release, 30 June 2010, http://wwf.panda.org/?194029/Real-emissions-cuts-in-Europe-preferable-to-dubious-offsets-elsewhere (accessed 30 June 2013).

72. K. Capoor and P. Ambrosi, *State and Trends of the Carbon Market 2008* (Washington, DC: World Bank, 2008).

73. 'U.N. Issues First Offsets to CDM Programme', *Point Carbon*, 28 December 2012.

74. A number of standardized procedures are available. In particular, the Greenhouse Gas Protocol for Project Accounting, developed by the World Resources Institute and World Business Council for Sustainable Development, and the ISO 14064, developed by the International Organization for Standardization, both provide a general framework for quantifying emissions reductions from offset projects. A truly standardized commodity for carbon offsets, however, requires elaborating these general requirements into 'methodologies', or protocols, aimed at specific types of project.

75. J. Goodward and A. Kelly, 'The Bottom Line on Offsets', *World Resource Institute*, Issue 17 (2010), www.wri.org/publication/bottom-line-offsets (accessed 30 June 2013).

76. See: http://cdm.unfccc.int/DOE/index.html (accessed 30 June 2013).

77. See: http://cdm.unfccc.int/Reference/Manuals/accr_stan01.pdf (accessed 30 June 2013).

78. D. Broekhoff and K. Zyla, 'Outside the Cap: Opportunities and Limitations of Greenhouse Gases Offsets', *Climate and Energy Policy Series*, World Resources Institute, December 2008, www.wri.org/publication/outside-the-cap (accessed 30 June 2013).

79. 'A Market Time Bomb in the Making?', *The Bottom Line: An Independent Voice for Canada's Accounting and Financial Professionals*, June 2009, www.thebottomlinenews.ca/index.php?section=article&articleid=386 (accessed 30 June 2013).

80. Ibid.

81. 'Real Emission Cuts in Europe Preferable to Dubious Offset Elsewhere', *WWF Global*, 30 June 2010, wwf.panda.org/?194029/Real-

emissions-cuts-in-Europe-preferable-to-dubious-offsets-elsewhere (accessed 30 June 2013).

82. 'Bad Grades for Offset Reviewers', WWF European Policy Office, 28 June 2010, www.wwf.eu/?194004/Bad-grades-for-carbon-offset-reviewers (accessed 30 June 2013). The report, prepared by the Institute for Applied Ecology in 2009, can be downloaded from: www.oeko.de/oekodoc/902/2009-020-en.pdf (accessed 30 June 2013).

83. 'UN Panel Suspends Two More Emissions Auditors', Reuters, 26 March 2010, http://uk.reuters.com/article/2010/03/26/us-carbon-un-suspensions-idUKTRE62P5E420100326 (accessed 30 June 2013).

84. Point Carbon, *Carbon 2012*, p. iii.

85. High-Level Panel on the CDM Policy Dialogue, *A Call to Action* (New York: UNFCCC, 2012).

86. J.A. Scholte, 'Civil Society and Financial Markets: What Is Not Happening and Why', in L. Fioramonti and E. Thumler (eds), *Citizens Vs. Markets: How Civil Society is Reshaping the Economy In a Time of Crises* (London: Routledge, 2013).

87. Transparency International, *Global Corruption Report: Climate Change* (London: Earthscan, 2011).

88. Ibid., p. xxvi.

89. Dunlap and McCright, 'Organized Climate Change Denial', p. 144.

90. Ibid.

91. Point Carbon, *Carbon 2012*.

92. European Commission, *Trends in Global CO_2 Emissions: 2012 Report* (Brussels: European Commission, 2012), p. 6, edgar.jrc.ec.europa.eu/CO2REPORT2012.pdf (accessed 30 June 2013).

CHAPTER 4

1. I have discussed these issues at length in a previous book: L. Fioramonti, *Gross Domestic Problem: The Politics Behind the World's Most Powerful Number* (London: Zed Books, 2013).

2. See H. Daly, 'Toward a Measure of Sustainable Net National Product', in Y. Ahmad, S. El Serafy and E. Lutz (eds), *Environmental Accounting for Sustainable Development* (Washington, DC: World Bank, 1989); A.M. Friend, 'UNEP/World Bank Expert Meeting on Environmental Accounting and the SNA, Paris, 21–22 November 1988', *Ecological Economics* 1 (1989): 283–5; A.M. Friend and D.J. Rapport, 'The Evolution of Information Systems for Sustainable Development', *Ecological Economics* 3 (1991): 59–76.

3. W.D. Nordhaus and E.C. Kokkelenberg (eds), *Nature's Numbers: Expanding the National Economic Accounts to Include the Environment* (Washington, DC: National Academy Press, 1999), p. 2.

4. Nordhaus and Kokkelenberg, *Nature's Numbers*, p. 3.

5. S. Hicks, *Value and Capital* (Oxford: Oxford University Press, 1946).
6. R. Repetto et al., *Wasting Assets: Natural Resources in the National Income Accounts* (Washington, DC: World Resources Institute, 1989), p. 2.
7. I. Kubiszewski et al., 'Beyond GDP: Measuring and Achieving Global Genuine Progress', *Ecological Economics* 93: 57–68.
8. See the history of the international programme The Economics of Ecosystems and Biodiversity (TEEB) at www.teebweb.org/about/overview/history (accessed 30 June 2013).
9. K.I. MacDonald and C. Corson, 'TEEB Begins Now': A Virtual Moment in the Production of Natural Capital', *Development and Change*, 43 (1) (2012): 159–84.
10. European Union, *The Economics of Ecosystems and Biodiversity: An Interim Report* (Brussels: European Commission, 2008), http://ec.europa.eu/environment/nature/biodiversity/economics (accessed 30 June 2013).
11. For more information, see: www.wavespartnership.org (accessed 30 June 2013).
12. This indicator was introduced by D.W. Pearce and G.D. Atkinson, 'Capital Theory and the Measurement of Weak Sustainable Development: An Indicator of Weak Sustainability', *Ecological Economics* 8 (1993): 103–8.
13. World Bank, *Where is the Wealth of Nations? Measuring Capital for the 21st Century* (Washington, DC: World Bank, 2006), p. xvi.
14. UN Statistical Commission et al., *System of Environmental-Economic Accounting* (New York: United Nations, 2012).
15. UN et al., *System of National Accounts 1993* (Brussels/Luxembourg, New York, Paris, Washington DC: UN, World Bank, International Monetary Fund, European Commission, OECD, 1993).
16. D. Blades, 'Revision of the System of National Accounts: A Note on Objectives and Key Issues', *OECD Economic Studies*, No. 12 (Paris: OECD, 1989), p. 214.
17. Ibid., p. 215.
18. UN et al. (2008) *System of National Accounts 2008* (Brussels/Luxembourg, New York, Paris, Washington DC: UN, World Bank, International Monetary Fund, European Commission, OECD), p. 7.
19. Ibid., p. 7.
20. More on this can be found in Fioramonti, *Gross Domestic Problem*.
21. UN Statistical Commission et al., *System of Environmental-Economic Accounting*, p. xi.
22. Ibid., p. 127.
23. Ibid., p. 140.
24. Ibid.
25. Ibid., p. 145.
26. Ibid., p. 27.
27. Ibid., p. 145.

28. R. Costanza et al., 'The Value of the World's Ecosystem Services and Natural Capital', *Nature* 387, 15 May 1997: 253–70.
29. Ibid., p. 258.
30. Ibid., p. 253.
31. A. Balmford 'Economic Reasons for Conserving Wild Nature', *Science*, 297 (5583) (2002): 950–53.
32. 'Ecological Economist Robert Costanza Puts a Price Tag on Nature', *Grist*, 9 April 2003, http://grist.org/article/what2 (accessed 30 June 2013).
33. Costanza et al., 'The Value of the World's Ecosystem Services and Natural Capital', p. 258.
34. Ibid.
35. M. Toman, 'Why Not to Calculate the Value of the World's Ecosystem Services and Natural Capital', Special Section: Forum on Valuation of Ecosystem Services, *Ecological Economics* 25 (1998): 58.
36. Costanza et al., 'The Value of the World's Ecosystem Services and Natural Capital'.
37. Toman, 'Why Not to Calculate the Value of the World's Ecosystem Services and Natural Capital'.
38. See R.K. Davis, 'Recreation Planning as an Economic Problem', *Natural Resources Journal*, 3 (2) (1963): 239–49; G.C. Blomquist, 'Self-Protection and Averting Behavior, Values of Statistical Lives, and Benefit Cost Analysis of Environmental Policy', *Review of the Economics of the Household*, 2 (1) (2004): 89–110.
39. W. Vickrey, 'Counterspeculation, Auctions, and Competitive Sealed Tenders', *Journal of Finance*, 16 (1) (1961): 8–37
40. This is also known as the BDM method, after the names of the authors of the first experiment in this field. See G.M. Becker, M.H. DeGroot and J. Marschal, 'Measuring Utility by a Single Response Sequential Method', *Behavioral Science*, 9 (3) (1964): 226–32.
41. C. Breidert, M. Hahsler and T. Reutterer, 'A Review of Methods for Measuring Willingness to Pay', *Innovative Marketing*, 2 (4) (2006), p. 13.
42. T.T. Nagle and R.K. Holden, *The Strategy and Tactics of Pricing* (Upper Saddle River, NJ: Prentice Hall, 2002), p. 344.
43. H. Nessim and R. Dodge, *Pricing-Policies and Procedures* (London: Macmillan, 1995), p. 72.
44. Y. Marbeau, 'What Value Pricing Research Today?' *Journal of the Market Research Society*, 29 (2) (1987): 153–82.
45. R.G. Stout, 'Developing Data to Estimate Price–Quantity Relationships', *Journal of Marketing*, 33 (2) (1969): 34–6.
46. Nessim and Dodge, *Pricing-Policies and Procedures*, p. 72.
47. T.C. Brown, P.A. Champ, R.C. Bishop and D.W. McCollum, 'Which Response Format Reveals the Truth About Donations to a Public Good?', *Land Economics*, 72 (2) 1996: 152–66.

48. R.C. Bishop and T.A. Heberlein, 'Measuring Values of Extra-Market Goods: Are Indirect Methods Biased?', *American Journal of Agricultural Economics*, 61 (5) (1979): 926–30.

49. Breidert, Hahsler and Reutterer, 'A Review of Methods for Measuring Willingness to Pay'.

50. R.C. Mitchell and R.T. Carson, *Using Surveys to Value Public Goods: The Contingent Valuation Method* (Washington, DC: Resources for the Future, 1989).

51. S.V. Ciriacy-Wantrup, 'Capital Returns from Soil Conservation Practices', *Journal of Farm Economics* 29 (November 1947): 1181–96.

52. Davis, 'Recreation Planning as an Economic Problem'; R. Ridker, *The Economic Cost of Air Pollution* (New York: Praeger, 1967); J. Hammack and G. Brown, *Waterfowl and Wetlands: Toward Bioeconomic Analysis* (Baltimore: Johns Hopkins University Press, 1974); R. Bishop and T. Heberlein, 'Measuring Values of Extramarket Goods: Are Indirect Measures Biased?', *American Journal of Agricultural Economics* 61 (1979): 926–30.

53. J. Acton, *Evaluating Public Progress to Save Lives: The Case of Heart Attacks*, RAND Research Report R-73-02 (Santa Monica: RAND Corporation, 1973); A. Krupnick and M. Cropper, 'The Effect of Information on Health Risk Valuation', *Journal of Risk and Uncertainty* 2 (1992): 29–48; D.G. Devine and B. Marion, 'The Influence of Consumer Price Information on Retail Pricing and Consumer Behavior', *American Journal of Agricultural Economics* 61 (1979): 228–37.

54. P.R. Portney, 'The Contingent Valuation Debate: Why Economists Should Care', *Journal of Economic Perspectives*, 8 (4) (1994): 3–17.

55. R. Carson et al., *A Contingent Valuation Study of Lost Passive Use Values Resulting From the Exxon Valdez Oil Spill*, Report to the Attorney General of the State of Alaska (La Jolla, CA: Natural Resource Damage Assessment, Inc., 1992).

56. W.H. Desvousges et al., *Measuring Nonuse Damages Using Contingent Valuation: An Experimental Evaluation of Accuracy* (Research Triangle Park, NC: RTI International, 2010 [1992]), www.rti.org/pubs/bk-0001-1009_web.pdf (accessed 30 June 2013).

57. R. Carson et al., *A Bibliography of Contingent Valuation Studies and Papers* (La Jolla, CA: Natural Resources Damage Assessment, Inc., 1994).

58. B. Weisbrod, 'Collective Consumption Services of Individual Consumption Goods', *Quarterly Journal of Economics*, 78 (3) (1964): 472.

59. Desvousges et al., *Measuring Nonuse Damages Using Contingent Valuation*.

60. Costanza et al., 'The Value of the World's Ecosystem Services and Natural Capital', p. 258.

61. Toman, 'Why Not to Calculate the Value of the World's Ecosystem Services and Natural Capital', p. 59.

62. Ibid., p. 57. For an overview of approaches based on individual utility

maximization, see D. Pearce, *Economic Values and the Natural World* (London: Earthscan, 1993).

63. R. Costanza, 'Social Goals and the Valuation of Natural Capital', *Environmental Monitoring and Assessment* 86 (2003): 24.

64. Ibid., p. 26.

65. Ibid.

66. Ibid.

67. UNEP, *In the Front Line: Shoreline Protection and Other Ecosystem Services From Mangroves and Coral Reefs* (Cambridge: UNEP World Conservation Monitoring Centre, 2006).

68. 'Bugs plug $57 billion into U.S. Economy', Associate Press, 1 April 2006, www.msnbc.msn.com/id/12103021/#.UNg_64X4bIU.

69. 'Growing on Trees: A Profitable Rainforest', *The Economist*, 18 May 2009.

70. See Canopy Capital's website at: http://canopycapital.co.uk/page.asp?p=5452 (accessed 30 June 2013).

71. For more info, see: www.globalcanopy.org (accessed 30 June 2013).

72. M. Cranford et al., *Unlocking Forest Bonds: A High-Level Workshop on Innovative Finance for Tropical Forests*, Workshop Report, WWF Forest & Climate Initiative, Global Canopy Programme and Climate Bonds Initiative, 2011.

73. See http://gdm.earthmind.net (accessed 30 June 2013)

74. 'A Green Development Mechanism for Bioversity', *Ecosystem Marketplace*, 21 October 2010, www.ecosystemmarketplace.com/pages/dynamic/article.page.php?page_id=7786 (accessed 30 June 2013).

75. Department of Environment and Climate Change NSW, *Biobanking: Biodiversity Banking and Offset Scheme* (Sidney: DECC NSW, 2007), www.environment.nsw.gov.au/resources/biobanking/biobankingoverview07528.pdf (accessed 30 June 2013)

76. See www.cpsl.cam.ac.uk/Business-Platforms/Natural-Capital-Leaders-Platform.aspx.

77. *The New Business Imperative: Valuing Natural Capital*, pp. 6, 9, www.corporateecoforum.com/valuingnaturalcapital/offline/download.pdf (accessed 30 June 2013).

78. The list of signatories includes: Athelia Ecosphere, ASN Bank, Banca Monte dei Paschi di Siena, Banco Multiva, Banco Pichincha, Banorte – Ixe, Caisse des Depots, Caixa Econômica Federal, Caledonia Wealth Management Ltd., Calvert Investments, CDC Climat, China Merchants Bank, CIBanco, Cyrte Investments, Financiera Rural, FIRA – Banco de Mexico, Fundación Social, Infraprev, International Finance Corporation, MN, Mongeral Aegon, Mutualista Pichincha, National Australia Bank, Nedbank, Oppenheim, PaxWorld Management, Rabobank Group, Robeco, Shenzhen Development Bank, SNS Asset Management, Société Forestière, Sovereign, Standard Chartered, Sumitomo Mitsui Trust

Holding, UniCredit, Vision Banco, Zevin Asset Management. See also 'Natural Capital Could Create a Market Value for Biodiversity', *Guardian*, 21 November 2012.

79. Besides a number of institutions belonging to the World Bank Group, signatories of the Natural Capital Declaration include private banks such as China Merchants Bank, Standard Chartered and Unicredit. See: www.naturalcapitaldeclaration.org (accessed 30 June 2013).

80. 'How Goldman Sachs Helped Greece to Mask Its True Debt', *Spiegel Online*, 8 February 2010, www.spiegel.de/international/europe/greek-debt-crisis-how-goldman-sachs-helped-greece-to-mask-its-true-debt-a-676634.html (accessed 30 June 2013).

81. 'Derivati, UniCredit Finisce alla Sbarra', *Il Fatto Quotidiano*, 29 September 2012, www.ilfattoquotidiano.it/2012/09/29/derivati-unicredit-finisce-alla-sbarra/367575 (accessed 30 June 2013).

82. 'Deutsche Bank Convicted in Italy in Widening Scandal', *EU Observer*, 20 December 2012, http://euobserver.com/economic/118581 (accessed 30 June 2013).

83. See the website of the group Baby Milk Action at http://info.babymilkaction.org (accessed 30 June 2013).

84. See Greenpeace's campaign 'Ask Nestlé to Give Rainforests a Break' at www.greenpeace.org/international/en/campaigns/climate-change/kitkat (accessed 30 June 2013). In 2012, Nestlé lost a court case in Brazil, which has now ordered the company to label genetically modified products. See more here: www.foodworldnews.com/articles/2017/20120827/brazil-court-rule-food-nestle-gm-monsanto.htm (accessed 30 June 2013).

85. You can view the documentary *We Feed The World* here: www.we-feed-the-world.at/en/film.htm (accessed 30 June 2013).

86. 'How a Global Web of Activists Gives Coke Problems in India', *Wall Street Journal*, 7 June 2005.

87. 'Dow Chemical: Liable for Bhopal?' *Bloomberg Business Week Magazine*, 27 May 2008, www.businessweek.com/stories/2008-05-27/dow-chemical-liable-for-bhopal (accessed 30 June 2013).

88. 'McKinsey's Close Relationship with Enron Raises Questions of Consultancy Liability', *Wall Street Journal*, 17 January 2002.

89. 'A Star Partner's Galleon Arrest Shakes up Ranks and McKinsey', *Wall Street Journal*, 21 October 2009.

90. 'McKinsey Implicated in Galleon Trial', *Guardian*, 14 March 2011.

91. For an introduction to McKinsey's Greenhouse Gas Abatement Cost Curve, see: www.mckinsey.com/client_service/sustainability/latest_thinking/greenhouse_gas_abatement_cost_curves (accessed 30 June 2013).

92. Greenpeace, *Bad Influence: How McKinsey-inspired Plans Lead to Rainforest Destruction* (Amsterdam: Greenpeace International, 2011), p. 11, www.greenpeace.org/international/en/publications/reports/Bad-Influence/?accept=d81175f13c50770ed778339fcb66d566 (accessed 30 June 2013).

93. Ibid., p. 11.
94. C. MacDonald, *Green, Inc.: An Environmental Insider Reveals How a Good Cause Has Gone Bad* (Guilford, CT: Lyons Press, 2008).
95. 'Environment: Market-based Conservation Brewing in Nairobi', *Inter Press Service*, 1 June 2010, www.ipsnews.net/2010/06/environment-market-based-conservation-brewing-in-nairobi (accessed 30 June 2013).
96. D. Brockington, *Celebrity and the Environment: Fame, Wealth and Power in Conservation* (London: Zed Books, 2009).
97. M. Dowie, *Conservation Refugees: The Hundred-year Conflict between Global Conservation and Native Peoples* (Cambridge, MA: MIT Press, 2009).
98. Brockington, *Celebrity and the Environment*.
99. M. Goldman, *Imperial Nature: The World Bank and Struggles for Social Justice in the Age of Globalization* (New Haven, CT: Yale University Press, 2005), p. 9.
100. J. Fairhead, M. Leach and I. Scoones 'Green Grabbing: A New Appropriation of Nature?', *Journal of Peasant Studies*, 39 (2) (2012): 237–61.
101. Ibid., p. 237.
102. C. Corson and K.I. MacDonald, 'Enclosing the Global Commons: The Convention on Biological Diversity and Green Grabbing', *Journal of Peasant Studies*, 39 (2) (2012): 263–83.
103. B. Büscher, S. Sullivan et al., 'Towards a Synthesized Critique of Neoliberal Biodiversity Conservation', *Capitalism Nature Socialism*, 23 (2) (2012): 4.
104. Ibid., p. 15.
105. 'Nature Inc.: A New Kind of TV Show', *Planet Green*, 8 October 2009, http://planetgreen.discovery.com/tv/nature-inc/nature-kind-show.html (accessed 30 June 2013).
106. M. Arsel and B. Büscher, 'Nature™ Inc.: Changes and Continuities in Neoliberal Conservation and Market-based Environmental Policy', *Development and Change*, 43 (1) (2012): 53–7.
107. D. Pearce, A. Markandya and E. Barbier, *Blueprint for a Green Economy* (London: Earthscan, 1989), p. 81.
108. 'Puma Scales up Environmental Profit and Loss Reporting to a Product Level', *Guardian*, 8 October 2012.
109. 'Natural Capital Could Create a Market Value for Biodiversity', *Guardian*, 21 November 2012.
110. K. MacAfee, 'Selling Nature to Save It? Biodiversity and Green Developmentalism', *Society and Space*, (17) 2 (1999): 203–19.
111. M. Hajer, *The Politics of Environmental Discourse: Ecological Modernization and the Policy Process* (Oxford: Oxford University Press, 1995).
112. R. Fletcher, 'Neoliberal Environmentality: Towards a Poststructural Political Ecology of the Conservation Debate', *Conservation and Society*, 8 (3) (2010): 171–81.

113. Costanza, 'Social Goals and the Valuation of Natural Capital', p. 26.
114. D. Ehrenfeld, 'Neoliberalization of Conservation', *Conservation Biology*, 22 (5) (2008): 1092.
115. The principle of weak sustainability is generally known in economics as the Hartwick's rule, which defines the amount of investment in produced capital that is necessary to offset declining stocks of non-renewable resources. This approach has informed, among others, a number of estimates of 'genuine saving' produced by the World Bank.
116. B. Caldecott and I. Dickie, *Habitat Banking: Scaling up Private Investment in the Protection and Restoration of Our Natural World* (London: CCC & eftec, 2011), www.climatechangecapital.com/news-and-events/press-releases/habitat-banking-scaling-up-private-investment-in-the-protection-and-restoration-of-our-natural-world.aspx (accessed 30 June 2013).
117. J. Kovel, *The Enemy of Nature: The End of Capitalism, or the End of the World?* (London: Zed Books, 2002).
118. Millennium Ecosystem Assessment, *Ecosystems and Human Well-being: Synthesis* (Washington, DC: Island Press, 2005).
119. C. Raudsepp-Hearne, 'Untangling the Environmentalist Paradox: Why Is Human Well-being Increasing as Ecosystem Services Degrade?', *Bio-Science*, 60 (8) (2010): 576–89.
120. Kaisa Kosonen, 'Beyond GDP: Measuring What Really Matters to Our Prosperity and Future' (Amsterdam: Greenpeace International, June 2012).
121. Ibid.
122. J.M. Keynes, 'National Self-Sufficiency', *Yale Review*, 22 (4) (June 1933): 755–69.

CHAPTER 5

1. The speech is reported by G. Rist, *The History of Development: From Western Origins to Global Faith*, 3rd edn (London: Zed Books, 2010 [1997]), p. 71.
2. Ibid., p. 71.
3. W.W. Rostow, *The Stages of Economic Growth: A Non-Communist Manifesto* (Cambridge: Cambridge University Press, 1960), p. 4.
4. Ibid., p. 9.
5. Ibid., p. 167.
6. Ibid., p. 1.
7. J. Vandemoortele, 'The MDGs: 'M' for Misunderstood?', World Institute for Development Economics Research (WIDER), UNU, No. 1 (2007), pp. 6–7, www.sarpn.org/documents/d0002652/WIDER_Angle_1_2007.pdf (accessed 30 June 2013).
8. W. Easterly, *The Elusive Quest for Growth: Economists' Adventures and*

Misadventures in the Tropics (Cambridge, MA: MIT Press, 2002).

9. D. Moyo, *Dead Aid: Why Aid Is Not Working and How There Is a Better Way for Africa* (New York and London: Allen Lane, 2009). The quotation is from D. Moyo, 'Aid Ironies: A Response to Jeffrey Sachs', *Huffington Post*, 26 May 2009, www.huffingtonpost.com/dambisa-moyo/aid-ironies-a-response-to_b_207772.html (accessed 30 June 2013).

10. P. Collier, *The Bottom Billion: Why the Poorest Countries Are Failing and What Can Be Done about It* (Oxford and New York: Oxford University Press, 2008). See also T. Wallace, L. Bornstein and J. Chapman, *The Aid Chain: Coercion and Commitment in NGO Development Funding* (Rugby: ITDG Press, 2006).

11. J. Sachs, *The End of Poverty: Economic Possibilities for Our Time* (New York: Penguin, 2005). See also J. Sachs, 'Aid Ironies', *Huffington Post*, 24 May 2009, www.huffingtonpost.com/jeffrey-sachs/aid-ironies_b_207181.html (accessed 30 June 2013).

12. M. Faraday, *Experimental Researches in Chemistry and Physics* (London: Taylor & Francis, 1859).

13. C. Darwin, The Effects of Cross- and Self-Fertilisation in the Vegetable Kingdom (London: John Murray, 1876).

14. J. Heckman and E. Vytlacil, 'Econometric Evaluation of Social Programs', in J. Heckman and E. Leamer (eds), *Handbook of Econometrics*, vol. 6 (Amsterdam: Elsevier, 2007); T. Koopmans, *Three Essays on the State of Economic Science* (New York: McGraw–Hill, 1957).

15. A.V. Banerjee and E. Duflo, *Poor Economics: A Radical Rethinking of the Way to Fight Global Poverty* (New York: Public Affairs, 2011), p. x.

16. E. Duflo and M. Kremer, 'Use of Randomization in the Evaluation of Development Effectiveness', paper prepared for the World Bank Operations Evaluation Department (OED) Conference on Evaluation and Development Effectiveness, Washington DC, 15–16 July 2003, p. 3.

17. 'Fighting Global Poverty with Hard Numbers', *Chicago Policy Review*, 4 April 2012, http://chicagopolicyreview.org/2012/04/04/fighting-global-poverty-with-hard-numbers (accessed 30 June 2013).

18. See IPA's website at: www.poverty-action.org/scaling-up-what-works (accessed 30 June 2013).

19. D. Karlan and J. Appel, *More than Good Intentions: How a New Economics is Helping Solve Global Problems* (New York: Dutton Press, 2011), p. 9.

20. Ibid., p. 5.

21. Ibid.

22. See www.poverty-action.org/provenimpact/investments/challenge (accessed 30 June 2013).

23. See www.givedirectly.org/evidence.php and http://blogs.hbr.org/cs/2013/03/want_to_help_people_just_give.html (accessed 30 June 2013).

24. See www.copenhagenconsensus.com/projects/copenhagen-consensus-2012/research/hunger-and-malnutrition (accessed 30 June 2013).

25. R. Patel, *Stuffed and Starved: The Hidden Battle for the World Food System* (New York and London: Melville House, 2007).
26. 'The GM Genocide: Thousands of Indian Farmers Are Committing Suicide after Using Genetically Modified Crops', *Daily Mail*, 3 November 2008, www.dailymail.co.uk/news/article-1082559/The-GM-genocide-Thousands-Indian-farmers-committing-suicide-using-genetically-modified-crops.html (accessed 30 June 2013).
27. Patel, *Stuffed and Starved*.
28. 'Nearly 2 lakh Farm Suicides since 1997', *India Together*, 25 January 2010, www.indiatogether.org/2010/jan/psa-suicides.htm (accessed 30 June 2013).
29. 'Farm Suicides Worse After 2001 – Study', *The Hindu*, 13 November 2001, www.hindu.com/2007/11/13/stories/2007111352250900.htm (accessed 30 June 2013).
30. ImechE, *Global Food Waste Not, Want Not* (London: Institution of Mechanical Engineers, 2013), www.imeche.org/knowledge/themes/environment/global-food (accessed 30 June 2013).
31. Ibid., p. 3.
32. M. Jerven, *Poor Numbers: How We Are Misled By African Development Statistics and What To Do About It* (Ithaca, NY: Cornell University Press 2013), p. 90.
33. See: www.philanthrocapitalism.net/about/synopsis (accessed 30 June 2013).
34. 'They Are Called the Good Club and They Want to Save the World', *Guardian*, 31 May 2009.
35. R. Rogers, 'Why Philanthro-policymaking Matters', *Society*, 48 (5) (2011): 378.
36. See www.gatesfoundation.org/Who-We-Are/General-Information/Letter-from-Bill-and-Melinda-Gates (accessed 30 June 2013).
37. See the Grand Challenges website: www.grandchallenges.org (accessed 30 June 2013).
38. B. Gates, 'My Plan to Fix the World's Biggest Problems', *Wall Street Journal*, 25 January 2013.
39. M. Edwards, *Just Another Emperor? The Myths and Realities of Philanthrocapitalism* (New York: Demos, 2008), p. 20.
40. 'A Businesslike Approach to Charity', *Financial Times*, 10 December 2007.
41. K.N. Ramdas, 'Philanthrocapitalism: Reflections on Politics and Policy Making', *Society*, 48 (5) (2011): 395.
42. Ibid.
43. 'A Businesslike Approach to Charity'.
44. S. Knack and A. Rahman, 'Donor Fragmentation and Bureaucratic Quality in Aid Recipient Countries', *Journal of Development Economics*, 83(1) (2007): 177.

45. A. Banerjee, *Making Aid Work* (Cambridge, MA: MIT Press, 2007).
46. Ibid., p. 21.
47. A. Banerjee and E. Duflo, 'The Experimental Approach to Development Economics', *Annual Review of Economics*, Annual Reviews 1 (1) (2009): 151–78.
48. A. Olofsgard, 'The Politics of Aid Effectiveness: Why Better Tools Can Make for Worse Outcomes', Working Paper No. 16 (2012), Stockholm Institute of Transition Economies, p. 11.
49. J.J. Heckman, 'Randomization and Social Policy Evaluation', in C.F. Manski and I. Garfinkel (eds), *Evaluating Welfare and Training Programs* (Cambridge, MA: Harvard University Press, 1992), p. 218.
50. See www.philanthrocapitalism.net/oldsite (accessed 30 June 2013).
51. W.R. Shadish and J.K. Luellen, 'Donald Campbell: The Accidental Evaluator', in M.C. Alkin (ed.), *Evaluation Roots: Tracing Theorists' Views and Influences* (London: Sage, 2004), p. 81.
52. See the MDRC's website at: www.mdrc.org/about/about-mdrc-history (accessed 30 June 2013).
53. See Jarrell's entry in the *Concise Encyclopaedia of Economics*, available online at: www.econlib.org/library/Enc1/TakeoversandLeveragedBuyouts.html (accessed 30 June 2013).
54. J. Thackaray, 'Leveraged Buyouts: The LBO Craze Flourishes Amid Warnings of Disaster', *Euromoney*, February 1986, www.euromoney.com/Article/1451496/Leveraged-buyouts-The-LBO-craze-flourishes-amid-warnings.html?single=true)&copyrightInfo=true (accessed 30 June 2013).
55. See *Time*, 132 (23), 5 December 1988.
56. J. Emerson and F. Twersky, *New Social Entrepreneurs: The Success, Challenge and Lessons of Non-profit Enterprise Creation* (San Francisco: Roberts Foundation, 1996).
57. N. Rotheroe and A. Richards, 'Social Return on Investment and Social Enterprise: Transparent Accountability for Sustainable Development', *Social Enterprise Journal*, 3 (1) (2007): 31–48.
58. R. Millar and K. Hall, 'Social Return on Investment (SROI) and Performance Management', *Public Management Review*, 14 (5) (2012).
59. Ibid., pp. 5–6.
60. J. Nicholls et al., *A Guide to Social Return on Investment* (London: SROI Network, 2012), p. 67.
61. Ibid.
62. New Philanthropy Capital, *Social Return on Investment Position Paper* (London: NPC, 2010), p. 2.
63. Ibid.
64. Ibid., pp. 3ff.
65. Ibid., p. 7.
66. See the SROI Network's seven principles at: www.thesroinetwork.org (accessed 30 June 2013).

67. CSI, 'Social Return': Eine sozioökonomische Mehrwertanalyse gemeinschaftlicher Wohnprojekte, Zukunft Quartier – Lebensräume zum Älterwerden, vol. 3 (Gütersloh: Bertelsmann Stiftung, 2009). See also V. Then et al., Creating Impact in Southern Norway: A Social Return on Investment Report to the Competence Development Fund of Southern Norway (Heidelberg: Centre for Social Investment, 2012) https://www.csi.uni-heidelberg.de/downloads/Creating_Impact_in_Southern_Norway.pdf (accessed 30 June 2013).

68. K. Sheridan, 'Measuring the Impact of Social Enterprise', British Journal of Healthcare Management, 17 (4) (2011): 152–6.

69. New Economics Foundation (NEF), Social Return on Investment: Valuing What Matters (London: New Economics Foundation, 2004).

70. P.W. Ryan and I. Lyne, 'Social Enterprise and the Measurement of Social Value: Methodological Issues with the Calculation and Application of the Social Return on Investment', Education, Knowledge and Economy, 2 (3) (2008): 223–337.

71. Millar and Hall, 'Social Return on Investment (SROI) and Performance Management', p. 6.

72. Goldman Sachs Foundation, Social Impact Assessment: A Discussion among Grantmakers (New York: Goldman Sachs, 2003).

73. Quotation from www.thinknpc.org/about-npc/our-history (accessed 30 June 2013).

74. S. Daly, 'Philanthropy, the Big Society and Emerging Philanthropic Relationships in the UK', Public Management Review, 13(8) (2011): 1077–94.

75. Cabinet Office, Growing the Social Investment Market: A Vision and Strategy (London: Cabinet Office, 2011).

76. See Phineo's website at: www.phineo.org (accessed 30 June 2013).

77. H. Husock, 'Stock Market for Nonprofits', Society, 44 (3) (2007): 16–23.

78. S. Goldberg, Billions of Drops in Millions of Buckets: Why Philanthropy Doesn't Advance Social Progress (Hoboken, NJ: Wiley, 2009).

79. M. Bishop and M. Green, 'The Man with a Plan', Philanthropy Magazine, Spring 2010, www.philanthropyroundtable.org/topic/excellence_in_philanthropy/the_man_with_a_plan (accessed 30 June 2013).

80. A.M. Eikenberry and J.D. Kluver, 'The Marketization of the Nonprofit Sector: Civil Society at Risk?', Public Administration Review, 64 (2) (2004): 132–40.

81. J. Steinbeck, The Log from the Sea of Cortez (London and New York: Penguin Books, 1941), p. 272.

82. C. Pozorski, 'Social Venture Partners: "Venture Capital" Grantmaking in Practice', Grantmanship Center Magazine, Fall 2000: 24.

83. Eikenberry and Kluver, 'The Marketization of the Nonprofit Sector', p. 134.

84. A.E. Birn, 'Gates's Grandest Challenge: Transcending Technology as Public Health Ideology', The Lancet, 366 (9484) (2005): 515.

85. Ibid.
86. See the Gates Foundation's scientific claims at: www.gatesfoundation. org/who-we-are/resources-and-media/annual-letters-list/annual-letter-2009 (accessed 30 June 2013).
87. 'Buffet Won't Judge Firms', *Los Angeles Times*, 7 May 2007, http://articles. latimes.com/2007/may/07/nation/na-berkshire7 (accessed 30 June 2013).
88. M. Edwards, 'Impact, Accountability and Philanthrocapitalism', *Society*, 48 (5) (2011): 390.
89. Edwards, *Just Another Emperor?*, p. 66.
90. 'Can Foundations Take the Long View Again?' *New York Times*, 6 January 2008.
91. Ibid.
92. P.M. Nickel and A.M. Eikenberry, 'A Critique of the Discourse of Marketized Philanthropy', *American Behavioral Scientist*, 52 (7) (2009): 975
93. Ibid.
94. Ibid.
95. 'America's Wealthiest Donors Slow their Giving', *Chronicle of Philanthropy*, 1 January 2013, http://philanthropy.com/article/America-s-Wealthiest-Donors/136405 (accessed 30 June 2013).
96. Ramdas, 'Philanthrocapitalism', p. 394.

CONCLUSION

1. T. Kuhn, *The Structure of Scientific Revolutions*, 3rd edn (Chicago: University of Chicago Press, 1996 [1962]).
2. H. Arendt, *The Human Condition* (Chicago: University of Chicago Press, 1958), p. 322.
3. M. Jerven, *Poor Numbers: How We Are Misled by African Development Statistics and What to Do About It* (Ithaca, NY: Cornell University Press, 2013).
4. 'How Did the Recent GDP Revisions Change the Picture of the 2007–2009 Recession and the Recovery?', Bureau of Economic Analysis, www. bea.gov/faq/index.cfm?faq_id=1004 (accessed 30 June 2013).
5. Bureau of Economic Analysis, 'Preview of the 2013 Comprehensive Revision of the National Income and Product Accounts', US Department of Commerce, March 2013, www.bea.gov/scb/pdf/2013/03%20March/0313_ nipa_comprehensive_revision_preview.pdf (accessed 30 June 2013).
6. 'Changes in GDP Measurement Create Growth Out of Thin Air', *Daily Caller*, 30 April 2013, http://dailycaller.com/2013/04/30/changes-in-gdp-measurement-create-growth-out-of-thin-air (accessed 30 June 2013).
7. D. Huff, *How to Lie With Statistics* (New York and London: W.W. Norton, 1954).
8. C. Seife, *Proofiness: The Dark Arts of Mathematical Deception* (Viking: New York, 2010), p. 236.

9. For a full account of this debate, see A. Kleiner, 'What are the Measures that Matter?' *Strategy + Business* 26 (2002): 1–6.

10. M. Power, *The Audit Society: Rituals of Verification* (Oxford and New York: Oxford University Press, 1997), p. 123.

11. Ibid., p. 13.

12. P. Genschel and B. Zangl, 'Transformations of the State: From Monopolist to Manager of Political Authority', TranState Working Papers no. 76 (2008), University of Bremen.

13. V.F. Heinrich and L. Fioramonti, *Global Survey of the State of Civil Society: Comparative Perspectives* (Bloomfield: Kumarian Press, 2007); L. Fioramonti and E. Thumler, 'Accountability, Democracy and Post-Growth: Civil Society Rethinking Political Economy and Finance', *Journal of Civil Society*, 9 (2) (2013): 117–28; L. Fioramonti and A. Fiori, 'Civil Society After Democracy: The Evolution of Civic Activism in South Africa and Korea', *Journal of Civil Society*, 6 (1) (2010): 25–40.

14. M. Edwards, *Civil Society* (Cambridge: Polity Press, 2004).

15. A.B. Seligman, *The Idea of Civil Society* (New York: MacMillan, 1992); C. Calhoun, 'Civil Society/Public Sphere: History of the Concept', in N.J. Smelser and P.B. Baltes (eds), *International Encyclopaedia of the Social and Behavioural Sciences* (Amsterdam: Elsevier, 2001).

16. R.D. Putnam, *Bowling Alone: The Collapse and Revival of American Community* (New York: Touchstone, 2001).

17. G. Hunt, 'The Development of the Concept of Civil Society in Marx', in B. Jessop and C. Malcolm-Brown (eds), *Karl Marx's Social and Political Thought: Critical Assessments* (London and New York: Routledge, 1990).

18. A. Gramsci, *Selections from the Prison Notebooks of Antonio Gramsci* (New York: International Publishers, 1971).

19. E. Gellner, *Conditions of Liberty: Civil Society and Its Rivals* (New York: Penguin Books, 1996).

20. J. Habermas, *Theory of Communicative Action*, vol. 2 (Boston, MA: Beacon Press, 1984).

21. G. Prins and S. Rayner, 'Time To Ditch Kyoto', *Nature* 449 (7165) (2007): 975.

22. M. Edwards, *Just Another Emperor? The Myths and Realities of Philanthrocapitalism* (New York: Demos, 2008), p. 107.

23. Kellogg Foundation, *Blurred Boundaries*, p. 26.

24. Seife, *Proofiness*, p. 236.

25. C. Lindblom, 'The Market as a Prison', *Journal of Politics* 44 (1982): 325–6.

26. S.P. Shapiro, 'The Social Control of Impersonal Trust', *American Journal of Sociology*, 93 (3) (1987): 645.

27. Ibid., p. 623.

28. D. Boyle, *The Tyranny of Numbers* (London: Flamingo, 2001), p. 39.

29. E. Ostrom, *Governing the Commons: The Evolution of Institutions for*

Collective Action (New York: Cambridge University Press, 1990).

30. R. Patel, *The Value of Nothing: How to Reshape Market Society and Redefine Democracy* (London: Portobello Books, 2009), p. 194.

Bibliography

Acton, J. (1973) 'Evaluating Public Progress to Save Lives: The Case of Heart Attacks', RAND Research Report R-73-02, Santa Monica: RAND Corporation.

Annual Review of Economics, Annual Reviews 1 (1): 151–78.

Arendt, H. (1958) *The Human Condition* (Chicago: University of Chicago Press).

Arsel, M., and Büscher, B. (2012) 'Nature™ Inc.: Changes and Continuities in Neoliberal Conservation and Market-based Environmental Policy', *Development and Change*, 43 (1): 53–7.

Asdal, K. (2011) 'The Office: Weakness of Numbers and the Production of Non-authority', *Accounting, Organizations and Society*, 36 (1): 1–9.

Baldwin, R. (2008) 'Regulation Lite: The Rise of Emissions Trading', *Regulation and Governance* 2: 193–215.

Baldwin, R., Cave, M., and Lodge, M. (2012) *Understanding Regulation: Theory, Strategy and Practice* (Oxford: Oxford University Press).

Balmford, A. (2002) 'Economic Reasons for Conserving Wild Nature', *Science*, 297 (5583): 950–53.

Banerjee, A. (2007) *Making Aid Work* (Cambridge, MA: MIT Press).

Banerjee, A., and Duflo, E. (2009) 'The Experimental Approach to Development Economics', *Annual Review of Economics* 1(1): 151–78.

Banerjee, A., and Duflo, E. (2011) *Poor Economics: A Radical Rethinking of the Way to Fight Global Poverty* (New York: Public Affairs).

Becker, B., and Milbourn, T. (2010) 'How Did Increased Competition Affect Credit Ratings?' Working Paper 09-051, Harvard Business School, Cambridge, MA.

Becker, G.M., DeGroot, M.H., and Marschal, J. (1964) 'Measuring Utility by a Single Response Sequential Method', *Behavioral Science*, 9 (3): 226–32.

Becker, P., and Clark, W. (eds) (2001) *Little Tools of Knowledge: Historical Essays on Academic and Bureaucratic Practices* (Ann Arbor: University of Michigan Press).

Best, J. (2001) *Damned Lies and Statistics: Untangling Numbers from the Media, Politicians and Activists* (Berkeley: University of California Press).

Birn, A.E. (2005) 'Gates's Grandest Challenge: Transcending Technology as Public Health Ideology', *The Lancet*, 366 (9484): 514–19.

Bishop, M., and Green, M. (2010) 'The Man with a Plan', *Philanthropy Magazine*, Spring.

Bishop, R.C., and Heberlein, T.A. (1979) 'Measuring Values of Extra-Market Goods: Are Indirect Methods Biased?' *American Journal of Agricultural Economics*, 61 (5): 926–30.

Blades, D. (1989) 'Revision of the System of National Accounts: A Note on Objectives and Key Issues', *OECD Economic Studies*, No. 12 (Paris: OECD).

Blastland, M., and Dilnot, A. (2009) *The Numbers Game: The Commonsense Guide to Understanding Numbers in the News, in Politics, and in Life* (New York: Gotham Books).

Blomquist, G.C. (2004) 'Self-Protection and Averting Behavior, Values of Statistical Lives, and Benefit Cost Analysis of Environmental Policy', *Review of the Economics of the Household*, 2 (1): 89–110.

Bolton, P., Freixas, X., and Shapiro, J. (2009) 'The Credit Ratings Game', Working Paper No. 14712, National Bureau for Economic Research, www.nber.org/papers/w14712.

Boyle, D. (2001) *The Tyranny of Numbers* (London: Flamingo).

Breidert, C., Hahsler, M., and Reutterer, T. (2006) 'A Review of Methods for Measuring Willingness to Pay', *Innovative Marketing*, 2 (4): 8–32.

Bridgman, B., et al. (2012) 'Accounting for Household Production in the National Accounts, 1965–2010', *Survey of Current Business*, 92 (5): 23–36.

Brockington, D. (2009) *Celebrity and the Environment: Fame, Wealth and Power in Conservation* (London: Zed Books).

Broekhoff, D., and Zyla, K. (2008) *Outside the Cap: Opportunities and Limitations of Greenhouse Gases Offsets*, Climate and Energy Policy Series (Washington, DC: World Resources Institute, December).

Brown, T.C., Champ, P.A., Bishop, R.C., and McCollum, D.W. (1996) 'Which Response Format Reveals the Truth About Donations to a Public Good?' *Land Economics*, 72 (2): 152–66.

Brunner, C., and Abdelal, R. (2005) 'To Judge Leviathan: Sovereign Credit Ratings, National Law and the World Economy', *Journal of Public Policy*, 25 (2): 191–217.

Buiter, W.H. (2007) 'Lessons from the 2007 Financial Crisis', CEPR, Policy Insight No. 18, December.

Bureau of Economic Analysis (2013) 'Preview of the 2013 Comprehensive Revision of the National Income and Product Accounts', US Department of Commerce, March.

Burtraw, D. (1996) 'Cost Savings Sans Allowance Trades? Evaluating the SO_2 Emission Trading Program to Date', Resources For the Future Discussion Paper 95-30-REV.

Büscher, B., and Sullivan, S., et al. (2012) 'Towards a Synthesized Critique of Neoliberal Biodiversity Conservation', *Capitalism Nature Socialism*, 23 (2): 4–30.

Butzengeiger, S., and Michaelowa, A. (2004) 'The EU Emissions Trading Scheme – Issues and Challenges', *Intereconomics*, May/June: 116–18.

Cabinet Office (2011) *Growing the Social Investment Market: A Vision and Strategy* (London: Cabinet Office).

Caldecott, B., and Dickie, I. (2011) *Habitat Banking: Scaling up Private Investment in the Protection and Restoration of Our Natural Torld* (London: CCC & eftec).

Calhoun, C. (2001) 'Civil Society/Public Sphere: History of the Concept', in N.J. Smelser and P.B. Baltes (eds), *International Encyclopaedia of the Social and Behavioural Sciences* (Amsterdam: Elsevier).

Canny, N. (1987) *From Reformation to Resistance: Ireland, 1534–1660* (Dublin: Helicon).

Capoor, K., and Ambrosi, P. (2008) *State and Trends of the Carbon Market 2008* (Washington, DC: World Bank).

Carson, R., et al. (1992) *A Contingent Valuation Study of Lost Passive Use Values Resulting From the Exxon Valdez Oil Spill*, Report to the Attorney General of the State of Alaska (La Jolla, CA: Natural Resource Damage Assessment, Inc.)

Carson, R., et al. (1994) *A Bibliography of Contingent Valuation Studies and Papers* (La Jolla, CA: Natural Resources Damage Assessment, Inc.).

Cashore, B. (2002) 'Legitimacy and the Privatization of Environmental Governance: How Non-State Market-Driven (NSMD) Governance Systems Gain Rule-Making Authority', *Governance: An International Journal of Policy, Administration, and Institutions*, 15 (4): 503–29.

CESR (2005) *Technical Advice to the European Commission on Possible Measures Concerning Credit Rating Agencies* (Paris: Committee of European Security Regulators).

Ciriacy-Wantrup, S.V. (1947) 'Capital Returns from Soil Conservation Practices', *Journal of Farm Economics*, 29 (November 1947): 1181–96.

Collier, P. (2008) *The Bottom Billion: Why the Poorest Countries Are Failing and What Can Be Done About It* (Oxford and New York: Oxford University Press).

Committee on Climate Change (2008) *Building a Low-Carbon Economy: The UK's Contribution to Tackling Climate Change* (London: CCC).

Corson, C., and MacDonald, K.I. (2012) 'Enclosing the Global Commons: The Convention on Biological Diversity and Green Grabbing', *Journal of Peasant Studies*, 39 (2): 263–83.

Costanza, R. (2003) 'Social Goals and the Valuation of Natural Capital', *Environmental Monitoring and Assessment* 86: 19–28.

Costanza, R., et al. (1997) 'The Value of the World's Ecosystem Services and Natural Capital', *Nature* 387 (15 May 1997): 253–70.

Cranford, M., et al. (2011) *Unlocking Forest Bonds: A High-Level Workshop on Innovative Finance for Tropical Forests*, Workshop Report. WWF Forest & Climate Initiative, Global Canopy Programme and Climate Bonds Initiative.

Crouch, C. (2010) 'The Global Firm: The Problem of the Giant Firm in Democratic Capitalism', in D. Coen, W. Grant and G.Wilson (eds), *Oxford Handbook of Business and Government* (Oxford: Oxford University Press).

CSI (2009) *'Social Return': Eine sozioökonomische Mehrwertanalyse gemeinschaftlicher Wohnprojekte, Zukunft Quartier – Lebensräume zum Älterwerden*, vol. 3 (Gütersloh: Bertelsmann Stiftung).

Cullen, M.J. (1975) *The Statistical Movement in Early Victorian Britain: The Foundations of Empirical Social Research* (Hassocks: Harvester Press).

Cutler, A.C., Haufler, V., and Porter, T. (eds) (1999) *Private Authority and International Affairs* (Albany, NY: State University of New York Press).

Cutler, A.C., Haufler, V., and Porter, T. (1999) 'The Contours and Significance of Private Authority in International Affairs', in A.C. Cutler, V. Haufler and T. Porter (eds), *Private Authority and International Affairs* (New York: State University of New York Press).

Daly, A. (2011) 'Philanthropy, the Big Society and Emerging Philanthropic Relationships in the UK', *Public Management Review*, 13 (8): 1077–94.

Daly, H. (1989) 'Toward a Measure of Sustainable Net National Product', in Y. Ahmad, S. El Serafy and E. Lutz (eds), *Environmental Accounting for Sustainable Development* (Washington, DC: World Bank).

Darwin, C. (1876) *The Effects of Cross- and Self-Fertilisation in the Vegetable Kingdom* (London: John Murray).

Davis, R.K. (1963) 'Recreation Planning as an Economic Problem', *Natural Resources Journal*, 3 (2): 239–49.

Day, P., and Klein, R. (1987) *Accountabilities: Five Public Services* (London: Tavistock).

Department of Environment and Climate Change NSW (2007) *Biobanking: Biodiversity Banking and Offset Scheme* (Sidney: DECC NSW).

Desvousges, W.H., et al. ([1992] 2010) *Measuring Nonuse Damages Using Contingent Valuation: An Experimental Evaluation of Accuracy* (Research Triangle Park, NC: RTI International).

Devine, D.G., and Marion, B. (1979) 'The Influence of Consumer Price Information on Retail Pricing and Consumer Behavior', *American Journal of Agricultural Economics* 61: 228–37.

Dietz, S., and Stern, N. (2008) 'Why Economic Analysis Supports Strong Action on Climate Change: A Response to the Stern Review's Critics', *Review of Environmental Economics and Policy*, 2 (1): 94–113.

Dowie, M. (2009) *Conservation Refugees: The Hundred-year Conflict Between Global Conservation and Native Peoples* (Cambridge, MA: MIT Press).

Duflo, E., and Kremer, M. (2003) 'Use of Randomization in the Evaluation of Development Effectiveness', paper prepared for the World Bank OED conference on Evaluation and Development Effectiveness, Washington, DC, 15–16 July.

Dunlap, R.E., and McCright, A.M. (2011) 'Organized Climate Change Denial', in J.S. Dryzek, R.B. Noorgard and D. Schlosberg (eds), *Oxford Handbook of Climate Change and Society* (Oxford and New York: Oxford University Press).

Easterly, W. (2002) *The Elusive Quest for Growth: Economists' Adventures and Misadventures in the Tropics* (Cambridge, MA: MIT Press).

Edwards, M. (2004) *Civil Society* (Cambridge: Polity Press).

Edwards, M. (2008) *Just Another Emperor? The Myths and Realities of Philanthrocapitalism* (New York: Demos).

Edwards, M. (2011) 'Impact, Accountability and Philanthrocapitalism', *Society*, 48 (5): 389–90.

Ehrenfeld, D. (2008) 'Neoliberalization of Conservation', *Conservation Biology*, 22 (5): 1091–2.

Eikenberry, A.M., and Kluver, J.D. (2004) 'The Marketization of the Nonprofit Sector: Civil Society at Risk?', *Public Administration Review*, 64 (2): 132–40.

Elkhoury, M. (2008) 'Credit Rating Agencies and their Potential Impact on Developing Countries', UNCTAD Discussion Paper 186.

Ellerman, D., Schmalensee, R., Bailey, F., Joskow, P., and Montero, J.-P. (2000) *Markets for Clean Air: The US Acid Rain Program* (Cambridge: Cambridge University Press).

Ellul, J. (1965) *Propaganda: The Formation of Men's Attitudes* (New York: Knopf).

Emerson, J.,and Twersky, F. (1996) *New Social Entrepreneurs: The Success, Challenge and Lessons of Non-profit Enterprise Creation* (San Francisco: Roberts Foundation).

European Commission (2012) *Trends in Global CO2 Emissions: 2012 Report* (Brussels: European Commission).

European Union (2008) *The Economics of Ecosystems and Biodiversity: An Interim Report* (Brussels: European Commission).

Fairhead, J., Leach, M., and Scoones, I. (2012) 'Green Grabbing: A New Appropriation of Nature?', *Journal of Peasant Studies*, 39 (2): 237–61.

Faraday, M. (1859) *Experimental Researches in Chemistry and Physics* (London: Taylor & Francis).

Financial Crisis Inquiry Commission (2011) *Final Report of the National Commission on the Causes of the Financial Crisis in the United States* (Washington, DC: Financial Crisis Inquiry Commission).

Fioramonti, L. (2013) *Gross Domestic Problem: The Politics Behind the World's Most Powerful Number* (London: Zed Books).

Fioramonti, L., and Fiori, A. (2010) 'Civil Society After Democracy: The Evolution of Civic Activism in South Africa and Korea', *Journal of Civil Society*, 6 (1): 25–40.

Fioramonti, L., and Thumler, E. (2013) 'Accountability, Democracy and Post-Growth: Civil Society Rethinking Political Economy and Finance', *Journal of Civil Society*, 9 (2): 117–28.

Fisher, R.A. (1954) 'The Expansion of Statistics', *American Scientist* 42: 275–82.

Fletcher, R. (2010) 'Neoliberal Environmentality: Towards a Poststructural Political Ecology of the Conservation Debate', *Conservation and Society*, 8 (3): 171–81.

Foucault, M. (1991) 'Governmentality', in G. Burchell, C. Gordon and P. Miller (eds), *The Foucalt Effect: Studies in Governmentality* (Chicago: University of Chicago Press).

Fougner, T. (2008) 'Neoliberal Governance of States: The Role of Competitiveness Indexing and Benchmarking', *Millennium: Journal of International Studies*, 37 (2): 303–26.

Friend, A.M. (1989) 'UNEP/World Bank Expert Meeting on Environmental Accounting and the SNA, Paris, 21–22 November 1988', *Ecological Economics* 1: 283–5.

Friend, A.M., and Rapport, D.J. (1991) 'The Evolution of Information Systems for Sustainable Development', *Ecological Economics* 3: 59–76.

Gates, B. (2013) 'My Plan to Fix the World's Biggest Problems', *Wall Street Journal*, 25 January.

Gavras, P. (2010) 'Regulatory Abdication as Public Policy: Government Failure and the Real Conflicts of Interest of Credit Rating Agencies', *Journal of Southeast European and Black Sea Studies*, 10 (4): 475–88.

Gellner, E. (1996) *Conditions of Liberty: Civil Society and Its Rivals* (New York: Penguin Books).

Genschel, P., and Zangl, B. (2008) 'Transformations of the State: From Monopolist to Manager of Political Authority', TranState Working Papers no. 76, University of Bremen.

Gigerenzer, G., et al. (1989) *The Empire of Chance: How Probability Changed Science and Everyday Life* (Cambridge: Cambridge University Press).

Goldberg, S. (2009) *Billions of Drops in Millions of Buckets: Why Philanthropy Doesn't Advance Social Progress* (Hoboken, NJ: Wiley).

Goldman, M. (2005) *Imperial Nature: The World Bank and Struggles for Social Justice in the Age of Globalization* (New Haven, CT: Yale University Press).

Goldman Sachs Foundation (2003) *Social Impact Assessment: A Discussion among Grantmakers* (New York: Goldman Sachs).

Goodward, J., and Kelly, A. (2010) 'The Bottom Line on Offsets', Issue 17 (Washington, DC: World Resources Institute).

Gramsci, A. (1971) *Selections from the Prison Notebooks of Antonio Gramsci* (New York: International Publishers).

Graz, J.C., and Nolke, A. (eds) (2008) *Transnational Private Governance and Its Limits* (London and New York: Routledge).

Greenpeace (2011) *Bad Influence: How McKinsey-inspired Plans Lead to Rainforest Destruction* (Amsterdam: Greenpeace International).

Habermas, J. (1984) *Theory of Communicative Action*, vol. 2 (Boston, MA: Beacon Press).

Hajer, M. (1995) *The Politics of Environmental Discourse: Ecological Modernization and the Policy Process* (Oxford: Oxford University Press).

Hall, R.B., and Biersteker, T.J. (eds) (2002) *The Emergence of Private Authority in Global Governance* (Cambridge: Cambridge University Press).

Hamilton, A., Jay, J., and Madison, J. (2006 [1787]) *The Federalist Papers* (New York: Cosimo Books).

Hammack, J., and Brown, G. (1974) *Waterfowl and Wetlands: Toward Bioeconomic Analysis* (Baltimore: Johns Hopkins University Press).

Hansen, H.K., and Mühlen-Schulte, A. (2012) The Power of Numbers in Global Governance', *Journal of International Relations and Development*, 15 (4): 455–65.

Hare, R.M. (1996 [1982]) *Plato* (Oxford: Oxford University Press).

Hayek, F.H. (1945) 'The Use of Knowledge in Society', *American Economic Review*, 35 (4): 519–30.

Heckman, J. (1992) 'Randomization and Social Policy Evaluation', in C.F. Manski and I. Garfinkel (eds), *Evaluating Welfare and Training Programs* (Cambridge, MA: Harvard University Press).

Heckman, J., and Vytlacil, E. (2007) 'Econometric Evaluation of Social Programs', in J. Heckman and E. Leamer (eds), *Handbook of Econometrics*, vol. 6 (Amsterdam: Elsevier).

Heinrich, V.F., and Fioramonti, L. (2007) *Global Survey of the State of Civil Society: Comparative Perspectives* (Bloomfield: Kumarian Press).

Herndon, T., Ash, M., and Pollin, R. (2013) 'Does High Public Debt Consistently Stifle Economic Growth? A Critique of Reinhart and Rogoff', Political Economy Research Institute Working Paper No. 322, April.

Hersh, A. (2011), 'The Folly of S&P', Center for American Progress, 12 August.

Hicks, S. (1946) *Value and Capital* (Oxford: Oxford University Press).

High-Level Panel on the CDM Policy Dialogue (2012) *A Call to Action* (New York: UNFCCC).

Hill, C.A. (2010) 'Why Did Rating Agencies Do Such a Bad Job Rating Subprime Securities?', Minnesota Legal Studies Research Paper no. 10–18.

Huff, D. (1954) *How to Lie with Statistics* (New York and London: W.W. Norton).

Hunt, G. (1990) 'The Development of the Concept of Civil Society in Marx', in B. Jessop and C. Malcolm-Brown (eds), *Karl Marx's Social and Political Thought: Critical Assessments* (London and New York: Routledge).

Husock, H. (2007) 'Stock Market for Nonprofits', *Society*, 44 (3): 16–23.

ImechE (2013) *Global Food: Waste Not, Want Not* (London: Institution of Mechanical Engineers).

IOSCO (2004) *Code of Conduct Fundamentals for Credit Rating Agencies* (Madrid: International Organization of Securities Commission).

Jerven, M. (2013) *Poor Numbers: How We Are Misled by African Development Statistics and What to Do About It* (Ithaca, NY: Cornell University Press).

Karlan, D., and Appel, J. (2011) *More than Good Intentions: How a New Economics is Helping Solve Global Problems* (New York: Dutton Press).

Katz, J., Salinas, E., and Stephanou, C. (2009) 'Credit Rating Agencies: No Easy Regulatory Solutions', *Crisis Response*, Note No. 8, October.

Kerwer, D. (2002) 'Standardising as Governance: The Case of Credit Rating

Agencies', in A. Heritier (ed.), *Common Goods: Reinventing European and International Governance* (Lanham, MD: Rowman & Littlefield).

Kerwer. D. (2005) 'Holding Global Regulators Accountable: The Case of Credit Rating Agencies', *Governance: An International Journal of Policy, Administration, and Institutions*, 18 (3): 453–75.

Kevles, D.J. (2000) *The Baltimore Case: A Trial of Politics, Science and Character* (New York: W.W. Norton).

Keynes, J.M. (1933) 'National Self-Sufficiency', *Yale Review*, 22 (4) (June): 755–69.

Keynes, J.M. (1979 [1921]) *Treatise on Probability* (London: Macmillan; AMS Press reprint).

Keynes, J.M. (1997 [1936]) *The General Theory of Employment, Interest and Money* (Buffalo, NY: Prometheus Books).

Kleiner, A. (2002) 'What Are the Measures that Matter?' *Strategy + Business*, 26: 1–6.

Knack, S., and Rahman, A. (2007) 'Donor Fragmentation and Bureaucratic Quality in Aid Recipient Countries', *Journal of Development Economics*, 83 (1): 176–97.

Knight, F. (1964 [1921]) *Risk, Uncertainty and Profit* (New York: A.M. Kelley).

Koopmans, T. (1957) *Three Essays on the State of Economic Science* (New York: McGraw–Hill).

Kosonen, Kaisa (2012) 'Beyond GDP: Measuring What Really Matters to Our Prosperity and Future' (Amsterdam: Greenpeace International).

Kovel, J. (2002) *The Enemy of Nature: The End of Capitalism, or the End of the World?* (London: Zed Books.)

Kruck, A. (2011) *Private Ratings, Public Regulations: Credit Rating Agencies and Global Financial Governance* (Basingstoke: Palgrave Macmillan).

Krupnick, A., and Cropper, M. (1992) 'The Effect of Information on Health Risk Valuation', *Journal of Risk and Uncertainty* 2: 29–48.

Kuhn, T. (1996 [1962]) *The Structure of Scientific Revolutions*, 3rd edn (Chicago: University of Chicago Press).

Leiserowitz, A.A., et al. (2010) 'Climategate, Public Opinion and the Loss of Trust', Working Paper of the Yale Project on Climate Change Communication, http://environment.yale.edu/climate/publications/climategate-public-opinion-and-the-loss-of-trust.

Lindblom, C. (1982) 'The Market as a Prison', *Journal of Politics* 44: 324–36.

Lomborg, B. (2012), 'An Economic Approach to the Environment', *Wall Street Journal*, 24 April.

Lowenheim, O. (2008) 'Examining the State: A Foucauldian Perspective on International "Governance Indicators"', *Third World Quarterly*, 29 (2): 255–74.

MacAfee, K. (1999) 'Selling Nature to Save It? Biodiversity and Green Developmentalism', *Society and Space*, 17 (2): 203–19.

MacDonald, C. (2008) *Green, Inc: An Environmental Insider Reveals How a Good Cause Has Gone Bad* (Guilford, CT: Lyons Press).

MacDonald, K.I., and Corson, C. (2012) 'TEEB Begins Now': A Virtual Moment in the Production of Natural Capital', *Development and Change*, 43 (1): 159–84.

Macey, J.R. (2002) 'Testimony before the U.S. Senate Committee on Governmental Affairs', 20 March, in *Rating the Raters: Enron and the Credit Rating Agencies, Hearings Before the Senate Committee on Governmental Affairs* (Washington, DC: Government Printing Office).

Mann, M.E., Bradley, R.S., and Hughes, M.K. (1998) 'Global Scale Temperature Patterns and Climate Forcing over the Past Six Centuries', *Nature* 392: 779–87.

Marbeau, Y. (1987) 'What Value Pricing Research Today?' *Journal of the Market Research Society*, 29 (2): 153–82.

Mathis, J., McAndrews, J., and Rochet, J.-C. (2009) 'Rating the Raters: Are Reputation Concerns Powerful Enough to Discipline Rating Agencies?' *Journal of Monetary Economics*, 56 (5): 657–74.

McClintock Ekins, E., and Calabria, M.A. (2012) 'Regulation, Market Structure, and the Role of Credit Rating Agencies', *Policy Analysis* 704, 1 August.

McIntyre, S., and McKitrick, R. (2003) 'Corrections to the Mann et al. (1998) Proxy Data Base and Northern Hemispheric Average Temperature Series', *Energy and Environment*, 14 (6): 751–71.

Meier, D., et al. (2004) *Many Children Left Behind* (Boston, MA: Beacon Press).

Mendelsohn, R. (2008) 'Comments on Simon Dietz and Nicholas Stern's *Why Economic Analysis Supports Strong Action on Climate Change: A Response to the Stern Review's Critics*', *Review of Environmental Economics and Policy*, 2 (2): 309–13.

Millar, R., and Hall, K. (2012) 'Social Return on Investment (SROI) and Performance Management', *Public Management Review* 14: 1–19.

Millennium Ecosystem Assessment (2005) *Ecosystems and Human Well-being: Synthesis* (Washington, DC: Island Press).

Miller, P. (1994) 'Accounting and Objectivity: The Invention of Calculating Selves and Calculable Spaces', in A. Megill (ed.), *Rethinking Objectivity* (Durham, NC: Duke University Press).

Mitchell, R.C., and Carson, R.T. (1989) *Using Surveys to Value Public Goods: The Contingent Valuation Method* (Washington, DC: Resources for the Future).

Monckton, C. (1987) 'AIDS: A British View', *American Spectator* 20 (1).

Monckton, C. (2009) *Caught Green-Handed: Cold Facts About the Hot Topic of Global Temperature Change After the Climategate Scandal* (Haymarket, VA: Science and Public Policy Institute).

Moyo, D. (2009) 'Aid Ironies: A Response to Jeffrey Sachs', *Huffington Post*, 26 May.

Moyo, D. (2009) *Dead Aid: Why Aid Is Not Working and How There Is a Better Way for Africa* (New York and London: Allen Lane).

Muegge, D. (2011) 'From Pragmatism to Dogmatism: EU Governance, Policy Paradigms and Financial Meltdown', *Journal of New Political Economy*, 16 (2): 185–206.

Mühlen-Schulte, A. (2012) 'Full Faith in Credit? The Power of Numbers in Rating Frontier Sovereigns and the Global Governance of Development by the UNDP', *Journal of International Relations and Development*, 15 (4): 466–85.

Nagle, T.T., and Holden, R.K. (2002) *The Strategy and Tactics of Pricing* (Upper Saddle River, NJ: Prentice Hall).

Nessim, H., and Dodge, R. (1995) *Pricing-Policies and Procedures* (London: Macmillan).

New Economics Foundation (NEF) (2004) *Social Return on Investment: Valuing What Matters* (London: New Economics Foundation).

New Philanthropy Capital (2010) *Social Return on Investment Position Paper* (London: NPC).

Nicholls, J., et al. (2012) *A Guide to Social Return on Investment* (London: SROI Network).

Nickel, P.M., and Eikenberry, A.M. (2009) 'A Critique of the Discourse of Marketized Philanthropy', *American Behavioral Scientist*, 52 (7): 974–89.

Nordhaus, W.D. (2006) 'The *Stern Review* on the Economics of Climate Change', National Bureau of Economic Research Working Paper No. 12741 (Cambridge, MA: National Bureau of Economic Research).

Nordhaus, W.D., and Boyer, J. (2003) *Warming the World: Economic Models for Global Warming* (Cambridge, MA: MIT Press).

Nordhaus, W.D., and Kokkelenberg, E.C. (eds) (1999) *Nature's Numbers: Expanding the National Economic Accounts to Include the Environment* (Washington, DC: National Academy Press).

Olofsgard, A. (2012) 'The Politics of Aid Effectiveness: Why Better Tools Can Make for Worse Outcomes', Working Paper No. 16, Stockholm Institute of Transition Economies.

Open Europe (2006) *The High Cost of Hot Air: Why the EU Emissions Trading Scheme is an Environmental and Economic Failure* (London: Open Europe).

Oreskes, N., and Conway, E.M. (2010) *Merchants of Doubt: How a Handful of Scientists Obscured the Truth on Issues from Tobacco Smoke to Global Warming* (New York: Bloomsbury).

Ostrom, E. (1990) *Governing the Commons: The Evolution of Institutions for Collective Action* (New York: Cambridge University Press).

Palan, R. (2006) *The Offshore World: Sovereign Markets, Virtual Places, and Nomad Millionaires* (Ithaca, NY: Cornell University Press).

Partnoy, F. (2003) *Infectious Greed: How Deceit and Risk Corrupted the Financial Markets* (New York: Times Books).

Partnoy, F. (2006) 'How and Why Credit Rating Agencies Are Not Like Other Gatekeepers', Legal Studies Research Paper Series, Research Paper No. 07–46, May 2006, University of San Diego, California.

Patel, R. (2007) *Stuffed and Starved: The Hidden Battle for the World Food System* (New York and London: Melville House).

Patel, R. (2009) *The Value of Nothing: How to Reshape Market Society and Redefine Democracy* (London: Portobello Books).

Pattberg, P. (2005) 'The Institutionalization of Private Governance: How Business and Nonprofit Organizations Agree on Transnational Rules', *Governance:*

An International Journal of Policy, Administration, and Institutions, 18 (4): 589–610.

Paudyn, B. (2010) 'The Analytics of Ratings: European Union Attempts to Regulate Credit Rating Agencies', paper presented at the International Studies Association annual convention, Montreal, 16–20 March 2010.

Pearce, D. (1993) *Economic Values and the Natural World* (London: Earthscan).

Pearce, D., Markandya, A., and Barbier, E. (1989) *Blueprint for a Green Economy* (London: Earthscan).

Pearce, D.W., and Atkinson, G.D. (1993) 'Capital Theory and the Measurement of Weak Sustainable Development: An Indicator of Weak Sustainability', *Ecological Economics* 8: 103–8.

Pearce, F. (2010) *The Climate Files: The Battle for the Truth about Global Warming* (London: Guardian Books).

Pearson, K. (2007 [1911]) *The Grammar of Science* (New York: Cosimo Books).

Poor, H.V. (1868) *Manual of the Railroads of the United States* (New York: H.V. & H.W. Poor).

Porter, T.M. (1986) *The Rise of Statistical Thinking, 1820–1900* (Princeton, NJ: Princeton University Press).

Porter, T.M. (1995) *Trust in Numbers: The Pursue of Objectivity in Science and Public Life* (Princeton, NJ: Princeton University Press).

Portney, P.R. (1994) 'The Contingent Valuation Debate: Why Economists Should Care', *Journal of Economic Perspectives*, 8 (4): 3–17.

Power, M. (1997) *The Audit Society. Rituals of Verification* (Oxford and New York: Oxford University Press).

Pozorski, C. (2000) 'Social Venture Partners: 'Venture Capital' Grantmaking in Practice', *Grantmanship Center Magazine*, Fall: 24–6.

Pratt, J.W., and Zeckhauser, R.J. (eds) *Principals and Agents: The Structure of Business* (Cambridge, MA: Harvard University Press).

Prins, G., and Rayner, S. (2007) 'Time To Ditch Kyoto', *Nature*, 449 (7165): 973–5.

Putnam, R.D. (2001) *Bowling Alone: The Collapse and Revival of American Community* (New York: Touchstone).

Quiggin, J. (2008) 'Stern and His Critics on Discounting and Climate Change: An Editorial Essay', *Climatic Change*, 89 (3–4): 195–205.

Ramdas, K.N. (2011) 'Philanthrocapitalism: Reflections on Politics and Policy Making', *Society*, 48 (5): 393–6.

Raudsepp-Hearne, C. (2010) 'Untangling the Environmentalist Paradox: Why Is Human Well-being Increasing as Ecosystem Services Degrade?', *BioScience*, 60 (8): 576–89.

Reddy, S. (1996) 'Claims to Expert Knowledge and the Subversion of Democracy: The Triumph of Risk over Uncertainty', *Economy and Society* 25 (2): 222–54.

Reinhart, C.M., and Rogoff, K.S. (2010) 'Growth in a Time of Debt', Working Paper 15639, National Bureau of Economic Research, January.

Reisen, H., Maltzan, J. von (1998) 'Sovereign Credit Ratings, Emerging Market Risk and Financial Market Volatility', *Intereconomics*, March/April: 73–82.

Repetto, R., et al. (1989) *Wasting Assets: Natural Resources in the National Income Accounts* (Washington, DC: World Resources Institute).

Ridker, R. (1967) *The Economic Cost of Air Pollution* (New York: Praeger).

Rist, G. (2010 [1997]) *The History of Development: From Western Origins to Global Faith*, 3rd edn (London: Zed Books).

Rogers, R. (2011) 'Why Philanthro-policymaking Matters', *Society*, 48 (5): 376–81.

Rom, M.C. (2009) 'The Credit Rating Agencies and the Subprime Mess: Greedy, Ignorant, and Stressed?', *Public Administration Review*, 69 (4): 640–50.

Roncaglia, A. (1985) *Petty: The Origins of Political Economy* (Armonk, NY: M.E. Sharpe).

Rostow, W.W. (1960) *The Stages of Economic Growth: A Non-Communist Manifesto* (Cambridge: Cambridge University Press).

Rotheroe, N., and Richards, A. (2007) 'Social Return on Investment and Social Enterprise: Transparent Accountability for Sustainable Development', *Social Enterprise Journal*, 3 (1): 31–48.

Russell, B. (1967) *A History of Western Philosophy* (New York: Simon & Schuster).

Ryan, P.W., and Lyne, I. (2008) 'Social Enterprise and the Measurement of Social Value: Methodological Issues with the Calculation and Application of the Social Return on Investment', *Education, Knowledge and Economy*, 2 (3): 223–337.

Sachs, J. (2005) *The End of Poverty: Economic Possibilities for Our Time* (New York: Penguin).

Sachs, J. (2009) 'Aid Ironies', *Huffington Post*, 24 May.

Sandel, M.J. (2012) *What Money Can't Buy: The Moral Limits of Markets* (New York: Farrar, Straus & Giroux).

Santos, J.A.C. (2003) 'Why Firm Access to the Bond Market Differs over the Business Cycle: A Theory and Some Evidence', *Journal of Banking and Finance*, 30 (10): 2715–36.

Scholte, J.A. (2013) 'Civil Society and Financial Markets: What Is Not Happening and Why', in L. Fioramonti and E. Thumler (eds), *Citizens vs. Markets: How Civil Society Is Reshaping the Economy in a Time of Crises* (London: Routledge).

Seabright, P. (2010) *The Company of Strangers: A Natural History of Economic Life*, rev. edn (Princeton, NJ: Princeton University Press).

Seife, C. (2010) *Proofiness: The Dark Arts of Mathematical Deception* (Viking: New York).

Seligman, A.B. (1992) *The Idea of Civil Society* (New York: Macmillan).

Shadish, W.R., and Luellen, J.K. (2004) 'Donald Campbell: The Accidental Evaluator', in M.C. Alkin (ed.), *Evaluation Roots: Tracing Theorists' Views and Influences* (London: Sage).

Shapiro, S.P. (1987) 'The Social Control of Impersonal Trust', *American Journal of Sociology*, 93 (3): 623–58.

Sharman, J.C. (2009) 'The Bark Is the Bite: International Organizations and Blacklisting', *Review of International Political Economy*, 16 (4): 573–96.

Sheridan, K. (2011) 'Measuring the Impact of Social Enterprise', *British Journal of Healthcare Management*, 17 (4): 152–6.

Sinclair, T.J. (1994) 'Passing Judgment: Credit Rating Processes as Regulatory Mechanisms of Governance in the Emerging World Order', *Review of International Political Economy*, 1 (1): 133–59.

Sinclair, T.J. (2001) 'The Infrastructure of Global Governance: Quasi-Regulatory Mechanisms and the New Global Finance', *Global Governance*, 7 (4): 441–51.

Sinclair, T.J. (2002) 'Private Makers of Public Policy: Bond Rating Agencies and the New Global Finance', in A. Héritier (ed.), *Common Goods and Governance* (Oxford: Rowman & Littlefield).

Sinclair, T.J. (2003) 'Global Monitor. Bond Rating Agencies', *New Political Economy*, 8 (1): 147–61.

Sinclair, T.J. (2005) *The New Masters of Capital: American Bond Rating Agencies and the Politics of Creditworthiness* (Ithaca, NY: Cornell University Press).

Sinclair, T.J. (2010) 'Round up the Usual Suspects: Blame and the Subprime Crisis', *Journal of New Political Economy*, 15 (1): 91–107.

Singer, S.F. (1979) *Cost–Benefit Analysis as an Aid to Environmental Decision-Making*, Report M77-106 (McLean,VA: Metrek Division, Mitre Corporation).

Singer, S.F. (1984) *Report of the Acid Rain Peer Review Panel: Final Report*, July, Office of Science and Technology Policy (Washington, DC: US Government Printing Office).

Stapel, D. (2012) *Ontsporing* (Amsterdam: Prometheus).

Starr, P. (1987) 'The Sociology of Official Statistics', in W. Alonso and P. Starr (eds), *The Politics of Numbers* (New York: Russell Sage Foundation).

Steinbeck, J. (1941) *The Log from the Sea of Cortez* (London and New York: Penguin Books).

Stiglitz, J., Ferri, G., and Liu, G. (1999) 'The Procyclical Role of Rating Agencies: Evidence from the East Asian Crisis', *Economic Notes*, 28 (3): 335–55.

Stout, R.G. (1969) 'Developing Data to Estimate Price-quantity Relationships', *Journal of Marketing*, 33 (2): 34–6.

Strange, S. (1996) *The Retreat of the State: The Diffusion of Power in the World Economy* (Cambridge: Cambridge University Press).

Strulik, T. (2002) 'Rating Agencies and Systemic Risk: Paradoxes of Governance', in A. Héritier (ed.), *Common Goods and Governance* (Oxford: Rowman & Littlefield).

Summers, L.H. (2004) Fourth Annual Marshall J. Seidman Lecture on Health Policy, 27 April, www.hcp.med.harvard.edu/files/SummersLecture.pdf (accessed 30 June 2013).

Svendsen, G. (2005) 'Lobbying and CO2 Trade in the EU', in B. Hansjurgens (ed.), *Emission Trading for Climate Policy* (New York: Cambridge University Press).

Sylla, R. (2002) 'An Historical Primer on the Business of Credit Rating', in R.M. Levich, G. Majnoni and C. Reinhart (eds), *Ratings, Rating Agencies and the Global Financial System* (Boston, MA: Kluwer Academic).

Taylor, J.B. (2009) 'The Financial Crisis and the Policy Responses: An Empirical Analysis of What Went Wrong', NBER Working Paper no. 14631, Cambridge MA.

Taylor, M., and Singleton, S. (1993) 'The Communal Resource: Transaction Costs and the Solution of Collective Action Problems', *Politics and Society*, 21 (2): 195–214.

Thackaray, J. (1986) 'Leveraged Buyouts: The LBO Craze Flourishes Amid Warnings of Disaster', *Euromoney*, February.

Then, V., et al. (2012) *Creating Impact in Southern Norway: A Social Return on Investment Report to the Competence Development Fund of Southern Norway*, Centre for Social Investment, Heidelberg.

Tietenberg, T. (1996) *Environmental and Natural Resource Economics* (New York: HarperCollins).

Toman, M. (1998) 'Why Not to Calculate the Value of the World's Ecosystem Services and Natural Capital', Special Section: Forum on Valuation of Ecosystem Services, *Ecological Economics* 25 (1998): 57–60.

Transparency International (2011) *Global Corruption Report: Climate Change* (London: Earthscan).

Tyrell, M., and Bannier, C. (2005) 'Modeling the Role of Credit Rating Agencies: Do They Spark Off a Virtuous Circle?' Working Papers Series in Finance and Accounting, Paper no. 160 (Frankfurt: Johann Wolfgang Goethe Universität).

UN et al. (1993) *System of National Accounts 1993* (Brussels/Luxembourg, New York, Paris, Washington, DC: UN, World Bank, International Monetary Fund, European Commission, OECD).

UN et al. (2008) *System of National Accounts 2008* (Brussels/Luxembourg, New York, Paris, Washington DC: UN, World Bank, International Monetary Fund, European Commission, OECD).

UN Statistical Commission et al. (2012) *System of Environmental-Economic Accounting* (New York: United Nations).

UNEP (2006) *In the Front Line: Shoreline Protection and Other Ecosystem Services From Mangroves and Coral Reefs* (Cambridge: UNEP World Conservation Monitoring Centre).

US Senate (2010) *United States Senate Report 'Consensus Exposed': The CRU Controversy*, US Senate Committee on Environment and Public Works, Minority Staff, Washington, DC.

US Senate (2011) *Wall Street and the Financial Crisis: Anatomy of a Financial Collapse*, Majority and Minority Staff Report of the Permanent Subcommittee on Investigations for the Committee on Homeland Security and Governmental Affairs, 14 April (Washington, DC: US Senate).

Van Maanen, J., and Pentland, B. (1994) 'Cops and Auditors: The Rhetoric of Records', in S.B. Sitkin and R.J. Bies (eds), *The Legalistic Organization* (Thousand Oaks, CA: Sage).

Vandemoortele, J. (2004) 'Credit Quality Moves Center Stage as African Countries Seek to Improve their Economic Performance', in Standard & Poor's, *Sovereign Ratings in Africa* (New York: Standard & Poor's).

Vandemoortele, J. (2007) 'The MDGs: "M" for Misunderstood?', World Institute for Development Economics Research (WIDER), UNU, No. 1.

Varian, H.R. (2006) 'Recalculating the Costs of Climate Change', *New York Times*, 14 December.

Véron, N. (2009) 'Rating Agencies: An Information Privilege Whose Time Has Passed', *Bruegel Policy Contribution*, issue 2009/01.

Véron, N. (2011) 'Rate Expectations: What Can and Cannot Be Done about Rating Agencies', *Bruegel Policy Contribution*, issue 2011/14.

Vickrey, W. (1961) 'Counterspeculation, Auctions, and Competitive Sealed Tenders', *Journal of Finance*, 16 (1): 8–37

Wallace, T., Bornstein, L., and Chapman, J. (2006) *The Aid Chain: Coercion and Commitment in NGO Development Funding* (Rugby: ITDG Press).

Weber, M. (1981 [1927]) *General Economic History* (New Brunswick, NJ: Transaction Books).

Weisbrod, B. (1964) 'Collective Consumption Services of Individual Consumption Goods', *Quarterly Journal of Economics*, 78 (3): 471–7.

White, H. (1985) 'Agency as Control', in J.W. Pratt and R.J. Zeckhauser (eds), *Principals and Agents: The Structure of Business* (Cambridge, MA: Harvard University Press).

White, L.J. (2009) 'The Credit-Rating Agencies and the Subprime Debacle', *Critical Review*, 21 (2–3): 389–99.

White, L.J. (2010) 'Markets: The Credit Rating Agencies', *Journal of Economic Perspectives*, 24 (2): 211–26.

Whitehead, J.M., and Mathis, H.S. (2007) 'Finding a Way Out of the Rating Agency Morass', statement submitted to the US House Financial Services Committee, Subcommittee on Capital Markets, Insurance, and Government Sponsored Enterprises, 27 September.

World Bank (2006) *Where Is the Wealth of Nations? Measuring Capital for the 21st Century* (Washington, DC: World Bank).

World Commission on Environment and Development (1987) *Our Common Future* (Oxford: Oxford University Press).

Yamey, B.S. (1949) 'Scientific Bookkeeping and the Rise of Capitalism', *Economic History Review*, 1 (2/3): 99–113.

Index